George Alagiah was born in   vas in Ghana where his parents n   ...tended secondary school in Portsmouth, England, and is a graduate of Durham University. He is married, has two sons and lives in north London.

George joined the BBC in 1989 after seven years in print journalism with *South Magazine*. He is currently a newscaster. Before that, he was one of the BBC's leading foreign correspondents, recognised throughout the industry for his reporting on some of the most significant events of the last decade. He is a specialist on Africa and the developing world. Between 1994 and 1998 he was based in Johannesburg as the BBC's Africa Correspondent.

George has won numerous awards, including the Critics Award and the Golden Nymph Award at the Monte Carlo Television Festival (1992); the award for Best International Report at the Royal Television Society (1993); a commendation from the British Academy of Film and Television Arts (1993); Amnesty International's Best TV Journalist Award (1994); the One World Broadcasting Trust Award (1994); the James Cameron Memorial Trust Award (1995); the Bayeux Award for War Reporting (1996); and in 1998, he was voted Media Personality of the Year at the Ethnic Minority Media Awards.

A Passage to Africa

GEORGE ALAGIAH

A *Time Warner* Paperback

First published in Great Britain in 2001 by
Little, Brown
This edition published by
Time Warner Paperbacks in 2002

A CIP catalogue record for this book
is available from the British Library

ISBN 0 7515 3214 2

Typeset in Goudy by M Rules
Printed and bound in Great Britain by
Clays Ltd, St Ives plc

Time Warner Paperbacks
An imprint of
Time Warner Books UK
Brettenham House
Lancaster Place
London WC2E 7EN

www.TimeWarnerBooks.co.uk

To my father, Donald Ratnarajah Alagiah, and in
memory of my mother, Therese Karunaiamma
Santiapillai. You opened the door to this huge
world of opportunity.

To my sisters, Mari, Rachel, Christine and
Jenny. Look back, see how far we have come.

To my nieces and nephews.
Stay well, stay together.

To Frances – a free spirit, friend and
fellow traveller.

To my sons, Adam and Matthew. So far you
have followed where we have led; we wait for the
day when you will walk in front, showing us
new things about our world.

Contents

Acknowledgements

Where to begin? Let me start with Charles – of whom more later – who first taught me about Africa and its people. Then the hundreds of other Africans – presidents and paupers, rogues and renegades, black and white – who, in most cases unwittingly, helped shape my views about their continent. Remember, all of you, these words from Ben Okri:

> We are the miracles that God made
> To taste the bitter fruit of Time.
> We are precious.
> And one day our suffering
> Will turn into the wonders of the earth.
>
> There are things that burn me now
> Which turn golden when I am happy.
> Do you see the mystery of our pain?
> That we bear poverty
> And are able to sing and dream sweet things.

Many of the experiences about which I have written were shared with other journalists. I have learned from them as, I hope, they have learned from me. Crammed into old taxis, waiting at a border post, sheltering under fire, propping up a bar and staying up too late – we have done it all together. To Allan Little, Milton Nkosi, Scott Peterson, Glenn Middleton, Richard Atkinson, Mike Purdy, Debbie Morgan, Peter Burdin, Kate Peyton, Tim Platt, Duncan Stone, Martin Seemungal, Sam Kiley, Alec Russell, Chris McGreal, Corine Dufka, Zara d'Abo, Steve Scott, Ferle Davis, Mark Huband, Karl Maier and many others: thank you.

Difficult and confusing places were made just that little less difficult and less confusing by many aid workers who gave of their time and resources. Some of them I have acknowledged in the following pages. Among those I have not are Samantha Bolton of MSF, Brenda Barton of WFP, Mike McDonagh of Concern, Steve Rifkin of SCF, Nina Winquist of ICRC and Panos Moumtis of UNHCR.

This manuscript has passed under the careful eyes of people whose judgement I respect and trust. Ama Annan, Rakiya Omaar, Hugh Lewin, Fiona Lloyd, Ofeibea Quist-Arcton, Cathy Watson, Humphrey Keenleyside and James Oporio-Ekwaro have improved this book immeasurably. Any failings that remain are entirely my responsibility.

From the day he first discussed my proposal with me Alan Samson, my publisher, has guided this whole venture with great intelligence and enthusiasm. Caroline North, editor at large with Little, Brown, honed the script and winkled out many little problems. My agent, Maggie Hanbury, saw a book in me long before I did.

Frances Robathan has probably read these pages as often as I have, from first, tentative draft to the finished product. That it was possible for me to write this book at all is due to the grace and patience with which she has let me pursue a career that has taken me away from home more times than I care to remember.

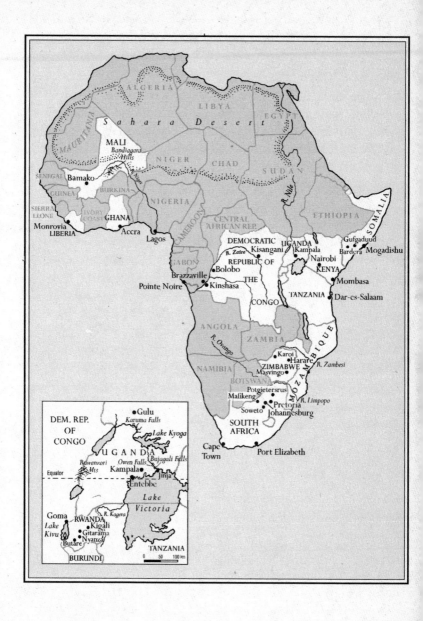

ALGERIA

LIBYA

EGYPT

MAURITANIA

Sahara Desert

MALI
Bandiagara
Hills

NIGER

CHAD

SUDAN

SENEGAL

Bamako

GUINEA

BURKINA

R. Niger

SIERRA
LEONE

IVORY
COAST

GHANA

NIGERIA

CAMEROON

ETHIOPIA

SOMALIA

Monrovia
LIBERIA

Accra

Lagos

R. Nile

GABON

DEMOCRATIC

R. Zaire   Kisangani

REPUBLIC OF

Bolobo

Brazzaville

THE

UGANDA
Kampala

Nairobi

KENYA

Gufgaduud
Bardera   Mogadishu

Mombasa

Pointe Noire

Kinshasa

CONGO

TANZANIA

Dar-es-Salaam

ANGOLA

ZAMBIA

R. Okavango

MOZAMBIQUE

Karoi

Harare

R. Zambesi

ZIMBABWE

NAMIBIA

Masvingo

BOTSWANA

Potgietersrus

Mafikeng

R. Limpopo

Soweto

Pretoria

Johannesburg

SOUTH
AFRICA

Cape
Town

Port Elizabeth

DEM. REP.
OF
CONGO

Gulu

Karuma Falls

Lake Kyoga

UGANDA

Rawenzori
Mts

Owen Falls

Bujagali Falls

Equator

Kampala

Jinja

Entebbe

Lake

Victoria

Goma
Lake
Kivu

RWANDA

R. Kagera

Kigali

Gitarama

Butare

Nyanza

TANZANIA

BURUNDI

0   50   100 km

Preface

The year 2002 has seen something of a revival of interest in Africa, at least in official circles in Britain. After roughly two decades during which Africa's fate – the odd famine or natural disaster aside – was largely relegated to the bottom of Whitehall's in-tray, the issue has now found itself rising towards the top. Three cabinet ministers, including the prime minister, and other junior ministers and politicians have made their way to Africa – and not merely for the quick, image-boosting photocall with Nelson Mandela that had become something of a ritual in the 1990s. Foreign secretary Jack Straw, for example, headed for conflict-ridden central Africa, not the place to go if scoring a few cheap and cheerful political points is the aim.

The Labour Party's traditional commitment to internationalism accounts, in part, for the tens of thousands of African air miles notched up by these politicians, but the new-found urgency with which they have pursued this policy can be traced back to a single day: 11 September 2001.

If the immediate reaction of the world's leaders, at least those in the rich world, was limited to the hunt for those responsible for the atrocities in New York and Washington, within a matter of weeks a few of them had turned their attention to some of the issues that drove those young men from apparently comfortable backgrounds towards terrorism in the first place. While George Bush's administration concentrated its efforts on the 'how did they do it?' question, Europe's leaders were as inclined to try to find an answer to the 'why did they do it?' problem.

As ever, the British prime minister, Tony Blair, stood somewhere in the middle. His quick promise to stand 'shoulder to shoulder' with America in its robust military response was complemented by the way he articulated Europe's desire to address not just terrorism, but the causes of terrorism as well.

His first major speech after the attacks on the World Trade Center and the Pentagon came at the Labour Party's annual conference on 2 October. Africa proved to be a central theme of his keynote address. Mindful of accusations that there was a stark contrast between the way the rich countries banded together after Americans had been killed and their political lethargy when those being murdered had been Africans, he had this to say: 'I tell you, if Rwanda happened today as it did in 1994, when a million people were slaughtered in cold blood, we would have a moral duty to act there also.'

Famously, he told conference delegates that 'the state of Africa is a scar on the conscience of the world'. Talk of 'conscience' suggested a moral purpose, but during this speech and in others that followed, he argued that dealing with 'chaos' abroad was in the rich world's own interests.

Just over a month later, in November 2001, Mr Blair expanded on this theme. He was speaking at the Lord Mayor's banquet, a white-tie occasion at which domestic affairs usually come to the fore. Not this time: 'One illusion has been shattered on 11 September – that we can have the good life of the West irrespective of the state of the rest of the world. Once chaos and strife have got a grip on a region or a country, trouble will soon be exported . . . The dragon's teeth are planted in the fertile soil of wrongs unrighted, of disputes left to fester for years or even decades, of failed states, of poverty and deprivation.'

I couldn't agree more. But why, why, why did it take the murderous assault on America to persuade mainstream politicians in the rich world to use the kind of language that Tony Blair employed? The fact is that the British prime minister was merely playing catch-up with what many others had been saying for years, even decades. I began my career in the 1980s at *South* magazine, which was dedicated to the notion that an unequal world was an unstable one. Such ideas were hardly restricted to the pages of the 'alternative' press. Listen to this: 'Widespread poverty and chaos lead to a collapse of existing political and social structures, which would inevitably invite the advance of totalitarianism into every weak and unstable area. Thus our own security would be endangered and our prosperity imperilled.' The speaker was one John F. Kennedy; the year was 1961. At the time he was arguing for a big increase in America's aid budget. But in the decades that followed the amount America spent on aid as a proportion of its national wealth shrank. It was a trend that persisted regardless of whether Republicans or Democrats were in charge of the purse-strings. Indeed, the steepest decline in the aid-to-wealth ratio occurred under Bill Clinton, arguably the most internationalist president of the modern era.

And long before Kennedy, in a classic work on decolonisation, *The Wretched of the Earth*, Frantz Fanon argued that oppression bred violence.

Going back to Mr Blair's definition of the conditions that breed violence, it is clear that Africa is home to more failed states, more poverty and more deprivation than any other continent on earth. If the wider lessons of September 11 are going to be learned, the foreign policies of the rich world will have to change. Men and women at the Foreign Office in London, at the Quai d'Orsay in Paris and at the State Department in Washington, to name but a few, will have to design policies that go beyond a projection of national interest and look to the global good.

Politicians like to talk vaguely about a global village, but if foreign policy is to be ethical as well as effective, it will have to recognise that conflict-resolution entails more than getting two sides around a table. In Africa, there has to be an acknowledgement that although Africans are primarily to blame for the decrepit state of their continent, the rich world has to shoulder its share of the blame. In the decades since decolonisation, Africa has been ill-served by those who claimed to be its friends.

Too often policy has been driven by a competition between various powerful nations over the continent's vast resources. We have argued for free trade when what we really meant was that Africans should open their doors to our goods while we continued to restrict their exports to us. Instead of extending the ideas of social justice that we take for granted, we have, all too often, allowed our companies to deny Africans those very standards. How fair is it that a cocoa farmer in Ghana should get less than one penny from the proceeds of a bar of chocolate that sells for 90p in Britain? Why did it take a court battle in South Africa in 2001 to persuade the great pharmaceutical businesses that some people simply couldn't afford their AIDS drugs?

In the aftermath of September 11 people were fond of saying that the 'world has changed'; that life would never be the same again. What they meant, of course, was that life in the rich world, and especially in America, had changed. In the poor world nothing much had changed at all – except that many more countries would be regarded with suspicion and many more of their citizens seen as potential terrorists. Very quickly, Somalia found itself on the list of those nations deemed to pose a threat to America's security. This is the country that the USA backed in the Cold War and then tried to save from famine in 1992.

The point is this: the world *should* change after September 11, but not simply in the way people suggested at the time of the attacks. If leaders like Tony Blair (and those who follow him) remain true to their words, then over the next forty years Africa might well look very different from the way I have had to portray it during the last forty years in the pages that follow.

A Passage to Africa has been a few months in the writing but virtually a lifetime in the making. While the events it covers reflect the preoccupations of a conventional, Western newsroom – where I have worked since early 1989 – my response to what I have witnessed is coloured by a much earlier experience. As a child, Africa was my home: my family moved from Ceylon, as it was then, to Ghana when I was six.

A few years ago I was asked to take part in a BBC World Service programme in which listeners were encouraged to question the reporters they had seen and heard over the years. It was an opportunity to criticise, praise, berate or applaud. I took many calls and e-mails that day, most of them about my views on the places that I had reported on – Liberia, Somalia, Rwanda, South Africa. But one listener stands out. This man wasn't interested in George Alagiah the journalist, he wanted to know about George Alagiah the person. 'I've seen you all over Africa and yet I hear you were born in Sri Lanka and now live in Britain,' he said. 'But where are you from, where's your home?' This inquiry, though it sounded innocent enough, had a sting to it, the hint of an accusation. What he was actually saying, as became apparent, was 'Where do you belong, where's your soul?'

This book is part of the answer to that question. It is, primarily, about Africa, but it is also about how I came to think about Africa in the way I do. The glib reply to that caller was simple enough: I am British – that is what it says on my passport – and my home is Britain. But the deeper answer, and the honest one, is that I am more than British. I am the sum of my experiences, and Africa is a huge element of that. I belong to Africa; or at least, a piece of me does.

Ghana was the continent's first independent nation, the first, that is, to shake off European colonialism. When we moved there in 1961, it was a time when all things seemed possible. Although we were immigrants, we were caught up in the air of optimism. It was contagious. Over three decades later I would end up in South Africa, the last country in Africa to free itself of the heavy weight of colonialism. This time I went as a professional observer, a foreign correspondent. By then Nelson Mandela's 'miracle' nation seemed to offer a rare glimmer of hope on a continent that otherwise appeared to be slipping into political and economic oblivion. From first to last, from beginning to end, those countries are bookends in a vast, often confusing library of experiences. There is talk now of an African Renaissance, an echo of the pan-Africanism of the 1960s. Africa has been through one of history's cycles and I have watched it happen, first as a boy, then as a man; once it was a playground, next a place of work.

You might argue that I am no different from scores of other foreign reporters who have passed their eager eyes over this continent. After all, I am a Brit and I work for that most British of institutions, the BBC. But sometimes it is where you come from, not where you end up, that marks you out. I look at it this way. In another era, some of my colleagues today might have been the foot soldiers of empire, and I would have been one of the eager-to-impress locals. We might have had the kind of relationship described in 1924 by E. M. Forster in A *Passage to India*. I might have been an Aziz to their Fielding, or worse, to their Turton. I would have worked hard and shown due deference during the day but, come the evening, I would have headed for my home across the bridge (the locals always lived across a bridge or a railway line) with a lingering sense of resentment. Inside me there would have been a knot of pent-up anger, a deepening sense of frustration fuelled by the knowledge that it was they, not me, who were calling the shots.

That sense of where I started out from – not just literally, but historically as well – has fashioned my reaction to the world I have reported on. I have listened in on enough conversations among the 'natives' to share something of their visceral disgust every time a foreign reporter reproaches the poor world in general, and Africa in particular. I have come to accept Africa for what it is. I have travelled its length and breadth, from Algeria to Zaire, Accra to Zanzibar. It is a journey that has left me gasping when facing the best the continent has to offer and in despair when confronted with its ugliness. The generosity of its people has left me humbled – in the most desolate of places, in the worst of times, I have been greeted with a warm heart and an open hand.

I have learned not to judge Africa by its worst excesses. Nor do I assume that its episodic yet startling achievements are representative of anything more than the time and place in which they have occurred. There are those who would argue that such a take-it-as-you-find-it attitude is at best naïve and at worst professionally negligent. My answer to them is that my relationship with this continent is different from that of some of my colleagues. It has never been merely a passing phase in my career, a stepping-stone to greater glory. Nelson Mandela, addressing reporters of the Johannesburg Foreign Correspondents' Association, once said: 'You are privileged people. You can observe from near but judge from afar.' And it is true that although the involvement of journalists in events can be intimate, we rarely have to cope with the emotional attachment that such intimacy normally entails. When, at the end of a day, we sit down in front of our laptops to write up the day's news, we do so as outsiders. We feel free to pass judgement, unhindered by any sense of belonging.

But that never has been, and never can be true of me. When I see injustice in Africa it hits me in the guts; every small victory notched up by the sons and daughters of this continent is one I celebrate with them. If I have trained my head to be dispassionate, my heart remains with Africa's people.

A *Passage to Africa* is not intended to be a definitive study of the continent. The countries featured are included not because they are the most important in any sense, but because they are the countries I have come to know well. My descriptions and judgements are therefore limited to the places I have seen for myself over a number of visits and understand best. There is no chapter on Kenya, for example, or on Mozambique or Angola, with their experience of Portuguese colonialism. And I have not dealt with Nigeria, Africa's giant – home to one in six Africans and to more ethnic groups and languages than any other country on the continent. To have included chapters on these countries would have been merely to offer my own interpretation of what others have seen, whereas what I wanted to write – and what I hope I have achieved – is a personal, intimate portrait of the continent that gives an insight into how it came to be what it is today.

George Alagiah
October 2002

1

Paradise Lost

Long, long before I came to know and love Africa as a place, I yearned for it as an idea. It was to be, for my family, a place of deliverance, a promised land. From that day in May 1961 when my father announced that we were to leave our island home, Ceylon, for the distant shores of Africa, it began to work a sort of magic on me.

In the seven months before our departure, I began to conjure up a vision of Africa and what it would mean for us. Even as a child of five I think I knew that it represented something better than the divided island we were about to leave. I was conscious that the reason we were going had something to do with us being different; that somehow we didn't fit in.

I knew this in the way a child knows these things. I learned from half-heard conversations between my parents that Ceylon was not somewhere that we Tamils would prosper. So Ceylon was bad; Africa was good. Now we were poor; in Africa we would be rich. Africa became one of my favourite things, like slurping buffalo curd laced with dark, sweet *kitul pani*, the nectar of the *kitul* palm tree, out of a cool, clay pot or beating my grandmother at *carom*, a tabletop game like billiards in which wooden discs are bounced into pockets with a flick of the finger. I was ready for Africa long before I knew where it was or how we would get there. I embraced it as only a child can – with the unquestioning certainty that everything will be all right in the morning.

Such optimism is shared, at varying levels of sophistication, by all those who have sought refuge in a new land. A migrant does much more than move from one place to another; his journey is a journey from despair to hope, from oppression to opportunity.

Of course, my parents never said we were leaving for ever. Very few people leave the land of their birth saying that they'll never return. Most people who head for new shores believe that one day they will be able to go back 'home'. That is what my parents told our relatives in Ceylon, partly because it was a way of alleviating the pain of separation but also because that is what they thought, perhaps even hoped would happen. It was not Ceylon we had rejected but what it had become. And that could change.

Actually, what happened was that we ourselves changed. It was true of all of us, but especially of my sisters and me. From the minute we were made aware of this place called Africa and the prospects it held in store, our young minds began to look forward, not backwards. Our mental horizons expanded as we got closer and closer to this new land of opportunity. Like Africa's vast, dawn-red sky, which we could see as our plane tilted towards Accra, our vision of what was now possible seemed limitless. Africa would be everything that Ceylon had not been: a place where we could start again. All of us, together, as a family.

So the thing I remember above all about the land of my birth is the fact that I left it. That is to say my parents left it, taking with them their five children: four girls and me, the only son. Other episodes do bob up to the surface, vestigial impressions of an early

childhood in Ceylon, but it's the leaving of the place that domi-
nates my recollections. It's a bit like trying to recall a dream:
wisps of unconscious thought float by but it's the image with
which you wake that sticks in your mind.

Yes, I can remember standing by the well at my grandfather's
home in the little eastern town of Kalmunai as he poured buckets
of cold water over me. From where I stood I'd look up to see this
vast expanse of belly hanging over the knot of a sarong and, further up, a kindly, indulgent face smiling down at me. There was
always a black cigar in his mouth, even, it seems, at bathtime.

And, yes, I remember our house in Colombo, the one with the
stinking gully running by its side. In the monsoon season the
gully would become a torrent of water into which we would throw
our paper boats. I recall how, as these fragile little constructions
were swept away, I thought of my Uncle John, who was in the
merchant navy. Was this what it was like for him? Please God, let
him be safe.

And there was the skinny, grizzled, filthy, smelly, half-naked old
man, or sometimes his wife, who would come to slop out our latrine
each morning. He was just one of a succession of people who came
to our home every day. I remember the sounds he made – the
squeak of his metal bucket as he walked up the path to our outside
loo, his footsteps on the way back and, finally, the clash of metal
against metal as he threw the contents of the bucket into the two-
wheeled tank. In a culture where everyone had a place in the
intricate and stifling hierarchy of caste, these people were the
lowest of the low. They were Tamils from south India, the untouch-
ables whom Mahatma Gandhi had vowed to liberate. Nobody in
Ceylon, not even the low-caste local Tamils, and certainly no
Sinhalese, would stoop so low as to clean out somebody else's toilet.

The *dhobi* collected our clothes for washing. I even remember
the mark by which our clothes were distinguished from all the
others that would be thrashed and dried next to some riverbed: a
cross with dots in each quarter.

Then there was the chap who came round to take the tiffin box to my father's workplace. This was takeaway service with home cooking. My mother would prepare a meal of rice and curries which was decanted into a stack of stainless-steel tins. These were collected by tiffin-carriers who, in bicycle relays, would ensure that food was delivered, still warm, to my father's office at the other end of town. The tins were held together by a clasp and stacked next to all the other boxes destined for men who couldn't do without the fruits of their wives' culinary talents.

But, as I say, more than anything else I remember the *frisson* of departure, the combination of fear and nerves that I sensed in my parents as they prepared us for emigration to Ghana.

From what I can tell, D. A. Seniveratne was a man of some means. He had once been a mayor of the upcountry city of Nuwara Eliya; by 1958 he was a planter in the Tamil-dominated east of the island. If he had at one time entertained political ambitions they were not in evidence at the tail end of the fifties. The lure of high office had given way to a more fatal attraction. No one I have asked can remember his first name, and very few remember him at all. But for a little moment of weakness, a lapse of judgement, Seniveratne would have passed through this life largely unnoticed and soon forgotten. And yet here he is at the start of my story.

It is one of the quirks of history that those who are judged to have played a pivotal role in a process are rarely aware of their contribution at the time. There are plenty of examples. Can that young student who stood in front of the long, menacing line of tanks in Tiananmen Square in 1989 have predicted that the image of his spontaneous act of protest would become an icon for all those who fight repression? Could Mr Quartus de Wet, judge president of the Transvaal in South Africa, have guessed, when he eschewed the option of a death penalty and instead sentenced Nelson Mandela to life imprisonment, that he was playing his part in the making of a twentieth-century legend? And whatever else Lee Harvey Oswald's motives were for gunning down John F. Kennedy, freeze-framing the president's life in youthful glory was surely not one of them.

That's the way it was with Seniveratne, or so I like to think. His part in the ethnic tension that has divided Ceylon for so long was accidental, but its consequences were tragic.

Seniveratne was a Sinhalese man living in the largely Tamil town of Batticaloa in the east of the island – the town, incidentally, where both my parents grew up. Seniveratne's people constituted the majority in the country as a whole, but here in the east he was in the minority. He would have done well to have appreciated the limits this ethnic imbalance placed on his tumescent aspirations.

There are certain things in life one can take for granted. One of them is a man's anger on discovering that he's been cuckolded. Having travelled far and wide, I can say with some certainty that this is an emotion that remains the same no matter how many frontiers one crosses. Whether he is a Texan or a Tamil, a man's deep-rooted insecurity over matters sexual will be exposed in much the same way. The loss of intimacy and the break-up of a friendship concern him far less than the affront to his manhood. One of the things that makes matters even worse is to have been cuckolded by the enemy. It's bad enough to discover that your wife has found comfort in the arms of another man, but when that other man turns out to be from a rival group, well, all hell breaks loose.

Nobody ever stops to ask what might have driven the woman from her marital bed, or what neglect pushed her towards the risk of an illicit tryst, or, as in this case, why ethnic background should play any part at all in relations between men and women. Foremost in the mind of the husband is the business of avenging his manhood, and in this he has the support of the male tribe. First they deal with the predator and then they turn their attention to the woman who slept with the enemy, that most heinous of crimes.

It's not known whether it was love or lust, but the object of Seniveratne's desire was a Tamil woman. And to the Tamils of Batticaloa, the Sinhalese were certainly the oppressors. Tamil integrity, not to say vanity, had been slighted, and in May 1958 the hapless Seniveratne paid for his error with his life. Though the murder itself does appear in several accounts of the period, the reasons for it tend to be glossed over. The nearest one gets to the full facts in any official document is an acknowledgement in parliamentary records that the killing had all the hallmarks of a vendetta. But what the historians omitted, word of mouth put right, and the locally accepted story of Seniveratne's death has been handed down through the generations.

That the matter was brought up at all in Parliament is a clue to the part it played in Ceylon's history. It became something of a *cause célèbre* among Sinhalese politicians. The murder was portrayed not as the crime of passion it probably was, but as a purely communal matter, evidence of incipient Tamil insurgency. Seniveratne became a martyr to the cause. In his classic account of Ceylon's communal tensions, *Emergency '58*, Tarzie Vittachi describes how the prime minister of the day attributed the murder to political motives. No mention was made of the private feud that Seniveratne had been caught up in.

His body was driven in a cortège from the Tamil east of the country to the Sinhala west. And whenever it passed through a town where the Tamils were in a minority there were ethnic disturbances as Sinhalese turned on their Tamil neighbours. Like a flaming torch dragged through the pre-monsoon grass, Seniveratne's posthumous and somewhat ostentatious progress through the hinterland ignited among Sinhalese a visceral desire to put one over on the Tamils.

There had been inter-communal strife before, but Seneviratne's murder took it to previously unknown heights. After this, the tensions that had largely been confined to isolated pockets spilled out on to the streets all over the island. People in Sri Lanka talk about the 'disturbances' of 1958 in much the same way as people in Britain blithely refer to the 'troubles' in Northern Ireland. Both are euphemisms for events that have disfigured the political and social landscape of the countries in question.

These so-called disturbances hardened the arteries of political discourse. For angry young men on both sides of the ethnic divide the events of 1958 provided the rationale for the decades of violence and distrust that have hobbled Sri Lanka's progress since its independence ten years earlier from over 500 years of colonialism.

But, looking back, one sees that the significance of Seniveratne's murder lay not in what it did to the hot-heads, the rebels merely waiting for the right cause. No, more important is the way it affected that huge army of people whose lives were framed not by political activism and high idealism, but the more pressing business of holding down a job and raising a family on its less-than-adequate returns. After 1958 a large proportion of educated Tamils, men and women who had believed that keeping their heads down was the best way to survive the Sinhala renaissance, began to rethink their lives. My parents were typical of them.

Those who thought they knew Donald Ratnarajah Alagiah regarded him as a model civil servant. In the Ceylon of the 1950s this meant that though he was a Tamil, he was not militantly so. In the Public Works Department at Ratmalana on the outskirts of the capital, Colombo, he was as popular with Sinhalese colleagues as he was with other Tamils. Indeed, having set up an informal loan scheme for PWD labourers, most of whom were Sinhalese, my father was something of a bridge between the two communities – at least as far as his workplace was concerned.

He had become an engineering apprentice in the department in 1943 and moved along quite smoothly under the watchful eye of one Tom Burns who, at that time, was chief engineer, Design. Burns was a Scotsman, one of those no-nonsense, avuncular types who made it tempting to think of colonialism as an essentially benevolent, if occasionally flawed enterprise, rather in the way that Ronnie Biggs gave highway robbery a pleasant, albeit somewhat rakish face. The truth, of course, is that kind people cannot disguise colonialism's true nature any more than Ronnie Biggs' ebullient disposition can hide the enormity of the crime he committed. Colonialism, whatever mask it wore, was about power and control over people who were never given the chance to say whether they wanted to be colonised or not.

My father would not necessarily agree with this. Respect, even a fondness, for the individuals he encountered made him more tolerant than you might expect. 'The Britishers', as he used to call them until he heeded our embarrassed corrections, 'were only behaving in a way that was right at that time. We would have done the same if the boot had been on the other foot.'

He has another theory about colonialism that I much prefer. This one has the gratifying whiff of comeuppance about it. 'Anyway, we're the ones who are doing the colonising now,' he says. Do I detect the tiniest smile, just a hint of self-satisfaction as he utters these words? 'What do you think is happening when all the corner shops and pharmacies in England are run by Patels from Gujarat? Look at how all the petrol stations in London are run by Tamil boys. This is reverse colonisation.'

The day the curse of Seniveratne cast its ugly shadow over the capital and my family was a working day, and Donald Alagiah looked the part in baggy white shorts that hovered just above the knee and white socks, folded over once, just under the knee. A starched white shirt, open-collared, with a fountain pen peeping out of the breast pocket, finished off the ensemble.

For British colonial civil servants all over the world, so much of it still coloured pink, these clothes were virtually a uniform. And very fetching they looked on the burly frame of the kind of Brit

who'd played in the first XV at his old, but minor, public school
back home. Men with calf muscles that stretched their long socks,
and forearms to match. As the young and aspiring locals worked
their way up the ranks it seemed only natural that they should
adopt the sartorial style of their colonial bosses, but no one
seemed to notice, or dared mention, that the kit looked faintly
ridiculous when the voluminous shorts delivered no more than a
pair of delicate little Asian legs. Nevertheless it remained the
dress of choice long after the stocky old colonials returned home
to Britain.

The day, then, began like any other. There had been news on
the 'wireless' about the riots in the interior but Colombo seemed
to have escaped the madness. My father set off early, having
arranged to drop off his car for a service. The garage owner's son
gave him a lift the rest of the way, an uneventful journey across
town to the PWD's Waterworks Department. He was, as it turned
out, very lucky. Other Tamils who arrived for work were full of
tales of harassment and worse. Anyone who sounded or looked
like a Tamil was being singled out for a thorough beating.
Sinhalese thugs were patrolling bus stops and train queues in
search of their prey.

Ethnic hatred comes with a ready-made checklist of signs that
identify the enemy. Years later, Rwandan Tutsis, Kosovan
Albanians and South African blacks would all tell me how they,
too, were persecuted for the way they looked. Tamils tend to be
darker and shorter than the Sinhalese. In a mixed crowd, they
keep themselves to themselves, fearful that their very demeanour
might expose them. The trick, of course, is not to be caught alone.
Knowing who is a Tamil is just as important to Tamils themselves.
In a throng you can gravitate towards your kind. Safety in
numbers. To this day, despite my peripatetic upbringing, I can
spot another Tamil across a room.

The Sinhalese hot-heads made their preliminary selection on
the basis of colour, moving on to other defining characteristics

once they had got their man. One of my father's Sinhalese colleagues was subjected to this filtering process. He was unusually
dark for a Sinhalese; dark enough, that is, to be mistaken for a
Tamil. His car was stopped by a group of youths who'd set up a
roadblock, one of many that had sprung up around Colombo. His
panic-stricken claims to a pure Sinhalese blood-line cut no ice.
Only his last-ditch and, in retrospect, inspired rendition of a
Buddhist *gutha* – roughly equivalent to a Christian hymn – saved
him from the beating being meted out to other hapless Tamils.
Tamils tended to be Hindus or, like us, Christians – certainly not
Buddhists.

This colour prejudice was not the exclusive province of
Sinhalese troublemakers. Matchmakers – both Tamil and
Sinhalese – were also, apparently, of the opinion that a dark skin
was inferior. A fair-skinned child, especially a girl, was assured a
somewhat easier ride when it came to finding a partner. Our more
traditional relatives would, I am told, look with some sadness at
my eldest sister, who is the darkest in our family. I might add that
she also happens to be one of the most beautiful women I know.

My mother was lucky that day, too. While hundreds of people
were being picked on for simply looking Tamil, she and her sister
Lily, who had gone to the *pettah* to buy a sari, were saved precisely
because they were obviously Tamil. They were both wearing a
potoo – a round dot of richly coloured powders pasted on to the
forehead – a Tamil habit. A sympathetic shopkeeper, noticing
their *potoos*, suggested that they might be better off doing their
shopping another day.

Back at the Waterworks Department on the other side of town,
the anxious engineers and clerks looked out of their windows. By
noon, telltale plumes of black smoke signalled the escalation of
the violence from intimidation to beating to the destruction of
goods and property.

Much of that afternoon was spent trying to work out how the
Tamils were going to get home. Sinhalese workers were sent off in

PWD vehicles as scouts. Their reports were not reassuring. One group had seen a Tamil they knew, a supplier of water pipes, lying in the gutter with his stomach cut open. They had been too scared to try to bring the man in. Calls to the police were being ignored. The prime minister, Solomon Bandaranaike, had not yet declared a state of emergency. The riots were to go on for two days and nights before the authorities took any decisive action.

As the afternoon wore on and the prospect of a dark and dangerous evening loomed, it was clear that the Tamils would have to be smuggled out. It was time to call in old favours. Wijenathan, one of the Tamils at the PWD, had a brother who was a lawyer, a man who had defended numerous Sinhalese, including one or two who had more than a fleeting acquaintance with Colombo's criminal classes. He agreed to organise a rescue mission.

Wijenathan's brother sent over his Humber Hawk, a fittingly ostentatious vehicle for a well-to-do lawyer. Three men came with the car, all of them Sinhalese. One was the driver; the other two were there just in case. They had taken the precaution of changing into red shirts. Red was the colour of revolution and many of the thugs were wearing some red garment or other. The men in the car hoped to pass as sympathisers if they were stopped.

The most brutal regimes often hide behind a show of revolutionary zeal. And the colour they choose as the badge of their radical credentials is nearly always red. A few years back I made a TV documentary on the systematic killing of students and intellectuals in Ethiopia during the 1970s. Mengistu Haile Mariam, then the leader of the self-styled revolutionary government, went as far as calling his campaign against the intellectuals the Red Terror. He launched this vile killing spree with a speech during which he smashed a bottle of blood on the parade ground (at least, that's what the rent-a-crowd in Addis Ababa thought it was when the red liquid splashed across the tarmac).

The hoodlums on Colombo's streets knew little about politics let alone revolution. They had mayhem on their minds, and wearing red was simply part of the costume.

Wijenathan and my father sat in the back between their red-shirted escorts, who took the window seats. As the Humber headed north towards our home they could see people being dragged out of buses and hammered. Whenever they got close to the action they cheered and shouted the right slogans. When in Rome . . .

At home we waited for my father. We lived in a rented house in Dehiwala in what one might politely describe as a modest neighbourhood, the kind of place that government servants could afford to live in. Though ethnically mixed, its defining feature was that most of the families in the area were Christians. The Catholic church was just down the road. In these early skirmishes between Tamils and Sinhalese, religion trumped ethnicity when it came to people's allegiances. Our neighbour across the road was Sinhalese. He came round to our house with a whistle. 'If anyone comes to your door, just blow hard. I'll watch out from my place. My gun is loaded,' he told my anxious mother.

I was three at the time, oblivious of the politics of hatred but, no doubt, conscious of the fear that was creeping around our home. My elder sisters knew something sinister was happening. They could hear the shouts of a crowd on the main road and knew the voices were raised in anger. But more telling was the look on my mother's face, her eyes betraying the fear she tried to hide with consoling words. There was no telephone. That would have been a luxury then. All we could do was wait: for the noise to die down, for my father to return, for the rage to ebb away.

Twenty-five miles east of Colombo, on the Kandy road, another aunt, Rose, was the only Tamil member of staff on the premises of the Holy Cross Convent where she taught. The school was in Gampaha, a very Sinhalese area. All the lay staff had been sent home. Auntie Rose was the only one left because the nuns thought it was too dangerous for her to try to get to Colombo. Worried that the thugs might search the teachers' quarters, the nuns waited till dark before taking her across the compound to the now-empty postulants' hostel. There she remained, blinds drawn, for a couple of days. Never has the rosary been recited with greater fervour.

My aunt in Gampaha, my mother at home in Dehiwala and my father at work in Ratmalana. One family but, on this day, separate and alone: three people caught in the web of hatred that had been spun around the city. When, finally, they were reunited, each knew that that day in May had changed their lives. My parents realised that it was time to get out. Only the how and when was uncertain. In the end it took three years for the right opportunity to present itself.

In May 1961, my father was on a tour of outlying stations. By now he had acquired the somewhat grand title of executive engineer, Maintenance and was responsible for water supply outside the capital.

He'd stopped in Anuradhapura, a city in the north-west which, for a thousand years, had been the seat of the Sinhala kings who ruled the island from about 400BC. Lunch was being served at the new government rest house, the old one, though it offered an unhindered view of the ancient ruins, being considered inferior. Just beyond the old rest house were the huge and ancient reservoirs that fed the irrigation system of a lost civilisation. The men from the PWD, men like my father, were the descendants of a long line of engineers that stretched back two millennia.

As he waited for his rice and curry – standard fare, whether the meal was being served in the morning, at noon or at night – the rest house keeper brought him a copy of that morning's *Ceylon Daily News*. The headline saw my father abandoning the rest of his trip and heading home. Three words in bold type – 'RIGHT TO

RETIRE' – would change the course of his life in ways he probably didn't even begin to understand at the time.

The 'right to retire' was the latest of a series of legislative measures enacted by post-independence governments, all of them Sinhalese-dominated, aimed at redressing the perceived imbalance between the island's two main ethnic groups. Taken together, they represented a formidable and systematic programme of social engineering.

In those post-independence days, Tamils made up about 18 per cent of the population. In fact the figure is not very different today. Yet, as is so often the case with minorities, there was a preponderance of Tamils in the higher echelons of the civil service. The Waterworks Department of the PWD was typical: the top six civil servants there were all Tamils. Their names were a giveaway: Rasiah, Loganathan, Peruminar, Alagiah, Wijenathan and Saravanabavan.

In Sri Lanka, or Ceylon as it was then, as in many other countries, you can make all sorts of assumptions about a person just from knowing his name. It's a bit like a signet ring on the little finger of a certain kind of Englishman – a tiny bit of jewellery that reveals a mountain of information about class and breeding. Those six names at the head of the PWD telephone directory, including my father's, were decidedly Tamil.

The reason you will be given for the high number of Tamils at the top levels of the civil service depends on who you ask. The Tamils will tell you that it is because they work hard and place more importance on the value of a good education. There is some truth in this. Sinhalese will tell you it's because the Tamils sucked up to the colonial masters and were rewarded with the plum jobs. There is some truth in this, too. After all, Ceylon would not be the only country where the British applied their tried and tested policy of divide and rule.

But there is – dare I say it – also a little something in the gene pool. There is a certain earnestness about Tamils, just as there is a certain breeziness about the Sinhalese. In a world of caricatures the Tamil would live in a shack and save all his money for a rainy day while the Sinhalese would live in a mansion he could not afford and not worry about the consequences.

There's a joke that illustrates the point: a Sinhalese man looks in the mirror one morning and notices a receding hairline. From then on he massages his scalp with various medicinal oils, consults a *vedamathaya*, a native doctor, and combs his hair to hide the bald patch. Across the road, his Tamil neighbour looks in the mirror and notices that he, too, is suffering from the same affliction. 'I won't be needing my comb much longer,' he says to himself. 'I wonder how much my brother would pay me for it?'

Although the rhetoric of unity and nation-building was much to the fore in the run-up to independence in 1948, the business of asserting Sinhala goals began pretty much straight away, despite the fact that some Tamil politicians had played a prominent role in the political agitation that led to Ceylon's independence. The United National Party, which formed the island's first government under prime minister Don Senanayake, included some Tamil politicians, but it turned out to be far from united and not very national in character.

One of its most significant and divisive legacies was the so-called resettlement scheme, whereby vast amounts of government money were pumped into projects to settle Sinhalese people on land bordering historically Tamil areas. The government called the building of houses and irrigation dams 'progress'; Tamils saw it as a thinly veiled attempt to tamper with the demography of the country.

By now, any Sinhalese readers might well be seething with indignation. They will doubtless see my interpretation of history as little more than Tamil propaganda. But if so, they miss the point: I have not set out to write the authoritative account of Sri Lanka's history, nor do I claim objectivity. All I'm trying to do is to explain why my family left and how it came to be that even the uncertainties of life in Africa seemed a better bet than what appeared to be in store for us in the country of our birth. Perception is everything. Whichever way you argue it, whatever perspective you impose on history, one thing is undeniable: thousands of Tamils were worried enough by what was happening in Ceylon to pack their bags and get out.

If there is room for debate over the exact nature of that first post-independence government, there is little doubt about the purpose of the one that followed. Solomon West Ridgeway Dias Bandaranaike sought office on an explicit pledge to give his people, the Sinhalese, their day in the sun. Bandaranaike was a nationalist *par excellence*, though this was not a role that came, shall we say, naturally to him. He had been educated at Oxford and was noted for his Western habits. Once back in Ceylon, he converted to Buddhism and adopted native dress in his quest for votes.

How amusing (or satisfying, from a colonial point of view) that this scion of the Sinhala cause should be saddled with names that bore such eloquent testimony to the country's history of subjugation. I assume he owed the first three to British dominance and the fourth to the Portuguese. Only the Dutch seem to have missed out. Many Sri Lankans have to cope with at least one foreign name handed down by their parents in the misguided belief that it was the civilised thing to do. As a result our given and family names symbolise the tensions that dominate so many colonised lives; the attempt to build a bridge from one culture to another without falling into the ravine in the middle in the process. It's the same for the migrant: heritage pulls you in one direction, assimilation in the other.

Even the way our names are ordered has been changed to accommodate Western customs. According to Tamil culture my father would be styled thus: Alagiah (his father's name) Donald (Christian name) Ratnarajah (given surname). This was apparently far too complicated for colonised Ceylon, so Donald Ratnarajah Alagiah is how he was addressed.

At election rallies Bandaranaike boasted of how, within twenty-four hours of taking office, he would establish Sinhalese as the official language of the country. Till then, English had been the language of government and commerce. Once in power, he set about delivering his commitment to Sinhala supremacy with alarming dedication. He duly made Sinhala the official language and, just in case anyone had any doubts about his intentions, he appointed Buddhism (the most common faith among Sinhalese) virtually, though not entirely, the state religion. At a stroke Tamils felt disenfranchised which, I suppose, is precisely what Mr Bandaranaike had in mind.

Up to that point my father had been taking Sinhala lessons and made a point of writing to Sinhalese colleagues in the out stations in their native language. After this he gave up the lessons and reverted to English in his correspondence. It was an early, if gentle, hint of the process of radicalisation that would eventually lead otherwise peace-loving and sane Tamils to believe that the indiscriminate violence of Tamil terrorists was justifiable.

Mr Bandaranaike eventually fell victim to the assassin's bullet, and it was his wife who was responsible for the particular piece of legislation that sent my family scurrying for cover in West Africa. Mrs Sirimavo Bandaranaike went into politics with very little in the way of political experience. But she did have one attribute that her opponents envied and could never emulate: she was a widow. Nothing galvanises an already partisan electorate like the sight of a tearful woman whose only wish is to finish off the work of a husband cut down in his prime. Mrs Bandaranaike duly won the election in 1960, becoming in the process the first woman to head a government. She it was who passed the 'right to retire' law that my father read about as he waited for his steaming white rice and beef curry at the Anuradhapura rest house.

A sleepless, sweaty night convinced my father that this was the chance he'd been waiting for. He abandoned the rest of his circuit and returned to Colombo, where my mother, a prudent and cautious woman, was greeted with the words no prudent and cautious woman wants to hear from her husband: 'Darling, I'm packing it all in.' By the next day he had handed in his notice to the PWD.

It was a clever piece of work, this 'right to retire' law. There was nothing coercive about it. On the contrary, it was an offer: it gave Tamils the opportunity to retire early with full benefits. And as a further sweetener, Mrs B. threw in an extra five years' pensionable service. The aim was to thin out the Tamils in the civil service to make room for more Sinhalese. It worked. Donald Ratnarajah Alagiah was probably the first Tamil to retire from the PWD under the new dispensation (it's difficult to imagine anyone else being quite as precipitate). In the years to come, thousands more who worked in the public sector would do the same.

It worked for two reasons. On the face of it, Tamils were being offered a generous package. And remember, no one spots a good deal like a Tamil. But the subliminal message was the more telling. By going to such great lengths to entice Tamils out of government service, Mrs Bandaranaike was making it clear that there was little future for them within it.

Ghana had been on my parents' minds for some time. My father's cousin, Thirugnanam Kathiravelupillai, also a civil engineer, had already gone out there and his reports had been encouraging. Ghana, he wrote back, was a place where you could build a future. The feeling, it seems, was mutual. So pleased was the fledgling Ghanaian government with its recruits from Sri Lanka that within a couple of months of the announcement of the right-to-retire policy, representatives of Ghana's own PWD (like Ceylon's, a legacy of the British) were being sent out to Colombo to look for more staff.

So it was that Donald Alagiah came to sit across the table from a Mr C. K. Annan, chief executive of Ghana's Water Department. Imagine, just for a minute, the rich symbolism of this meeting.

Here, in this air-conditioned room at the Ghana High Commission in Colombo, one tiny component of a changing world order was being put in place. An African was recruiting an Asian. There was no white man at the table mediating between his erstwhile charges. Indeed, the whole point of the exercise was to ensure that the colonial classes would never again hold sway. The new order was asserting itself over the old.

C. K. Annan was impressed enough to offer my father a job. 'When can you start?' he asked.

'Any time,' replied my father with the urgency of a man who had already given up his job and had a wife and five children to support.

There runs through Asian society a thick vein of racism, and Ceylon in the late fifties and early sixties was no exception. Colour, as I said earlier, was, and still is, an issue, and the caste system tended to reflect this. The low-caste Tamil man who used to come to our house to slop out the contents of our latrine was blacker than most Africans. Add to this entirely home-grown aversion to dark skin the imported prejudices of colonial literature and practice, and you have a pretty solid foundation for some alarmingly racist ideas.

My grandmother, Ammamma, we called her, was typical. 'At least leave the children here,' she pleaded when my parents broke the news of our impending departure for Ghana. 'Why do you want to take them all that way just to be eaten by the *karpili*?' She was serious. Cannibalism, not career advancement, was what Africa meant to her. The nearest translation of *karpili* would be the word *kaffir*, which many white South Africans used (and still do, though *sotto voce* nowadays) when referring to their black countrymen.

Others took a more sanguine view of the enterprise. 'Little brother, you'll be earning more than the perm. sec. gets here,' was the reaction of my father's eldest brother, Archibald.

While my mother's parents seem to have had an uncontrollable

desire to call their children after flowers – I had an Auntie Daisy
as well as Lily and Rose – my father's demonstrated an inexplica-
ble obsession with names ending in '-bald'. Archibald was
followed by Theobald, and when my father was born, my paternal
grandparents, apparently stumped, had intended to name him
Donaldbald. Happily for him, they were persuaded that since
Donald already contained three letters of their favourite suffix
they might as well leave it at that. But they found it a difficult
habit to break and a fourth son, who sadly died in infancy, was
duly named Haribald.

Friends and colleagues, too, were interested in my father's
enhanced potential as a breadwinner. In those days, and even
more so now, having a relative outside the country was a bit like
winning the lottery. It meant the prospect of money flowing into
the family coffers. All those debts that could be paid off, the
stream of imported goods, the dowries that could be funded in the
hope of a better catch.

People's responses revealed their own visions of what life in a
newly independent African state would be like. My Aunt Lily and
her husband, Lawrence, were the most worldly-wise in the family.
Uncle Lawrence worked in the commercial sector. As a rising
star in Carson Cumberbatch, a trading company established in
colonial times, he moved in circles my parents didn't get close to.
Auntie Lily's job was to sort out my mother's wardrobe, such as it
was. 'Acca,' she said, using a term of respect for an elder sister, 'you
have to wear slacks. You can't be running around in saris there.'
And so it was that my mother showed the shape of her legs for the
first time in her adulthood. She bought those tight-fitting, tapered
precursors to leggings, the ones with the little loops at the ends to
slip under your feet.

Uncle Lawrie took Dad to the tailor and had him kitted out in
white dinner jacket, dress trousers and cummerbund. It turned out
to be a case of getting all dressed up with nowhere to go.
Although my parents enjoyed a full social life when they

eventually got to Ghana, it was hardly at the kind of places that insisted on dress suits.

With all this talk of more money and sophisticated wardrobes you can imagine how it was that we, the children, began to conjure up the vision of Ghana as a sort of paradise.

The last week or so was devoted to a tour of the country as we bade farewell to our relatives. All seven of us piled into my father's car, a black Morris Oxford, registration number EY1391. It had one of those split windscreens at the front and an indicator that popped out like a finger from the side. Advertisements for the model used to boast about its 'fingertip steering'. Ours was, however, eleven years old and had rather lost its much-vaunted lightness of touch.

The journey to the east, the largely Tamil region where my parents had grown up, took the best part of a day. All I remember of it is a succession of meals. This was competitive hospitality, with each family trying to outdo the last. When all the lunch and dinner slots were accounted for, my parents accepted invitations to breakfast. Imagine a day's intake. Egg pancakes, *kiri-bath* (milk rice), *lunu-miris* (chili relish) and fried fish in the morning. For lunch there would be mutton curry, chicken curry, *pittu* (layers of steamed flour and coconut flakes) and boiled rice. And to finish off in the evening devilled crab curry, prawn *sodhi* (soup), brinjal *pahee* (ratatouille) and *iddi-appam* (steamed vermicelli coils).

Protest was pointless. To have refused any one of these courses would have been a snub to our hosts. The women of the house hovered around the table, watching over our shoulders, ladles of curry or rice at the ready. 'Eat, will you, child,' they insisted. It might sound like an invitation but it was more of an order.

The highlight of the trip was a visit to one of my father's cousins, who was married to Rasiah Muthiah, a great bull of a man and prosperous with it. Here was a Tamil who had made it. Rasiah was an overseer. He held the local contract for maintaining PWD roads and buildings. He had a 'modern' house, a codeword that signified it had a flush toilet. Though we lived in the capital we had yet to enjoy the convenience of such sewerage. In Rasiah's kitchen there was a fridge, something my parents only dreamed of owning. The house itself was opposite the Hindu temple in Batticaloa, a prime location if ever there was one. Rasiah drove a huge American Chevrolet which he'd had converted to run on paraffin, cheaper than petrol at the time. Just think of it: so important that he could change the way an American car worked. That's how it seemed to us.

All this and more would be ours, we told ourselves, when we got to Africa. With that thought uppermost in our minds, we gathered at Ratmalana Airport in Colombo. It was November 1961. The whole extended family was there: grandparents, uncles, aunts, cousins and second cousins. Friends and work colleagues showed up, too. One of the reasons Asian airports are always so overcrowded is that there are always at least ten people there to see off every passenger.

Even Ammamma, who had virtually stopped speaking to my mother after being told of our departure, broke her silence. She was there too, the matriarch fussing over the grandchildren who were being taken away to God knows what sort of fate.

Everybody hugged and kissed everyone else, the women weeping openly, the men swallowing hard, forcing down the emotions to which their wives gave vent. I moved from one auntie to the next, my face buried in a mixture of sari cloth and bare midriff. I remember the heady cocktail of smells: cheap eau de cologne, talcum powder and nervous perspiration.

And then it was time to board the plane, an Air Ceylon DC3 that would take us to our first stop, Madras. From Madras to Bombay, then Rome; from Rome to Cairo, and finally to Accra. Stepping-stones to a new life.

2

A Passage to Africa

The Ceylon government's travel allowance for emigrants was the equivalent of £3 2s per person in sterling. Today it would be about £60. Not a lot on which to start a new life.

There were two other Tamil families on the plane in similar circumstances. They were also bound for Ghana. The Subramaniams had two daughters, and Mr Subramaniam was unusually fair – for a Tamil, I mean. That colour thing again. Then there was Mr Gunaratnam, his wife and two children, also both girls. Gunam, as my parents called him, was reassuringly dark. The other thing I remember about Mr Gunaratnam was the way he habitually ran his tongue along the bottom of his top teeth. The procedure seemed to start somewhere in the region of his molars and culminate in the periodic appearance of his pink and fleshy tongue out of the corner – always the same corner – of his mouth. I spent most of the flight to Madras, which in those days would have taken about three hours, trying to work out what it was he was chewing, and then, when I realised it was his tongue, wondering whether he had an itch on it.

Gunaratnam and Subramaniam were engineers too. They specialised in irrigation, my father in water supply. Together they represented a trickle of talent that would grow into a full-scale brain-drain. We were all part of the beginning of the Tamil diaspora. And virtually every man who left was a professional: a doctor, a teacher, an engineer – I say man because, in those days, there were very few, if any, Tamil women who emigrated on their own account.

So worried was the Ceylonese government when it realised what a haemorrhage of talent it had unleashed that, just three weeks before we left the country, it had impounded our passports. We only got them back after the Ghanaian High Commissioner in Colombo lodged a formal complaint. It was a telling episode. Having to seek the help of an African government to sort out a mess created by your own rammed home the sense of alienation felt by so many Tamils.

Over the next decade or so literally thousands of Tamil families left the island. As word spread and old favours were called in, more and more found jobs abroad. Such was the demand that what was an escape for Tamils became a boom for the travel industry as travel agents started wooing them with special offers. All of a sudden clerks who were more used to booking passengers on the overnight sleeper to Jaffna, the Tamil heartland in the north of the country, found themselves having to price tickets to places like Accra, Lusaka and Lagos. They would discover these previously unknown capitals in Africa.

All over the African continent at this time, in country after country, the last bugle of empire was sounding. Down came the flag, up went the white-gloved salutes. Pretty soon it became like a play you saw over and over again: the script remained the same, and only the actors changed. The once-reviled nationalist leader, usually with a few years in jail behind him, would, with great magnanimity, embrace (metaphorically if not physically) the departing governor who, in turn, would behave as if this was exactly what Britain had hoped for all along when it had overrun the territory all those years previously. The pale-skinned wives of the colonial servants would sit under canvas awnings, fanning themselves with freshly printed copies of the independent country's new national anthem. Women who had once had nightmares about the passions the nationalist leader was stirring up now began to talk about him fondly as the 'old man'. Dr Kwame Nkrumah of Ghana was the first leading man in this play. A generation later, Nelson Mandela would perform the same role, to rave reviews.

At the end of the last act came the exit of the colonials. The real purpose of all the pomp and ceremony was simply to try to find an elegant way to retreat, to head home to Britain. That, after all, was the point of the exercise. As E. M. Forster put it in *A Passage to India*, his refreshingly honest account of colonialism on another continent, 'Soon they would retire to some suburban villa, and die exiled from glory.'

But now who would run the ministries? How would the roads be maintained? Where were the doctors who would ensure health for all? That is where the migrant professionals came in – Indians, Poles, Filipinos, Ceylonese and Czechs. A new breed of British came, too. But they were different. These were the expats, the technical advisers who worked with the local government rather than for it. The distinction was crucial, not least in terms of prestige and remuneration.

So Britain's loss was, without question, our gain. Ghana needed us. Tamil professionals could do the jobs left behind by the Brits unencumbered by colonial baggage. Tamils were ideal employees: they weren't going to rock the boat. There would be no attitude problem when the new bosses started giving their orders. Do the work and bank the money was the Tamils' philosophy.

First stop for our Air Ceylon DC3 was Madras (now Chenai),

the capital of Tamil Nadu which, as its name implies, is home to a large population of Tamils, some 50 million, in fact. None of us had ever set foot outside Ceylon but Madras had a comforting sense of familiarity about it. They speak a different dialect of Tamil there, close enough, though, to make communication possible.

However, it wasn't communication so much as barter that my parents were interested in. With impending cash-flow problems in mind – all we had to last us was that modest travel allowance – they had brought along some desirable goodies. It was, apparently, well known in Ceylon that Indians were keen on malt drinks like Ovaltine and Horlicks, a taste made all the keener for the fact that these were not available on their side of the Palk Strait, the 20-mile-odd stretch of water that separates the teardrop of Ceylon from its giant neighbour. India, in those days, had far more stringent regulations on what could be imported. So bottles of these quintessentially colonial night-time beverages were handed over to sundry hotel staff in return for Indian rupees which, in turn, paid for our hotel expenses at our first staging-post en route to Africa.

Next stop was Bombay. The plane approached the airport after dark. None of us had ever flown over a city at night. Come to think of it, none of us, except perhaps my father, had ever been on a plane at all. Beneath us were a thousand twinkling lights, like the candles lining the temple grounds back home, but on a scale we could never have imagined: a huge carpet of lights that stretched out into the unseen horizon. Darkness robs you of a sense of proportion, makes everything seem distant, far away, mysterious. There's no point of reference for the mind's compass, nothing to latch on to, nothing visible about which you could ever genuinely say: 'Ah, but that's just like the one at home.'

For my parents this was a moment of revelation. The way my father tells it, it was here, hanging over this hidden city, that for the first time the sheer scale of the gamble he had taken really hit him. He looked across the aisle at my mother and was met by a wordless reflection of the knot of panic that had struck him. The precariousness of the enterprise seemed all the greater as the DC3 was buffeted this way and that, rising and falling on a trade wind that might have come all the way from the eastern shores of Africa.

Bombay was an international airport. Here we would make our connection with a Transworld Airlines plane bound for Cairo, and the rules about what the airline was willing to pay for would change. Our overnight stay at a hotel would be courtesy of TWA. Or at least, it would have been if any of our party had had the nerve to claim the complimentary hospitality.

'The hotel shuttle will take you into town,' said TWA's rep at the airport, words that had reassured thousands of passengers before and millions since. 'Don't worry,' replied my father, with studied nonchalance, mentally calculating what would be left of his meagre funds after paying for accommodation for a family of seven, 'we'll just while away the time here.' The Subramaniams and Gunaratnams had reached the same conclusion, everybody making it sound for all the world as if laying a troupe of irritable children to sleep on airport-hard benches was just the kind of thing they'd been looking forward to.

Whenever I think back to this scene at Bombay Airport I am amazed at how people who were too diffident to query overnight arrangements for a flight to Accra could have had the courage to consider moving to Africa in the first place. The truth is that my parents were timid travellers driven more by the need to escape rather than the desire to arrive. From the moment we set foot on the plane, everything we did, we did for the first time.

It's difficult to convey how awesome the obstacles seemed when travel has become such a mundane business these days. Even fastening a seatbelt represented a skill to be mastered. The belt is stuck, twisted around the arm rest. Pulling is no good, you've got to unwind it. Quick! The steward is coming down the aisle! He's checking every single person, making sure they know how to do this. Everyone else seems to be able to do it, why can't I? There, it's free. But now the two ends won't reach across. I can't click the buckle into place. Oh God, the pilot won't take off if I don't get this right. I mustn't look up – all the other passengers are staring at me. That was me, that was us.

Each leg of our journey to Africa took us further away from what we knew and closer to something we could only imagine. The greater the distance we were from home, the more powerful was the urge to huddle close, to hold tight to the one thing we were sure of – the family. So a night at Bombay Airport was solace, not hardship. The two youngest girls slept on a *jamakalam*, a rug, spread on the floor. I was where I was always most secure and comfortable, my head on my mother's lap, cosseted in the silk-soft folds and pleats of her sari. The two elder girls were curled up in their chairs. My father paced up and down the departure hall, holding off the exhaustion that threatened to overwhelm him. Now, this was familiar. This was like old times. This we had done before on any number of railway platforms in Ceylon.

By the time our plane touched down in Rome we were old hands at the travelling game. It is incredible how quickly and comprehensively people absorb and accept what was once strange and new. During the flight my father had found out what he'd been too shy even to ask about before: that the hotel stay in Bombay had, indeed, been free of charge. It would be the same in Rome. Armed with this information the three Tamil families disembarked in Rome determined to make up for their reticence in Bombay.

The airline official at the airport went through the arrangements for the rest of our trip to Accra. His remarks were addressed to the three men in English – at least, they thought it was English. They all nodded in unison, grinning inanely, before turning to each other. 'Can't understand what the fellow was saying, something about being at the desk pronto,' said Mr Subramaniam.

'Anyway, where the devil is Pronto?' asked my father.

'Give me the tickets, will you?' Gunam called to his wife. They pored over the itinerary, compared it with what they thought the man had said and worked out that it was going to be an early start in the morning. The one thing everyone was clear about was that there would be taxis to take us to the airport.

We checked into our hotel in the city. The Gunaratnams and Subramaniams got a 'family' room each. We, the Alagiahs, were given two adjoining rooms. Another night beckoned. But who could sleep? Our first night in Europe. All three families congregated in the biggest room. We played hide and seek – in between turning the taps on and off. How strange the taps seemed, all silver and shiny. The ones at home were a brass colour. And you got hot water out of these. 'How many times have I told you not to waste the hot water?' my mother shouted, to no avail. I remain convinced that my subsequent and long-lasting frugality with hot water stems from these formative moments in a three-star hotel room in Rome. When we were not playing hide and seek, or turning the taps on and off, we were lying on the fitted carpets. What luxury compared to the straw mats in Ceylon!

The men were getting bored. They were also beginning to get cocky. It is always a lethal combination in the male of the species.

'Shall we get a bit of fresh air?' suggested Subramaniam. What he meant, of course, was: 'I'm getting tired of all this noise, let's get the hell out of here.'

'Yes, why not?' my father agreed. 'We could get some fruit or something for the children.' Offering to do something for the children is the oldest ploy in the book, but that has never stopped men from using it. My mother, like all women, did not so much fall for it as indulge it.

'We'll be back soon,' promised Gunam, weaving a path between umpteen bags and children.

And then they were gone. And they stayed gone, hour after hour. At first it was treated as something of a joke. 'My! Knowing those fellows, they must have got lost by now,' said Mrs Gunaratnam. But mirth soon gave way to impatience and impatience to blind panic as it dawned on the women that something had, indeed, gone badly wrong. Their worst fears were confirmed when the telephone rang and the caller said something about a taxi. It was time to go. Where on earth were the men?

As it turned out, they were not so very far away. In fact they were finally located in one of the other rooms. Physically close but otherwise, well, they were not altogether with it. The search for fresh air had ended rather abruptly with the acquisition of a flagon of cheap Chianti. It was a strange purchase given that none of them were particularly keen drinkers, and they were certainly not used to wine. In fact my father was virtually a teetotaller. But, as I said, having finally availed themselves of a night in a hotel free of charge, all three had been in robust mood. One glass had led to another, one hour had turned into two, each story had been capped by a better one until the whole thing melted together, leaving them with only a dim awareness of the task in hand.

It was a very ashamed and decidedly wobbly species of Tamil manhood that was dragged from the hotel room. The bravado of just a few hours earlier was gone, and in its place was meekness bordering on subservience. Like little boys caught with their fingers in the pudding, they tried to make up for their misdemeanour with overexaggerated co-operation in rounding up the troupe.

By the time the whole party got to the hotel lobby even the taxi drivers looked nervous. And when Italian taxi drivers are nervous, you know you're in trouble. It was going to be an extremely close call.

I was only six at the time, but I remember the journey to Rome Airport as if it were yesterday. We drove in convoy, each driver pushing the one in front of him into ever more risky manoeuvres. The whole scene comes back to me like one of those time-lapse photographs of a busy traffic intersection – full of red streaks, a

combination of the brake lights of the car ahead and the red traffic lights our convoy ignored.

My mother's face revealed a battle of emotions, her contempt
for the behaviour of the men duelling with a rising fear that our
journey to a brave new life would end in a mangled heap on a
Roman road. She said nothing, clutching my infant sister to her
bosom as the car, a humble Fiat, lurched from side to side.

I took my cue from her. Those eyes which, when smiling, could
fill me with elation, now imbued me with a sense of foreboding.
Even the surreptitious glances of lovers across a crowded room
cannot convey as much meaning as the exchange of feelings
between a parent and child. Now, as a father, I am studiously
aware that my mood can pass, as if by some osmotic transfer of
thoughts, to my sons. Then, as a child, I received and absorbed my
mother's incipient fear. All the childish anticipation evaporated,
the thrill of travel disappeared. I wanted to be back home, I
wanted to be at the airport, I wanted to be in Ghana – I wanted
to be anywhere but in that car. More than anything, I wanted my
mother to smile for me again.

We made it to the airport. We even made it on to the plane.
We were lucky: the airport staff rushed us through the formalities
and shoved us on to an aircraft that had, fortuitously, been
delayed for some unrelated reason. We would not have been able
to board the plane had it departed on schedule.

And in the morning, as we touched down on African soil, my
mother smiled again. Africa beckoned. Our new life had begun.

3

Land of Milk and Honey

I want you to do me a favour. Before you start reading this chapter, I'd like you to try to forget what you know or think you know about Africa today. If impressions are based on my own reports on some African famine or civil war, set them aside. I want to try to paint a picture of an African country that is full of hope and optimism rather than of the Africa now synonymous with chaos and disaster. In the theatre it's called the suspension of disbelief. You put aside your scepticism and let your imagination run with the plot. Try to do the same now.

All it takes is for us to turn back the clock. Back to December 1961, about the time a Tamil family arrives in the newly independent state of Ghana. It is only four years since it gained its freedom from Britain, the first country in 'black' Africa to shake off the yoke of European colonialism.

Dr Kwame Nkrumah, Ghana's first president, has his critics inside and outside the country but he is, all the same, recognised as a statesman of international standing. The way he managed the transition from colony to nationhood is still fresh in people's minds. As he consolidates his leadership, the first African in modern times to run an African state, he seems to bear the imperial power that once imprisoned him no ill will. Ghana, having been in the front line of the battle for freedom, has a pivotal role in the process of decolonisation.

The Alagiahs arrive in a country still basking in the glory of its achievement. The promise of liberation is there to be fulfilled and the desire to succeed boundless. Everything and anything is possible.

Let's take a drive down to the Ambassador Hotel, the place to be seen. The road is in great condition, the verges neatly trimmed. When you park at the hotel you lock the car, but the action is not the obsession it will later become. Vehicle break-ins aren't a huge problem and the nightwatchman is perfectly reliable. As you walk under the *neem* trees rustling to and fro in the cool evening breeze, you can just hear the brassy sound of 'hi-life' music drifting across from the hotel.

It could be E. T. Mensah and his Tempos Dance Band. What's he playing? Perhaps 'Onipa' which means 'people', sung in the Fanti language of the coast. Or it might be 'Ghana-Guinea-Mali', which celebrates the recent economic union between the three countries. Hardly the stuff for an easy evening on the town, you may think to yourself. But you'd be wrong. The song is not about economics but about unity and destiny, the unity of Africa and the destiny of its people.

Just listen to the words. They're a bit hard to catch at first because Mensah and his band have chosen to sing in pidgin English.

> *Ghana-Guinea-Mali*
> *Africa's strongest foundation.*
> *Soon it will be all Africa*
> *The achievement of our great destiny.*

Africa is now awakened;
That unity can save her.
All leaders of Mother Africa
Are called to join this great union.

Nobody's laughing. There are no hoots of derision from bored and cynical expatriates. The fact is, it seems plausible. The Organisation of African Unity will be formed in a couple of years. It's going to be the first step towards continent-wide unity.

There's just one vacant table on the hotel terrace. It's Friday night. Ghana's new élite is shaking off the burdens of the week and enjoying the fruits of freedom. The waiters are attentive. Their uniforms are crisp and clean. You order a round of Club beers. It's doesn't have the hint of sweetness that is the hallmark of the rival Star beer. Club is brewed here in Accra; Star is brought down from Kumasi, the ancient seat of Ashanti chiefs and the country's second city. Accra, the seat of modern power, and Kumasi, the centre of an older authority – rivals even in the brewing of beer. People say the sharpness of Club beer comes from the quinine they put in it. True or not, that's what every newcomer is told by the old-timers.

There is an eclectic mixture of people here, straight out of those streetside hoardings you see all over the developing world on which companies advertise the good life. Elegance, wealth, confidence are the words they bring to mind. The Ghanaians are carefree and expansive. They have every reason to be. They are proving they can run the country. There's a little talk of corruption, but it has yet to undermine the country. Many of the foreign businessmen who feed this incipient cancer with their dollops of money paid into numbered accounts abroad still think it's all rather amusing. In years to come they will rue the day they ever started this, accusing Africa's sons and daughters of greed and forgetting that their own greed played a part in it all.

But in 1961 the foreign diplomatic missions don't seem to be unduly worried. In fact they are virtually competing to help Ghana. In return, the Ghanaians are happy to see so many expatriates enjoying themselves: resentment at the failed interference of outsiders is a long way in the future. The presence of so many foreigners in their midst is a sign of success, a symbol of just how important their country is to the rest of the world.

For their part, the expatriates exhibit all the enthusiasm of children at a party. And, indeed, it is something of a party for them. The government has yet to start taxing them; there are holidays home every other year if they work for the government and annually if they are employed in the private sector; lazy afternoons by the pool and no one watching over their shoulder in the office. Back home in Britain, in some dreary suburb, there would be all the drudgery of running a house. Here there's someone else to do all that.

There is an English couple with their Ghanaian friends at that table rather too near the band. The Englishman is in banking and his wife is a paid-up member of the leisured classes. She plans to do some charity work eventually but for now she wants to get to know Africa, meet some real Africans. What with the music and the problem of accents, they're finding it just a little bit difficult to understand the Ghanaian couple they've invited out to dinner. The two wives smile at each other. The men contrive a conversation about work that could wait till next week, but they have little else in common. It's not ideal, but these are early days. It's all going to get better, easier. Business is booming and friendship will follow in its wake.

Some Lebanese families have pulled a few tables together. The men wear their shirts open to the third or even fourth button. The gold medallions that sit on their chests, gleaming through the mass of thick, black hair, speak volumes for their business acumen if not for their taste. They are the deal-makers, the buyers and sellers – the people who know how to make serious money in Africa. In *The Heart of the Matter*, Graham Greene called them the Syrians. Their wives are elegant, fragrant. You wonder what they are doing with these men. The Lebanese need so many tables because, unlike the rest of the crowd, they have their children with them. The kids are indulged, running this way and that between the tables. They will not want for anything.

One group of people is conspicuous by its absence – the Asians. There are certainly some of them wealthy enough to afford an evening at the Ambassador: not just in Ghana, but all over Africa, Asian trading families are involved in the retail business. But, in what will prove to be a hallmark of their presence in Africa, they don't flaunt their wealth as ostentatiously as the Lebanese do. The other type of Asians in Africa are the professionals – people like the Alagiahs. But this group, too, keeps itself to itself. Not because of some false modesty, but because its members don't fit in to this new high society. They are at the bottom of the expatriate pile. Most of them work for the government on less favourable terms than those enjoyed by people employed in the commercial sector. This is decidedly not their social *milieu*.

Right in the middle, in the thick of it all is another table of racially mixed couples. But unlike the banking foursome, this lot are having huge fun and are utterly comfortable with each other. There's something about them that strikes you as unusual, though you don't pick it up straight away. And then you see it. All the women are white, mostly with English accents. All the men are black. They are Ghanaians, but have the nonchalant air of those who have lived abroad. These are the men who studied in Britain and who were courted by the British establishment while they were there. They are not intimidated at all by the white women around them. That's because they know them intimately: these are relationships forged in exile. These are lovers who first exchanged glances across the lecture theatres of universities in the UK. One day, not very long from now, the women will talk to each other about how their husbands seemed to change once they were back in their home country. How they became, well, Ghanaian again.

For now, though, they just roll their heads back and laugh. Now is the time to enjoy being in the vanguard. This is the moment to revel in being different, the place to unleash your dreams. This is Africa, and it's jumping. Let's dance.

For me, the earliest evidence of our new, elevated status was the acquisition of our first car in Ghana. In Ceylon, as I've said, my father had driven an old Morris Oxford. We couldn't afford anything brand new here, either, but the choice was a whole lot better.

We were all at home when the phone rang. It was my father to say he'd found the car of his dreams – a Mercedes-Benz. It was a 190D which, I suppose, is a less useful piece of information than the fact that it was shaped like those cars German officers used in Second World War movies. All my mother wanted to know was what colour it was. 'Oh, powder blue,' my father replied, with the confidence of an interior decorator.

So there we were at the bottom of the steps leading up to the front door, waiting for this powder-blue apparition to come up the driveway. 'This car is bigger than Rasiah Uncle's American car,' I told the girls knowledgeably, although I had never been near a Mercedes-Benz before. Our house – a temporary home till we'd found something to rent – belonged to the Water Department, with whom we shared the front drive. It was called simply Mile 4 Rest House. We never did work out where it was four miles away from. There was many a false alarm as sundry government vehicles came and went. And then, at last, crunching the gravel under its wheels, a Mercedes-Benz made its sedate progress towards us. But there was something wrong. There are many ways you could describe the colour of the car my father stepped out of, but powder blue, with its suggestion of a light, pastel hue, was certainly not one of them. Try battleship grey and you'd be nearer the mark.

Our initial disappointment was as palpable as our subsequent joy once we'd opened the doors and clambered in. I can remember something about every car we ever owned as a family, and with this one it was its smell, a mixture of well-worn leather and diesel. In my mind the steering wheel seems as big as a boat's helm. There was an inner chrome wheel attached to it – the horn. I pressed it. Panic at first from my sisters, and then shrieks of delight. We did it again and again.

The racket brought my parents back out of the house, both of them freshened up and at ease with the world. 'Who wants to go for a drive in a Mercedes-Benz?' asked my father with a heavy emphasis on the make of the car.

So off we headed down the airport road, my father driving, my mother and my youngest sister in the front, the rest of us in the back. It was a moment to be freeze-framed; a moment of unalloyed joy. My father seemed as relaxed as he'd ever been, my mother as content as she ever allowed herself to be, my sisters were excited and happy. I just stuck my head out of the window and let Africa's hot, urgent air rush over me.

I can't remember exactly what it was I was thinking about but, as I look back, I know this to have been a life-changing occasion. People talk about knowing exactly what they were doing and thinking the day President Kennedy was shot, or when Nelson Mandela was released from prison. Well, for me, this first drive in our new car is on a par with those momentous events. It sounds ridiculous, but it's true. It marked a subtle but significant shift in my view of the world. What greater proof could there be, for a boy of six, of Africa's vast opportunities than to be driving through its streets in a Mercedes-Benz just days after setting foot on the continent? From this point on I wanted to be identified with this new place. Like the snakes we found in our compound, I was eager to shake off one skin and climb into another.

Many people know how to travel, how to get from A to B.

They're good at the physical process. But their minds often stay put, stuck in the place they have left. It was as true of the English in India who dressed for dinner, just as they would have done at home, in the pre-monsoon heat of the Raj as it is for the lager louts and laddettes who crave nothing more than an ersatz pub when they holiday in Ibiza. The migrant's psychological journey is much less arduous for children. They are more trusting, more open to different experiences. I have watched my own sons transfer their allegiances from England to South Africa and back again without difficulty. For them it is an unconscious, spontaneous shift. For me, too. Seven years later, by the time I was sent off to boarding school in England, I was calling Ghana my home. Not only that, I sounded like a Ghanaian and thought like a Ghanaian. I would come to know more about my adopted country than about the country of my birth.

The learning process started with a man named Charles. Well, to be accurate, he wasn't actually a man and his name wasn't really Charles, but he was, I suppose, my first African friend. In fact, he was my first friend, period.

Charles became our house worker, though in those days he was probably called houseboy. And, in truth, he was a boy. He was sixteen or so when a colleague of my father's brought him to our house.

'Tell the mastah what be your name,' my father's friend said in the broken English most expatriates used to their domestic staff.

'George, sah,' came the reply.

'Oh, we have a George, too,' commented my father, in what he thought was an amusing aside.

'George no good,' said the friend, turning to the bemused teenager. 'There be a George for this house already. He be the small mastah. What be your father's name?'

'Charles, sah.'

'OK, from today Charles be your name. You understand?'

'Yes, sah.'

And that was it, really. From that day, this teenager who for some sixteen years had answered to the name George started responding to the name Charles. It was as simple as that. It makes me cringe now to think that I was the reason an unsuspecting boy looking for a job ended up having his name changed. We talk about it in the family now and again. 'I can't believe you let that happen, Dad,' is my usual line of attack. My father says simply that his friend seemed to know what he was doing.

Today it would be considered outrageous, of course. Anywhere in Africa it would make the newspapers. You can see the first paragraph: 'An expatriate civil engineer will appear before an industrial tribunal today after forcing a house worker to change his name. The employer, a Sri Lankan national with a wife and five children, is believed to have objected to the fact that the house worker had the same name as his only son . . .'

Put in such contemporary terms, it sounds truly ghastly. What can I say? It's not a defence, but things like this were probably happening all over the place a generation ago. I hope Charles was not scarred by the experience. And if he was, I hope he has found it in himself to forgive us. He'd be pushing sixty now. Perhaps he's gone back to calling himself George. For the rest of this chapter, however, he will be Charles, as he was then.

The first thing Charles taught me was how to act like a soldier. He used to perform this little sequence he'd seen in a film. Here's how it went. Charles would stand at the top of the steps leading up to our front door, pretending to be in the back of a military truck. He'd flick an imaginary canvas flap over the top of the truck and peer out. From there he would jump to the ground, landing nimbly, perfectly balanced, with a make-believe gun held ready for action. He'd take one or two careful, deliberate steps. Then: '*Kwa, kwa, kwaaa.*' Enemy fire. Charles would fall to the ground and roll across the sand, firing his gun as he did so. '*Thuthuf, thuf, thuf thuthuf.*' Then he'd grin – a huge, great grin that exposed the big gap between his two front teeth. After that we'd do it together, except that I'd start from one of the lower steps.

I will never forget Charles's face and its gap-toothed grin. It is as clear to me as the faces of my closest friends. His skin was the colour of copper, and his facial features were long. One of the Afrikaners I would meet later in life would have described him thus: 'Naa, man, he was quite fair. And his face was not round like some of these blecks. No, it was long. Not your typical Bantu.'

Charles knew how to dress. He came with us to Sunday mass, shedding the shorts and ill-fitting T-shirts he wore to work and re-emerging from his 'quarters', as we called the two-room annexe in which he lived at the bottom of our garden, resplendent in fine clothes. Tight, slightly shiny drainpipe trousers; a white, long-sleeved shirt. My mother used to say she felt compelled to dress us more grandly than was her inclination for fear of her children looking shabby next to the boy employed to look after them. Best of all was Charles's selection of shoes. My favourites were the white ones. They were pointed and the uppers were a tight lattice of woven leather. He would brush his hair to the front so that it formed a sort of shelf over his forehead. On the collection of African barbers' advertising signs I have at home, the style Charles adopted is known as 'fast-forward'. It just about sums him up: he was fast and he was forward. Just the kind of guy an impressionable Tamil boy would look up to.

Charles was the perfect antidote to the hoary vision of Africans seeded in our minds by the likes of my grandmother. Her African was as black as night with rolling, lascivious eyes. But Charles was the same colour as me and his interest in my sisters was the kind you might expect from an older cousin. So concerned had my parents initially been about the effects of all these girls on Charles's adolescent libido that they employed a series of women to look after them. But none of them matched Charles for energy or imagination and, by a process of elimination, Charles emerged as the prototype male nanny.

My youngest sister, who was just fifteen months old when we arrived in Ghana, probably enjoyed the most intimate relationship with Charles. Jenny took her first steps with him. During the day, while the rest of us were at school or nursery, she was at home with Charles and my mother. And since my mother's mornings were largely taken up with preparing food, it was Charles with whom Jenny spent most of her time, following him around the house as he attended to his chores.

Charles's morning started at seven with tea, bread and jam provided by my mother. At around ten he would take a break for a snack bought from one of the many hawkers who went from house to house selling food. A favourite of his was *kenke* (heavy, slightly sour balls of fermented maize flour steamed in plantain or maize leaves) and smoked fish with a hot relish of chili, onions and tomato on the side. Another was roast plantain and groundnuts. Charles and Jenny would sit opposite each other in the shade of the porch outside the kitchen, their legs spread out in front of them, bare feet touching. The food would be in the middle, on a page of the previous day's *Ghanaian Times*. Every now and then Charles would pull off a bit of *kenke* and hand it to my sister. She would dip it into the hot relish before eating it with gusto.

For those of us at school, the mid-morning break meant pyramid-shaped cartons of chocolate milk. The contents were fantastic to drink but even better to squirt over the girls. Our first school was Christ the King in Accra. It was more or less opposite Flagstaff House, which was in those days the president's office.

The alternatives, it has to be said, were not exhaustive. Among them was the International School. These schools still prosper wherever there is a large concentration of expatriates. They are aimed at foreign parents who like the idea of living somewhere exotic but draw the line at enrolling their children at a school where, heaven forbid, local kids might actually be in the majority. These are the same people who will tell you glibly how they love Africa. What they mean is that they love what Africa stands for in their imaginations, rather than the reality. Like the chattering classes in Western capitals who are right behind the idea of multiculturalism but make sure they live as far away as possible from those parts of the city where the cultures actually mix and, sometimes, clash.

International schools usually make a point of advertising the fact that most of their teachers are trained abroad – a not-so-subtle way of implying that local teachers can't be any good. They are stuffed to the brim with the children of ambassadors, multinational executives and so-called development experts. And always there is a smattering of pupils from the local élite, who end up developing views and accents that are utterly at odds with the nation they are being groomed to run. These are the people Frantz Fanon wrote about, so tellingly, in *Black Skins, White Masks*, his book about the false dawn of decolonisation.

The products of these schools are a part of a new world class – not an upper or lower class, not even middle, but what I like to call the global class. They inhabit a new space outside national boundaries and conventional measures of social standing. Though they may carry the passport of a particular country, their allegiance is more to a way of life, a standard of living. These people are not to be confused with the international jet set, which is made up of those fortunate enough to have come into some serious money. Though comparatively well off, the global class is not necessarily cash-rich.

Whether its members are born in New York or New Delhi, they will have more in common with each other than they will with their kith and kin. When politicians eulogise about the global village they conjure up an image of peoples linked together in some cosy, communal way. Actually, the peasants of South Africa have little, if anything, in common with workers in Sweden. But some people in South Africa – the wealthy and mobile – and some people in Sweden have an awful lot in common.

Don't get me wrong. Christ the King was not exactly your township school. It had plenty of foreign pupils. However, the prevailing ethos was Ghanaian. Many, probably most, of the teachers and the children were Ghanaian. Given income distribution at the time of independence, our Ghanaian classmates certainly belonged to the privileged few. Their parents made up the new and burgeoning African middle class. Many had themselves been educated abroad and had returned to take up pivotal positions in the public services. Their children were born, like me, at or around independence. They were freedom's children, the first generation of boys and girls to start school imbued with the idea that to be African was once again to be free: free of colonialism, and free to choose whatever path their talents suggested.

That, at any rate, was the theory. My passage through Africa some thirty years later as a foreign correspondent would be a chronicle of what freedom's children had made of themselves and their continent. But at the time, as the suffocating walls of subjugation came down, a landscape of unrivalled beauty and unlimited opportunity was revealed. Obviously, that's not how we would have described it as children, but it was the way we felt, the way we were taught to feel. This was the first generation on the continent who could ask their parents: 'What will I be when I grow up?' and be told: 'Whatever you want to be, my child.'

These sentiments were infectious. They had a special appeal to us, Tamils who had escaped the ethnic straitjacket into which the government of Ceylon would have forced us. My parents had left their homeland because they could see that they would not have been able to give the same answer as those Ghanaian parents were giving their children. It was in Ghana and because of Ghana that my parents could do what all parents want to do for their children: allow them to grow unhindered by the curse of ethnicity and unencumbered by the confidence-sapping weight of social derision.

Whatever prejudices I might have brought with me to Ghana evaporated in the classrooms and playgrounds of the various schools I attended over the next seven years. We moved on to the provincial towns of Takoradi and Kumasi before returning to Accra in 1965. There's nothing like a classroom full of bright African kids to dispel any stereotypical notions of the correlation between race and aptitude. I learned very early on that when Mother Nature dispenses talent she does so with a blindfold over her eyes. Indeed, I began to see the Ghanaians as a people blessed by birth and privileged by circumstance.

Our first forays as a family into Accra's city centre confirmed that view. These were exhilarating excursions. It was here, taking turns to push a trolley between the aisles at the Kingsway department store, that we began to realise just how wide was the gulf of opportunity and wealth that we had crossed. It was here that I first ran up and down an escalator. We would dawdle in front of the deli counter, something we'd never heard of before. We'd never tasted ham or salami: now we were presented with umpteen varieties. And shelves full of chocolate bars. Some with nuts, some with raisins, others with both. Was there no end to this country's bounty?

Back in Ceylon we had not been department-store people, we'd been market people. The way we shopped was as good an indicator as any of what Ghana meant to us. In Ceylon my mother had shopped daily, either walking to the market herself or sending the servant to fetch whatever was needed for that day's meals. And if neither of them could get to the market, she would buy produce from the old men and women who wheeled it around the suburbs, their sarongs tucked between their skinny, bandy legs. There was no point in stocking up on anything perishable because we didn't have a fridge to store it in.

In Ghana we began that great ritual of the rich world, the weekly shopping trip. You know those United Nations tables that compare countries according to gross national product per capita or hospital beds per thousand people? Well, I'd like to offer a new, and just as meaningful, category: the number of shopping trips per family per year. Only relatively rich people can be sure enough of their income next week to blow a whole load of cash this week on food. Only people wealthy enough to have their own transport or to pay for a taxi can manage to get all those goodies back home. And only those with money will have fridges and freezers to keep what they've bought fresh enough to be consumed days later.

I know it's not very scientific, but it works. Not simply as a measure of the difference in wealth between countries, but also within countries. You can test this theory in any British borough where rich (though they would never call themselves that) and poor live close to each other and shop at the same supermarket. Some people buy so much they can hardly see over their trolleys. Others walk out with no more than one plastic bag packed with some bread, a carton of milk, some cereal, a tin of spaghetti hoops and a packet of cigarettes. Look at how old people on meagre state pensions shop a little at a time. It's not because that's all they can carry (though that may also be true), but because it's all they can afford. Refugees shop in the same way.

So when we started shopping at Kingsway we moved up from the world of poor people to the world of rich people.

In global terms, if you have a roof over your head, food on the table, a doctor who will not charge you when you're ill and a school place that does not depend on your ability to pay, then, my friend, you are rich. That is what every British citizen has of right. So many of the civil wars and conflicts I have reported could be solved if the states concerned could deliver anything like the kind of life we in Europe take for granted. People who have the opportunity to make a living and to pass on the benefits to their children are unlikely to be seduced by the blandishments of class warriors or the peddlers of ethnic solutions to economic inequality. Ethnicity has been a favoured tool of politicians for as long as there have been politicians. Africans didn't start the business of exploiting ethnic differences, although I would readily concede that they have done much to perfect the art.

But it wasn't like that in the 1960s. Then the old, sometimes ancient, animosities between one group and another were set aside, first in the struggle for freedom and, soon afterwards, in the attempt to forge a pan-African identity. Whether you were part of the Ashanti nation in the West African hinterland or owed allegiance to chiefs in the coastal belt was less important than the fact that you were a Ghanaian and you wanted to be free. In continental terms, the differences between people who lived in the Sahel and worshipped God in his Islamic form and those who grew up in the deep interior and revered her in her ancestral guise were not as significant as the fact that they were all Africans.

Kwame Nkrumah, our president, embodied this ideal. Some might disagree with this contention, but what can't be denied is that his was the boldest, most audacious vision of Africa's future. To be a Ghanaian in those days meant being an African. The two were synonymous in a way that has not been possible since. Very soon the Cold War, the competition for scarce investments, the clash of presidential vanities all did their bit to divide one African country from another. But being a Ghanaian in 1961 was like subscribing to an idea: the idea that Africa's time had come. A period of its history that began in 1483 with the landing of Portuguese seamen in the kingdom of Kongo, which extended southwards from what is now the Congo River estuary, was coming to an end.

We believed with a passion that Ghana's freedom was incomplete until all Africa was both free and united. As a goal it felt real and noble, even to children. Especially to children. When we sang the national anthem at school each morning it was with youthful vigour and innocent belief.

Lift high the flag of Ghana
The gay star shining in the sky . . .

And in the third verse:

> *This be our vow, O Ghana,*
> *To live as one in unity*
> *And in your strength, O Ghana,*
> *To build a new fraternity!*
> *Africa waits, in the night of the clouded years,*
> *For the spreading light that now appears*
> *To give us all a place beneath the sun*
> *The destined ending of a task well done.*

I felt the potency of this huge, African aspiration in a very personal way. I became embarrassed by the fact that while my friends could call this vast and varied land of Africa their own, all I had to offer was the small, seemingly insignificant island of Ceylon. And what was more, we were the trampled people of Ceylon. We had run away. While Ghanaians paraded the triumph of independence, I dragged around the legacy of Tamil defeat. By the mid-sixties I'd found a way out, or so it seemed to me. When asked where I was from I would routinely reply, 'Oh I'm from Asia,' laying claim to an area that was, in geographical terms, at least, as rich and robust as Africa. Later still, I simply abandoned Asia and cleaved to Africa, both the place and the aspiration.

The Organisation of African Unity (OAU) was part of that aspiration. It was established in May 1963 at a conference of thirty-two leaders in Addis Ababa, the capital of Ethiopia. Despite his imperial (though that is disputed), and some would say despotic lineage, Emperor Haile Selassie of Ethiopia was in the vanguard of the drive towards some form of continental unity. Right from the start there had been opposition to Nkrumah's vision of a United States of Africa, which was part of the reason why Addis, and not Accra, was chosen as the organisation's headquarters. The issue was complex, but the problem was not so much a rejection of the idea itself as a distrust of the people who might have led the union. Still, after a second gathering in Cairo, Ghana got to host the OAU's third summit, the first in 'black' Africa, in October 1965. Africa, in all its nascent glory, was coming to town and would parade itself literally on our doorstep.

Having done a tour of the regions my father was posted, once again, to the capital. We lived at 10, Second Avenue, a massive house built in what might loosely be called the colonial style. There were verandas everywhere. In the rainy season I used to go out on to the front veranda to await one of nature's most potent displays. I could smell the rain coming. Actually, it was the smell of dust, kicked up by distant droplets and carried on the advancing wind. My skin would turn goose-pimply, partly because the temperature began to drop but also in anticipation of the imminent thrill. Soon I'd see the curtain of water coming nearer and nearer, bouncing off rooftops, bending the branches of once-sturdy trees. Finally, that climactic moment when a million raindrops, released from a thunderous African sky, crashed into the corrugated metal roof above the veranda like arrows hammered into a shield. The noise spoke of power and destruction; the veranda offered safety and security. There was something magical about being so close to all that turbulent energy without being harmed by it.

The house sat on a half-acre plot. We shared one perimeter wall with what became known to everyone in Ghana as 'Job 600'. The number itself was not significant – it merely identified the latest in a sequence of construction projects under the supervision of the PWD. But this building was certainly different. It was the most ambitious government construction scheme of the post-independence era. Once finished, it would serve as a temporary home to African leaders attending the OAU summit.

Today Job 600 would be seen as yet another white elephant, a venture with no purpose other than to satisfy the pretensions of a vain president in search of dubious glory. But then, of course, it was a matter of national, even continental pride. As the scaffolding pushed ever skywards it acquired a totemic quality, becoming a symbol of Ghana's soaring ambitions.

We had a personal interest in the project. My father's cousin, Thirugnanam Kathiravelupillai, was the engineer in charge of Job 600. There was no room for failure. Presidential honour depended on the building being ready and functioning on time. In public, the Ceylonese community took vicarious pleasure in one of its own having been chosen for such an important job. In private the adults muttered to each other about what might happen to Thiru if the lifts failed to work with the president on board.

Thiru Uncle, as we called him, wasn't the only Ceylonese immigrant involved in a showcase project. Another Tamil engineer, A. C. Visvalingam (nobody seems to know what his first name was – he was always known simply as Visva), a friend of my parents, was working on the Akosombo Dam across the River Volta, then one of the biggest hydro-electric facilities in existence. The dam created the massive Volta Lake, an artificial water mass of 8,480 square kilometres. My father, too, had been promoted beyond expectation. By the time of the summit he was acting deputy and later head of the Water Supplies division of the Ghana Water and Sewerage Corporation. In his field, you could go no higher. Opportunities such as these vindicated the migration to Africa.

As the date of the summit drew closer it was clear that Job 600 was falling behind schedule. Thiru Uncle had had thirteen floors to build in eleven months, not to mention the conference hall itself. He established a night shift, the first time such a thing had been ordered on a civic project. But nobody was going to argue: this was the president's baby, after all. From our front veranda, we could see the floodlights shining on into the night. Sometimes you'd see a smaller light, perhaps a torch, moving across the dark interior of the building. Occasionally it would disappear for a few seconds, only to reappear somewhere else, like a firefly flitting from one place to another. I used to imagine poor old Thiru Uncle walking through that building night after night, finishing off jobs left undone by others.

And he made it; he met the deadline. So Job 600, formally renamed State House, was ready in time for the biggest, most spectacular political gathering Africa had ever seen.

At school we talked constantly about our new USA, the United States of Africa. And, naturally, our president, Kwame Nkrumah, would be the continent's first leader. That made us rather special. Of course, all Africans were going to be equal but, hey, some of us would be slightly more equal than others. How were we to know that men like Julius Nyerere of Tanzania, suspicious of our president's motives, had already put the mockers on a new USA? Besides, who cared? All this was far too good to let politics interfere with it.

Despite our relatively privileged backgrounds, when we discussed these things – indeed, whatever we talked about – we adopted a mock pidgin dialect.

'My faddah knows the president,' my classmate Beema would say in a nudge-nudge tone. I remember Beema well. Partly because he was, shall we say, rounder than the rest of us, and partly because he once brought in a chart displaying various coital positions for us to gloat over when Mr Mason, the class teacher, wasn't looking. 'He's going to aks my faddah to go and run Togo for him.'

'Beema, you're a fool, man.' This was Peter, bespectacled Peter who read a lot and knew a lot. 'Your faddah can't speak French. Those Togolese people will throw him out.'

'They can try,' retorted Beema, his chest expanding with patriotic fervour. 'If they aggravate us, hmmm, Ghana is going to give them one. If these people want unity, they have to speak English.'

Not all of our ambitions for the continent involved Ghana's martial and political superiority over other African countries. This was, of course, the era of the US–USSR space race. In 1962 John Glenn had become the third man (the first were Yuri Gagarin and Gherman Titov of the Soviet Union) to orbit the planet. Soon afterwards, the American Embassy in Accra had exhibited a full-size model of John Glenn's space capsule at the Accra International Trade Fair. It fired our boyish imaginations. We discussed it all in our playground pidgin.

'What of an African rocket,' began Richard. In the idiom this was more statement than question. 'If the Americans can send one, we can also send one.'

Technical limitations were ignored; financial considerations weren't even mentioned. Our biggest problem was what to call the rocket.

'We can call it the African Spacecraft,' offered Ivor, but not very convincingly.

'Thas not a name,' Beema scoffed. 'Look at the Americans, eh, they have Gemini. The Rossians call theirs Sputnik. Thas a name. And you, you want the African Spacecraft. They are going to laff at us. Do you want them to laff at us?'

In the end we settled for Black Star. It was on our flag and it stood for Africa: black and proud.

These were heady times, glory days. It was like election night and the World Cup final rolled into one exhilarating event, part politics, part spectacle – and we had a ringside view. As the visiting delegations arrived they had to drive past 10, Second Avenue to get to State House.

After school, my sisters, our friends and I would hang around on our front veranda waiting for the telltale sound of police sirens. Whoever heard it first would alert the others. We'd sprint the twenty yards or so down the drive, kicking up red dust as we hurtled towards the main road. First there'd be just one or two police outriders. They'd slow down at each intersection and stare through their darkened goggles at the traffic on either side. The message was clear: 'Stay where you are.' Jesus, they looked good. Forget about becoming an astronaut – this was what I wanted to be.

Then, in the distance, you could just make out the main body of the convoy. In the heat haze the whole tableau, the mass of blue flashing lights and shiny black limousines, seemed to be melting into the hot tarmac. So hot that those of us who weren't wearing shoes were forced to hop from one foot to the other. I longed to have feet like Charles. He could run over gravel, stand on hot sand or step on a thorn without feeling a thing. He stood there with us, four square on both feet, holding on to the younger ones.

The presidential cars were Chevrolet Impalas. Their bonnets stretched way out in front and the back ends curved towards the ground like old-fashioned Coke bottles on their sides. These people were so important that they didn't need number plates, just the name of their country where the registration number would normally have been. The trick was to shout out the name of whichever president was gliding past. And we knew them all: they were far more familiar to us than the names of Europe's leaders might be to British children today. They were icons of liberation, important to us because they were the first to wear the mantle of leadership in Africa. Less than ten years into independence, it was still possible to regard these men as freedom fighters. In years to come new, more famous, names would emerge. In 1965, very few people had even heard of Nelson Mandela, for example. Rhodesia was still ruled by Ian Smith and it would be another ten years before the Portuguese pulled out of Africa altogether.

Once the summit had started, the leaders disappeared from view. What they said to each other behind closed doors didn't matter to us as much as the fact that they were behind closed doors in the first place. After all, when you're plotting the creation of a new world power you can't be sitting in the open under mango trees, discussing your plans for everyone to hear. You've got to do it secretly in the conference centre. We assumed that this was why our own president didn't actually tell us about the new USA at the end of the conference. The president was clever, and if he decided to keep things to himself for the moment, that was fine. He knew what he was doing.

And so the summit came and went. The delegates returned to their respective countries and the national flags we had been able to see from our house were pulled down. The lightbulbs that sat on our shared wall with State House started to burn out and no one replaced them. The grass round the perimeter of the complex grew tall and untidy and nobody bothered to cut it back.

For weeks after the summit, a watchman at one of the gates used to let me into the compound to ride my bike. Sometimes, as a special favour, he took me up in the lifts (fortunately they had all worked, and Thiru Uncle was duly rewarded) to the top floor. All of Accra was there in front of me. It must have been a spectacular view, the only one like it in the whole city, and yet the view is not what I remember. What sticks in my mind from those surreptitious visits to the thirteenth-floor penthouses was their utter emptiness. How could something as important as an all-Africa summit leave so little trace of its existence? Only the odd cigarette butt and the leftover staleness of rooms that had once been air-conditioned betrayed the fact that anyone at all had been here.

I did not think it then, but I now see that emptiness as an apt metaphor for what was to happen to my beloved Africa. I had no way of knowing this at the time, but Africa's unity would turn out to be a shell of an idea with nothing much inside it, just like the building on our doorstep. The little cracks I saw in the plaster of those cavernous, echoing rooms signalled far greater schisms in Africa's political edifice. I was destined to spend my adulthood dispelling the dream I had nurtured so carefully as a child. The journalist would retell the story first conceived by the boy.

For that year, 1965, was something of a watershed for the continent. Within twelve months of the OAU summit, Kwame Nkrumah would be deposed in a military coup.

4

The Fallen Star

On weekday mornings the routine was always the same. Breakfast usually consisted of thick wedges of white, fluffy bread with sweet jam. Occasionally my mother would give us a treat: pancakes with a filling of mung dahl, shaved coconut and brown sugar.

By 1966 my father's status entitled him to an official vehicle to take him to work, and we had the family car for the school run. It was a Peugeot 404, the model used by the *gendarmerie* in the Pink Panther films. Outside, our driver, Al Hassan, would be polishing the paint off it. I used to watch as the little beads of sweat formed on his brow. He'd mop them off with the cloth he was using to clean the vehicle.

The only thing he allowed to interrupt him was his morning prayer. He would take his mat, which he kept rolled up in the boot, and lay it out under our mango tree. Collecting some water in the empty Cow & Gate milk tin he kept specifically for the purpose, he would perform the ablutions set out in the Koran.

Then he would kneel and touch his head on the mat, whispering something I could never understand.

'What are you saying?' I would ask.

'I'm talking to God,' he replied simply.

'Yes, but what are you saying to Him?'

'I'm not saying anything. I'm not telling him anything. Just that I am here to serve him.'

'Don't you ask him for anything? I asked God for a new bike. Maybe you can ask him for a new car.'

'No. I just want him to keep us safe.'

Years later, as I travelled through the Muslim Sahel, I would see this ritual in progress a thousand times, perhaps at the ancient mosque in Timbuktu or in the shadow of a petrol tanker on the road to the north of Nigeria. I still cannot watch this simple act of Muslim worship without being aware of a wonderful sense of continuity. It's the absence of any ceremonial props that has always fascinated me. One man in communion with his God; no fuss, no bother. It was like that in 1966 for Al Hassan; it is the same for hundreds of millions of others today.

This early and close-range familiarity with Islam is, I think, one of the reasons why I have never been tempted to accept the fanatical adherents of the religion as truly representative of the whole. In my mind Islam has always been a religion of quiet purpose and private worship; a religion that aims to help in the pursuit of personal fulfilment and communal advancement. Indeed, a religion that tries to balance the ambition required for the former with the restraint necessary to achieve the latter. Al Hassan's Islam never seemed threatening when I was a child and I refuse to feel threatened by it now.

My mother always told us to wait till Al Hassan had finished his prayers before going out to the car. As we piled into it Al Hassan would walk over to us, unfolding his handkerchief. In the middle there would be a few pieces of cola nut. They looked like bits of cork and tasted as bitter as the beer the grown-ups used to drink. Even worse, come to think of it. My parents knew I'd tried the beer but I don't think they knew I'd sampled Al Hassan's cola nut – a favourite with drivers all over West Africa because of its caffeine-like properties. All we were told was that it was fine for Al Hassan, but not for us. He'd pop a couple of pieces into his mouth, pull the gear lever on the steering column into reverse, wave to the gardener and head out of the compound.

On 24 February 1966 the morning routine was no different. It was what had happened by the time the sun set over the Atlantic that marks out that day as a day to be remembered; a day that changed Africa.

We hadn't gone very far before Al Hassan was looking troubled. This wasn't the tut-tut irritation he reserved for other drivers who got in his way or – the worst sin in his book – the pedestrians who left their fingermarks on the car when we stopped at a crossroads. This was more serious. He chewed his cola nut ever more furiously and kept looking in the rear-view mirror. 'Whas goin' on?' he muttered to himself. 'Ahh no, somtin' is happening.' My sister Kitto and I just sat there.

What was happening was a coup. The black star of Africa had fallen.

To get to Christ the King School, you had to turn right off the main road opposite Flagstaff House. As we approached the inter-section we saw soldiers all over the road. One of them stopped the car and looked in. Al Hassan spoke to him before turning the car round. 'The school is closed,' he explained to us in a manner that suggested he was not about to tell us anything more. I don't remember being frightened.

At home, my mother had heard the news from friends. Leela, the wife of the man who'd been in charge of Job 600, had phoned to warn her to keep us at home – too late, as it turned out. My father was out of town, visiting the remote station of Bolgatanga in the north of the country. He tells me that memories of that ear-lier separation during the riots of 1958 in Colombo came flooding back. As his official Mercedes-Benz (a newer model than the one we'd started out with) sped south, he had visions of turmoil in Accra. His fears were dispelled when Kwesi, the driver, slowed down at the first of many roadblocks. This time, happily, whether or not my father was a Tamil was utterly irrelevant. The soldiers were only interested in those who might be associated with the now deposed president.

Back in Accra, as Al Hassan turned the car down our driveway, my mother came running out of the house. She'd been waiting at the window. 'Go inside quickly!' she shouted, practically pulling us out of the car. As we hurried in we heard her ask Al Hassan what was happening. From the kitchen window we could see the two of them talking. We didn't have to hear what they were saying to know that something bad had happened. I could tell when Al Hassan had got to the bit where we were stopped by the soldiers and had to turn round, because as he described the scene he shaped his fingers like a gun. My mother came in and locked the doors.

At the same time, I locked away one Ghana and prepared to accept another. The Ghana of playground hopes gave way to something less certain, less shiny. Suddenly I began to hear conversations among the adults that they had never dared to raise in public before. 'He got what he deserved,' someone would say of Nkrumah. 'Imagine spending all that money on the palace in Aburi.' What palace, what money? Nobody had told me about these things before.

Even his marriage to Fatia, an Egyptian woman, was, it seemed, a sham. 'Well, everybody knew he never loved her,' one of my parents' friends declared, as if he had been on intimate terms with the presidential couple. 'No, the only reason he married her was so that President Nasser would get the Arabs to support him in the OAU.'

Beyond the walls of 10, Second Avenue history was being made. As we huddled together in my parents' bedroom, wondering when my father would return, a whole nation was wondering where its future lay. How often does this happen? How often do we retreat into the cocoon of personal survival, shutting out the tremors of historical change? Ghana's carefree days were over. Suddenly the world did not look quite such a secure place.

Beyond Ghana's borders a continent watched in dismay. If it can happen in Nkrumah's Ghana, they muttered, it can happen anywhere. They looked on as the men in uniform stripped away the patina of power that had surrounded Nkrumah. The rejoicing of the Ghanaian people sent a collective shiver down the spines of presidents all over Africa. Not in my country, they said. They resolved to concentrate even more power in their own hands, precisely the option that would convince yet more soldiers that democracy was a failed experiment. All that talk of African unity, it turned out, was just so much hot air. Form had been allowed to surpass substance, words had replaced meaning, and ideals had given way to shabby politics.

Nkrumah fled into bewildered exile in Guinea. The champion of a greater Africa had been so out of touch he hadn't realised that his people were having to queue for milk. There has always been talk that America's CIA had a hand in his downfall. It would not surprise me – as the Americans proved elsewhere on the continent, they found socialist leanings like Nkrumah's difficult to swallow. But you cannot engineer a coup if you cannot find anyone on the ground who will go along with the idea. And in Ghana in 1966 there was no shortage of volunteers.

If Ghana's independence in 1957 had been a milestone for Africa, so, too, was this coup. Independence had marked the end of a history of subjugation. The coup signified the start of a new era for this continent of changing fortunes. The seventies and eighties were what I call Africa's lost years. I'm not even sure that she has even now emerged from this long season of chaos, though the road out of troubled times is clearer than it has been for decades.

Since that coup in Ghana the continent has seen many more.

There have been over eighty violent or unconstitutional changes of government; nearly ninety leaders have been deposed; at least twenty-five heads of government have been killed in political violence. Thirty-one countries have been plagued by the violent overthrow of government, and in twenty of them this kind of political turmoil has occurred more than once. Benin had six coups, five different constitutions and twelve heads of state all within the first ten years of independence. It is a measure of Africa's volatile politics that some of these statistics will almost certainly be out of date by the time you read this book.

As telling as these figures are, they describe only part of the story, like headlines without a following report. What they hide is the relentless, gruelling, dispiriting, demoralising, enervating, corrupting, painful slide into the disgrace of poverty, ignorance and ill health that has disfigured virtually every family in Africa. No longer can the parents of this continent turn to their children and say with any assurance: 'Be whatever you want to be.' These days, the message from father to daughter, mother to son is more likely to be something along the lines of 'Take what is on offer today, for tomorrow there may be even less.' A generation now in its twenties has grown up hobbled by low expectations and a lack of belief in either itself or the continent.

For me, too, it was a time of change. My own transition from childhood to adolescence was mirrored by what was happening to my country. My world would never, ever seem so simple again. Within a few months I would be preparing for a journey out of Africa, another step in the migrant's progress. Partly prompted by the uncertainties raised by the coup and its implications for the prospects of a decent education in Ghana, my parents decided to send me to boarding school in Britain.

There I would strive again to fit in, discarding my West African pidgin for the unmistakable tones of middle-class England. It was not, however, a case of replacing one culture with another. All I did was hide the old layer under a new one in the interests of the migrant's need to conform. The African in me re-emerged every time I returned to the continent to join my family for the long summer holidays. It always felt like home, even when my parents eventually moved on to Nigeria and then Zimbabwe, and when I too took up a posting in Harare: my first job as a foreign correspondent, for the now-defunct *South* magazine.

And it is still like that today. There is no place in Africa about which I say to myself, 'This feels strange, this feels wrong.' There is always a sense of umbilical connection as I step off a plane and into the hot, often humid, air that caresses the continent. 'I know this,' I say to myself. 'Here I am comfortable.'

Travelling through Africa in recent years as a professional observer, paid to pass on my thoughts, I have never quite managed to do it utterly dispassionately. When the phone rings and one of my editors at the BBC points me towards Ethiopia or South Africa, Mozambique or Zimbabwe, for me it's more than just another assignment: it is the chance of a passage back to Africa.

When I joined the BBC, arguably the Western world's most influential broadcaster, I told myself I would avoid the clichés. If I took pictures of the starving, I would try to preserve their dignity; if I showed footage of conflict I would try to explain where all the anger and hatred came from. I wanted to challenge the image of Africa as a place of tribal savagery and greedy, callous leaders.

But Africa didn't help me. All too often it was difficult to make sense of what I saw. That's the way it has been since the BBC sent me back to Africa for the first time. Liberia was a bad place from which to attempt to rebuild the continent's tarnished reputation. Two and a half decades after I had left for boarding school in England, Africa was in worse shape than I could ever have imagined.

5

My Room with a View

The pilot threw the plane into a sharp, gravity-defying left turn, away from the sea and in towards the runway. I peered out of the window. Just for an instant, it felt as if Africa had rotated onto its side. For a split second it seemed that we were upright and it was the land below us that was about to slide into the lead-grey Atlantic, a continent sinking like a wrecked ship, swallowed by the hungry ocean around it. And then the plane straightened up and below me a much more familiar Africa began to take shape. The rust-red tin roofs atop their garishly coloured clapboard shacks. The tall palm trees waving their herringbone leaves in a lazy welcome. As we lost height I could even make out the 'mammy wagons' loaded with little regard for either safety or comfort. It was all there except for the hot, sickly-sweet air of the west coast – and that I could conjure for myself, for it was ingrained in my memory.

In my heart I wished the continent below me could be the land of my childhood. I wanted it to be the continent Kuki

Galman describes in her eulogy to Africa, *Night of the Lions*: a land 'of gentle, handsome, intelligent people, who protect the young and respect the old'. If only I were back in Africa to confirm the hopes of my generation, freedom's children. But I was a TV journalist now and I was returning to record the truth: that Africa's new children faced a much harsher world than they deserved. As the ageing Antonov shuddered to a stop I told myself to put away childish thoughts. I emerged from the plane, a reporter prepared to portray Africa not as I wanted it to be, but as I found it.

The noon heat bounced off the tarmac of Spriggs Paine Airport in Monrovia. It was December 1990. The civil war in Liberia was a year old. It would go on for another seven.

I didn't have to venture far to get a glimpse of what lay in store for me. At the bottom of the airstrip a soldier from the West African peacekeeping force picked his way through what looked like a pile of rubbish. On closer inspection it turned out to be a heap of bleached and broken bones. He stepped gingerly, taking care not to disturb the skeletons. The soldier, a Nigerian, was showing them in death the respect they had been denied in life.

Later I would find out that just over sixty bodies had been dumped here. They were all hospital workers, doctors and nurses included. Troops loyal to the former government had killed them because they had done what they were trained to do: treated the sick and wounded irrespective of whether or not their patients supported the government. That, in the Liberia of 1990, was a crime punishable by summary execution. No courts, no Red Cross, no Geneva Convention – just a bullet in the back.

Liberia was the first African country to which I travelled in my capacity as a reporter for the BBC. Over the next decade I went to many more 'trouble spots'. Sometimes, as in the case of Liberia, more than once. In those ten years I talked to people who no longer hoped for the grand vision of the early sixties. They had settled for much simpler aspirations: a night without the crack of gunfire; a morning with enough food to eat; an afternoon when the rain falls like it used to; an evening filled with the laughter of children by the river. For too many people even these little things are no longer guaranteed.

There is a tragic poignancy about Liberia's decline. This, of all places in Africa, was supposed to be a land free of oppression. The state was founded by former slaves from America and so escaped the French and British colonisation that was to befall its neighbours. The abolition of slavery in the northern United States in 1808, and the presence of free slaves in the southern states, where slavery was still legal, had given rise to unexpected social tensions. The American Colonisation Society's plan to repatriate former slaves to Africa was an attempt to shift the problem. This was a 'send them back home' policy in the guise of philanthropy. On 31 January 1820, the good ship *Elizabeth* duly set forth from New York on the society's inaugural voyage.

Many former slaves jumped at the chance to re-establish their lives in the land of their ancestors. Hope ran strong despite the terrible toll of tropical disease. In *Crossing the River*, Caryl Phillips' novel about the African diaspora, former slave Nash Williams writes to his master back in America: 'Liberia is a fine place to live in. Liberia, the beautiful land of my forefathers, is a place where persons of colour may enjoy their freedom. Its laws are founded upon justice and equality and here we may sit under the palm tree and enjoy the same privileges as our white brethren in America. It is truly our only home.' Though the words are fictitious, they bear faithful testament to the spirit of the time.

But the Americo-Liberians, as they came to be called, recreated in their new home the same inequality from which they had fled. Slowly they accumulated all the political and economic power, freezing out the indigenous people. By 1900 some 20,000 Americo-Liberians lorded it over about 1.5 million Africans – the people who spoke the languages of the Mande, Kru and Atlantic Mel groups, who had settled these lands over a thousand years earlier. By the middle of the twentieth century, power was even more concentrated: some twenty-five Americo-Liberian families effectively controlled the country.

Africans, as they have proved so often, are a patient people. But even so a time comes when enough is enough. In Liberia it came in 1980, when a gang of low-ranking soldiers, disgruntled about their pay and conditions, overwhelmed the Executive Mansion and murdered President William Tolbert, bringing Americo-Liberian rule to a violent end. Among the soldiers was a semi-literate master sergeant named Samuel Kenyon Doe. He claimed to be a reluctant leader but it didn't take him long to acquire a taste for power and its trappings. He promoted himself to the rank of a general, arranged for an honorary doctorate to be awarded to him and indulged a fondness for Mercedes-Benzes. He rigged the elections in 1985 and a little later adjusted the constitution so that he wouldn't have to face them again. He was now president for life.

There is a pattern to this kind of behaviour, which some have called Africa's 'big man' syndrome, and a certain inevitability to what it results in, namely rebellion and civil war. That came in Liberia in December 1989, when a former cabinet minister turned rebel commander, Charles Taylor, launched a military campaign that would take him to the edge of the capital within a year. But the privilege of presiding over President Doe's demise evaded Mr Taylor. It fell instead to another rebel leader, Prince Johnson, like his predecessor eager for the comforts of the Executive Mansion.

In September 1990, some weeks before my first trip to Liberia, President Doe was assassinated in a particularly vicious manner. It is said that before he was killed his ear was cut off and he was made to eat it. I met Prince Johnson on that first trip, at his base on the outskirts of the capital, Monrovia, where he had been confined by the West African peacekeeping force. He showed me the chair on which Doe had been beaten and tortured. He seemed proud of what he had achieved. He called himself a freedom fighter and in the same breath he urged me to buy a videotape of Doe's last, painful hours.

There were seven more years of civil war before Charles Taylor finally consolidated his hold over the country. I met him on another trip to Liberia in 1996, by which time he was a member of the so-called State Council, a curiously named body given that there was no Liberian state – at least, not one you or I would recognise as such. His retinue of aides habitually referred to him as Mr President, though nobody had actually elected him to that office. Mr Taylor talked about good government, about economic recovery, about law and order. All this without the slightest hint of irony. He feigned ignorance of the fact that virtually all the vehicles in the 'presidential' compound belonged elsewhere and that the house he'd taken to describing as his official residence was the home of a foreign diplomat. Mr Taylor was leader of the pack in a city that had become a play-ground for delinquents.

I could see it all from my hotel, the Mamba Point. 'I'll give you a room with a view,' Shawi, the Lebanese hotel manager, had said. It was the line he'd used in those far-off days when his guests drank ice-cold gins on the balcony as the Atlantic rollers thrashed the West African coast and the sun settled beneath the dancing palms. In 1996 those guests had gone and it wasn't the tropical seascape that caught the eye.

The prematurely balding Shawi stayed on when most of those who could pulled out. 'Where would I go?' he asked, shrugging his shoulders and holding out his hands. 'Look at what the Israelis are doing to Lebanon.' (They were bombing it.) 'I could join my wife and her family, but they are from Northern Ireland. I'll take my chances here!'

In fact, he left nothing to chance. He knew which commander to pay off and which egos needed to be massaged. It was no more than what the Lebanese had been doing in West Africa for decades. They are the archetypal middlemen, taking their cut on both sides. They buy for a good price and sell for an even better one.

Shawi would shuffle around the little hotel with a walkie-talkie glued to his left ear. He knew the frequencies used by the Nigerian peacekeepers, ineffective though they were most of the time, and gathered his own intelligence about just how risky life at Mamba Point was becoming.

Shawi had a sidekick, the ever-present, ever-useful Mr Ming. I assumed he was Chinese, though I never thought to ask. He, too, was virtually bald, but he made the most of what little hair he had, combing strands of it over his head from one side to the other in the Bobby Charlton style. He was short with bandy legs that curled out of billowing, grease-stained shorts. Ming, as clever with a screwdriver as he was with a wok, doubled as handyman and chef. Between them, Shawi and Ming ministered to our every need, whether it was a car for a day or for a message to be sent to a faction leader.

In 1996 there were three types of people staying at the Mamba Point. Those, like we journalists, there in the line of duty; those who knew how to turn a profit in a situation in which everybody else was making a loss; and those who couldn't think of anywhere else to go.

The German who propped up the bar from time to time fell into the last category. I've found people like him all over the continent; men ready to pour out their life stories for the price of a bottle of beer. Once they were young and full of drive and ambition, convinced they could plunder Africa and return home to plaudits and the hand of an impressionable bride. But a poor business deal here, a failed relationship there, and they end up sour of breath and mind. They will tell you it is all Africa's fault. But they never leave her shores because back home, where they'd have to shave again, looking in the mirror, they'd see failure staring back at them. So they stay with Africa. She is like a tolerant mistress, slow to rebuke and blind to their faults.

Then there was the chap with a Greek-sounding name who had once lived in South Africa. He had got out when the blacks moved in, though he made a point of telling me that there was absolutely no link between the two events. When the fighting came to Monrovia, he'd been in the middle of a business deal that would have made him rich. Now he was trying to cut his losses. He, too, cursed Africa, forgetting that it was Africa's riches that had paid for the house he now owned in Europe.

From my room with a view, I could see the battle raging. It was like having a seat in the stalls in a theatre of the absurd. Just a few hundred metres from my perch, a man in an orange wig emptied his rifle as if he were spraying a garden with a hosepipe. Nearby a boy tottered under the weight of a grenade-launcher. When he pulled the trigger, the backblast sent him rolling across the sand. His friends jeered and made a grab for the weapon: it was their turn to have some fun. One of them wore a filigree doily over his head and face. I assumed he could see through the patterned holes but after observing the way he unleashed his bullets, I couldn't be sure. If I'd watched for long enough I might have seen the Butt Naked Brigade, fighters who stripped off their clothes before heading into battle.

There are some academics who will tell you that there is a reason for this strange behaviour, that it is a modern mutation of much older rituals. They may be right. On the other hand, it may simply be what people do when they have lost their way, forgotten their sense of who they are and what they are here for. Or it might just be the booze and drugs. Because there was plenty of that, too.

Every now and then we'd don our bullet-proof vests and walk the streets. It was on one of these forays that I bumped into General Do or Die. I had the idea of filming him and his colleagues for a 'day in the life of . . .' kind of piece. In times like these you have to grab your chances when they come. 'I'm doing a story on the various factions in the Liberian civil war, and I wondered whether I could have an interview with you?' He didn't accept my handshake. It was not a good sign. The general was not a soldier in the accepted sense. There were no stars on his cap or stripes on his epaulette. That's because his army had no uniform. This was a very irregular war in a very irregular country.

'Doin' a story on what? Fashions? Wha's that, man?' He turned to the sergeant. 'Let's go, man. We ain't got time for this crap.' The accent was a cross between something you'd hear on the streets of Harlem and West African pidgin. I can understand the Harlem slang (or at least, the version of it they use in the films), and I used to speak pidgin myself, but the combination of the two was a challenge to the ear.

'Oh, I'm sorry. I meant the different sides in the civil war.'

'There ain't no sides, man. There's winners and losers. And I ain't no loser.' He smiled at the sergeant. The routine was well rehearsed.

'Well, that's exactly why I've been looking for you. I've been told your unit has been one of the most successful and courageous in the conflict.' I hadn't been told anything of the sort but, at times like this, flattery is called for.

'Yeah, we've been in some tough operations, but we come through OK,' he said, all puffed up with the thought that his dubious exploits had been recognised. I knew I had him then. The interview was in the bag. He was like a child who'd been given a gold star for good work. And that is exactly what he was: a child. A child at play. But his was a deadly game.

General Do or Die. It wasn't his real name, of course, but the one he'd adopted and used ever since he'd got involved in the killing business some five years earlier. At fifteen – that's right, fifteen – General Do or Die was something of a veteran, an old hand compared to the soldiers under his command. Sergeant Snake, his sidekick, couldn't have been more than twelve or thirteen, though he lied when I asked him how old he was.

It occurred to me that General Do or Die was about the same

age that Charles, our house-worker, would have been when we first employed him in those halcyon days in Ghana. How things had changed. Then, Charles and I had pretended to be at war. Here in Liberia, General Do or Die was a living embodiment of war, the real thing, up close and personal. There was no sham. Except for his name, of course. But in this, too, there were uneasy parallels with those bygone years. We had given Charles his new name so that he would fit in with our family. In Liberia, this young boy gave himself a new name so that he could melt into his new world, find a place in an environment where there was no room for weakness or childishness.

General Do or Die said he was tired, and it was too hot to talk outside. If we wanted an interview, it would have to be at his headquarters down the road. We walked there. Leading the way in his rolled-up jeans, battle-green sleeveless vest and spotted bandana, the general looked as if he might break into a rap routine at any moment.

Liberia is one of the most humid places on earth. Glenn Middleton, my South African cameraman, dripped sweat from every pore of his body. The dark stain under his armpits was slowly spreading across his shirt, which made it look as if an attempt to dye it had ended in disaster.

Watching Glenn as we moved around Africa was like watching a prisoner who had been released into a community he'd forgotten he was a part of. Nothing in the upbringing of a white boy from Northcliff, a working-class district of Johannesburg, could have prepared him for what lay beyond the Limpopo River in the north. Like so many of his generation, Glenn had served his time in an army dedicated to keeping the rest of Africa at bay. Good looks, a boyish charm and a sharp eye had ensured that his toughest assignments had been to take portraits of his commander's wife in his capacity as regimental photographer. Glenn might not have gone around trying to kill black Africans in the bush but he was, nevertheless, a product of the system that wanted them dead.

Given that so much of what we saw apparently confirmed Apartheid's propaganda about the black Africans' inability to rule themselves, it would not have been at all surprising if Glenn had adopted an I-told-you-so air. But he didn't. Instead he ranged over the continent with an openmindedness that belied his roots. His universal greeting – 'How's it my china?' – was almost always followed by a conversation about Bafana Bafana, South Africa's national football team. It was a joy to watch.

Monrovia in 1996 was a capital without a country. We struggled through the cloying, wet heat of a West African afternoon, picking our way along streets strewn with rubble. A United Nations Jeep lay on its side, its insides still smouldering. Nothing and no one was exempt from the violence. This was not a war that respected an aid worker's neutrality. The houses had been blasted to bits, their walls blown away by the random trajectories of mortars to reveal interiors where people had once led ordinary lives. There was a touch of prurience about the way we peered at what lay exposed. The glint of a tube of lipstick caught my eye. It didn't look a whole lot different from a high-calibre bullet casing. With one you enhance beauty; with the other you destroy it.

All the shops had been looted. Here and there a few desperate people searched through the debris, looking for something, anything, that might have been neglected by others. They were like modern-day hunter-gatherers, rummaging through a landscape of broken concrete and bent steel.

We got to Do or Die's redoubt, a three-storey building at the seedier end of a town which he described as a hotel. The general and Sergeant Snake rented a room on the first floor at $20 a month. The corridor was dark; Monrovia hadn't had electricity for months. The whole place reeked of stale sweat and untreated excrement. Every now and again the general would poke his head through a half-open door and bark some instructions. He wanted us to know who was boss.

In between times, he slumped down on a bed. The state of the mattress suggested that sleeping was the last thing people did on these beds. And here was this boy in the middle of it all. He affected the war-weariness of a man, but when he pulled off his bandana you could see just how young he was.

Children are killed in wars all the time, but when you find one in which it's the children who do the killing, you know that the people involved have breached a psychological threshold beyond which there is no longer any guarantee of social cohesion. All the factions in the Liberian civil war used children. It is thought that they represented about a third of the 150,000 people who lost their lives during the seven years of fighting. By the mid-1990s, the United Nations children's fund (UNICEF) put the number sent into battle at over 20,000. Some of those I saw were as young as nine or ten.

When I was that age, a pupil at Christ the King School in Ghana, the most violent act committed by my classmates and me was the destruction of a termite hill with a pickaxe and rocks. Whereas we dreamed of putting an African into space, these children in Liberia talked about putting the enemy into an early and shallow grave. Kids who should have been learning to write with pencils were finding out what it was like to kill with guns.

I have come across nothing so dangerous as a child with a weapon. Moods can change in as little time as it takes a teenager to throw a tantrum. Humiliate a child and you end up with tears; humiliate a child soldier and you may well end up with a bullet. They are young enough to be my children but powerful enough to tell me what to do. They brandish their weapons with the same abandon shown by our children playing with their toy guns. Bang, bang, you're dead. In Africa it's for real. I have seen them not just in Liberia, but in neighbouring Sierra Leone, in far away Mozambique and in Uganda.

The warlords of Africa know all about the power of formative experiences. The details may vary, but there is a definite pattern to the way in which children are initiated into the killing game.

A child psychologist once told me that you can get a child to kill in a far more cruel way than any adult would countenance. First they have to be brutalised, their nascent sense of what is right and what is wrong erased. It is an evil corruption of the apocryphal Jesuit boast that if you give them a child for the first seven years, you may do as you like with him afterwards. Forced to do something that leaves them overcome by guilt and self-loathing, they subsequently shut out reason and emotion. In this numb state they will do their masters' bidding, however gruesome the task.

I remember Paulo Simbini, who I met at the Don Bosco Centre in Maputo, Mozambique. He was captured by the RENAMO, the South African-backed rebels who fought the socialist and anti-Apartheid government. Paulo spoke of a friend of his who had rounded up his own family, barricaded them into a hut and set light to it. The friend had been made to stand there, listening to the screams of his mother and infant sister. Afterwards, the carers at the centre told me it was Paulo himself who'd committed the atrocity, though he had never been able to speak of it in anything other than the third person.

I remember Rosemary and her sister in northern Uganda. They had been captured by the so-called Lord's Resistance Army. Both of them had been raped repeatedly. Afterwards, along with other seized children, they were forced to stab corpses. They were only allowed to stop when their captor decided he had seen enough blood spurting on to their clothes and bodies.

With tears in their eyes, these children, and many, many more, told me about the barbarous acts they went on to commit. Sometimes, when it was too difficult to talk, they showed me drawings depicting their tortured lives. Those were the days when I wondered if I wanted to be a foreign correspondent at all; the times when I had nightmares in which I saw my own children crying for help, unable to see that I was reaching out for them. Those were the occasions when I did not want to be robust and professional, when I wanted someone to tell me it was OK to weep.

Yet these children were the lucky ones. I talked to most of them in rehabilitation centres, in orphanages, in schools. They had been found. What about all the others who will never get a chance to exorcise their demons? I have seen them, too. They are the ones you spot in a crowd, the boys who stare into nothingness. Look at their faces and you see a child; look into their eyes and you see the loss of innocence. When a thief steals your car it can be recovered and returned, but when a childhood has been robbed it cannot be replaced. It is gone for ever.

All over the continent there are children old beyond their years. For some, like the child soldiers of Liberia, it happens suddenly in that terrifying moment when they first kill another human being. Many others simply never have the opportunity to indulge in childish pursuits. When you have to help till the soil, or look after your younger siblings, or fetch water from a river two hours away, there is not much time left for play or to explore the world of make-believe. When even the youngest member is needed to contribute to a family's survival from one season to the next, there is little energy left for textbooks and tests.

A smaller percentage of children completes the first stage of education in Africa than in any other part of the poor world. And of those who manage to get through primary school, the proportion who go on to secondary school is only a little over half of that in the rest of the developing world.

Of the 7 million children across the world who die before they reach their fifth birthday, over two thirds are in Africa. This is partly because no more than about half are immunised against childhood diseases. And when children do get sick, their chances of being seen by a doctor are slimmer than in any other part of the world. There is only one doctor for every 20,000 people in Africa. And since most of those are in the cities, the prospects of getting a diagnosis in time in rural Africa are very remote indeed.

If all that were not bad enough, Africa is unique in the developing world in that it is the only continent where so many social indicators show a downward trend. While Asia and Latin America have their problems, on the whole life has been getting steadily better for people there. In Africa the standard of living today is worse than it was twenty years ago. Per capita income in 2000 was 10 per cent below the level reached in 1980. And the incomes of the poorest fifth have been hit hardest, dropping by an average of 2 per cent every single year. Whichever way you want to measure it, Africa performs worse than any other part of the world. In 1957, when Ghana won its independence from Britain, it was more prosperous than South Korea. Today South Korea's economy is six times larger than Ghana's. In 1965 Nigeria and Indonesia had similar economies. Three decades later, Indonesia's economic output was three times bigger than Nigeria's.

Africa has the highest proportion of people living below the international poverty line, in other words, surviving on less than a dollar a day. Life expectancy at birth is a mere 48.8 years. The continent's economy is the least sophisticated in the world. It still relies heavily on exporting primary products, and prices for some of these on the international markets have plummeted. Coffee, for example – exported by Tanzania, Ethiopia and Uganda, among others – has seen a 70 per cent price fall since 1997. If South Africa is taken out of the equation, there is virtually nothing in the way of manufactured exports. Africa now accounts for just 1.3 per cent of world trade, having lost a quarter of its world market share in the 1990s alone.

What's more, unjust international trade rules give Africa little hope of increasing its share by adding value to its exports by, say, turning cocoa beans into chocolate or coffee beans into processed granules. When Ghanaian farmers export raw cocoa beans into the European Union, they face a tariff (effectively a tax on trade) of 3 per cent. If they tried to export processed chocolate, the tax would rise to 27 per cent. The message is simple: don't get too clever. You can see why, for so many Africans, globalisation remains a dirty word. A recent study by Oxfam showed that the poorest countries – most of which are in Africa – faced the highest trade barriers.

Well over 80 per cent of those people who have died from AIDS around the world come from Africa. At the end of 2000, just over 25 million people in sub-Saharan Africa were living with HIV or AIDS. In parts of the south, the number of sufferers has increased by 50 per cent since 1999. According to a study in South Africa in 2001, some 7 million people in that country will die from the disease by the end of the decade. So far there have been nearly 14 million deaths attributable to the disease in Africa as a whole.

Almost all of the victims are parents in their thirties and forties. At first their children were looked after by relatives, but now those relatives, in turn, have been hit by the scourge, or else have become too poor to extend the hand of kinship that has taken care of Africa's vulnerable through the ages. From Kano to Kinshasa, Dar es Salaam to Durban, a generation is growing up alienated from the ancient sense of community that thrives in African hearts as it does nowhere else on Earth.

This is the world from which General Do or Die escapes every time he ties on his bandana, slings an assault rifle over his shoulder and heads into town, looking for trouble. He is a social misfit. But we must not pretend he is a uniquely African phenomenon. We in the rich world have our social outcasts. The English hooligans who like to bait foreign football supporters and the German neo-Nazis who think it is fun to kick someone to death are also men without hope. The only difference is that it's all so much more brutal in Africa. For all his swagger and back-alley bravado, General Do or Die and boys like him as far afield as Somalia and Congo are a product of a sick society, the victims of a continent that has failed to provide for its most vulnerable people.

6

A Year of Living Dangerously

It was as if we'd been plucked from our top-storey Victorian con-
version in Hackney and plonked into a scene from a Bond movie.
One grimy February morning in 1993, my wife, Frances, was
scrabbling around in her top drawer looking for a pair of black
tights that didn't have a hole in them; the same afternoon we
were being ushered across the tarmac at Nice Airport in the south
of France. 'There's a helicopter waiting for you,' said the woman
in the exotic accent obligatory for Bond girls. In fact, she was an
employee of the Monte Carlo Television Festival, for which we
were headed.

'Here we go,' said the pilot, directing his Ray-Ban-shrouded
eyes at Frances. The Jet Ranger rose a few feet in the air, hovered,
pitched forward and then pulled away to the right, each manoeuvre carried out rather more sharply than I would judge necessary
if getting from A to B was the only point of the exercise. Which,
of course, it wasn't. These chaps can spot an impressionable
English lass a mile off and Frances duly played her role, clinging to

her soft leather armrest in the kind of helpless way these men love.

On our left, as we gathered speed, a mosaic of terracotta roofs flashed past, broken every now and then by the rippling turquoise of a sun-soaked swimming pool. The rich at play.

At the heliport in Monte Carlo, another woman from central casting shepherded us to 'our' car. It was a Mercedes-Benz. S class, of course. What else? 'The chauffeur knows where to take you,' she said. 'You'll have time to freshen up at the hotel before the reception.'

L'Hermitage in Monte Carlo is the kind of hotel where your budget for the whole weekend gets blown away on a few *citron pressés* and 15 per cent service charges. Luckily, we were not paying. Our suite, with a balcony overlooking the marina, was one of the perks accorded to award-winners.

So it was that I came to stand on the stage in the Salle d'Etoiles with several other journalists, all of us looking rather ill at ease in crisp dress suits that still gave off a whiff of chemically induced cleanliness. Down below, Frances made small talk with an actress from the American TV series *Santa Barbara*. She even looked interested. Sacha Distel was meant to be on our table, but he didn't show up.

It was a good night for me. No, it was a great night for me. I was about to collect not one but two awards for my coverage of the civil war and subsequent famine in Somalia. However many times you tell yourself to keep these things in perspective, vanity always wins the day.

One of the stars of another American soap opera, *Dynasty*, who was presenting the awards, made her way along the winners' line. She had a little something to say to each recipient. I rehearsed a couple of replies. 'Keep it light,' I told myself.

'It must have been terrible,' she said when she got to me. 'Yes,' I replied lamely.

Inside I felt like making a sharp retort to pierce the showbiz veneer. But it would have been a cheap shot, and wholly unwarranted. How could she be expected to know what it was like? She was only doing her job. It was just that, at the back of my mind, even as I was enjoying the fruits of my labour, I was aware of the horribly unsettling juxtaposition of a night out in Monte Carlo and the badlands of Somalia.

I saw a thousand hungry, lean, scared and betrayed faces as I criss-crossed Somalia between the end of 1991 and December 1992, but there is one I will never forget.

I was in a little hamlet just outside Gufgaduud, a village in the back of beyond, a place the aid agencies had yet to reach. In my notebook I had jotted down instructions on how to get there. 'Take the Badale Road for a few kilometres till the end of the tarmac, turn right on to a dirt track, stay on it for about forty-five minutes – Gufgaduud. Go another fifteen minutes approx. – like a ghost village.' It was my dispatches from Gufgaduud that would be recognised by the panel of judges in Monte Carlo the following year.

In the ghoulish manner of journalists on the hunt for the most striking pictures, my cameraman on that trip, Ian Dabbs, and I tramped from one hut to another. What might have appalled us when we'd started our trip just a few days before no longer impressed us much. The search for the shocking is like the craving for a drug: you require heavier and more frequent doses the longer you're at it. Pictures that stun the editors one day are written off as the same old stuff the next. This sounds callous, but it is just a fact of life. It's how we collect and compile the images that so move people in the comfort of their sitting rooms back home.

There was Amina Abdirahman, who had gone out that morning in search of wild, edible roots, leaving her two young girls lying on the dirt floor of their hut. They had been sick for days, and were reaching the final, enervating stages of terminal hunger. Habiba was ten years old and her sister, Ayaan, was nine. By the time Amina returned, she had only one daughter. Habiba had died. No rage, no whimpering, just a passing away – that simple, frictionless, motionless deliverance from a state of half-life to death itself. It was, as I said at the time in my dispatch, a vision of 'famine away from the headlines, a famine of quiet suffering and lonely death'.

There was the old woman who lay in her hut, abandoned by relations who were too weak to carry her on their journey to find food. It was the smell that drew me to her doorway: the smell of decaying flesh. Where her shinbone should have been there was a festering wound the size of my hand. She'd been shot in the leg as the retreating army of the deposed dictator, Siad Barre, took revenge on whoever it found in its way. The shattered leg had fused into the gentle V-shape of a boomerang. It was rotting; she was rotting. You could see it in her sick, yellow eyes and smell it in the putrid air she recycled with every struggling breath she took.

And then there was the face I will never forget.

My reaction to everyone else I met that day was a mixture of pity and revulsion. Yes, revulsion. The degeneration of the human body, sucked of its natural vitality by the twin evils of hunger and disease, is a disgusting thing. We never say so in our TV reports. It's a taboo that has yet to be breached. To be in a feeding centre is to hear and smell the excretion of fluids by people who are beyond controlling their bodily functions. To be in a feeding centre is surreptitiously to wipe your hands on the back of your trousers after you've held the clammy palm of a mother who has just cleaned vomit from her child's mouth.

There's pity, too, because even in this state of utter despair they aspire to a dignity that is almost impossible to achieve. An old woman will cover her shrivelled body with a soiled cloth as your gaze turns towards her. Or the old and dying man who keeps his hoe next to the mat with which, one day soon, they will shroud his corpse, as if he means to go out and till the soil once all this is over.

I saw that face for only a few seconds, a fleeting meeting of eyes before the face turned away, as its owner retreated into the darkness of another hut. In those brief moments there had been a smile, not from me, but from the face. It was not a smile of greeting, it was not a smile of joy – how could it be? – but it was a smile nonetheless. It touched me in a way I could not explain. It moved me in a way that went beyond pity or revulsion.

What was it about that smile? I had to find out. I urged my translator to ask the man why he had smiled. He came back with an answer. 'It's just that he was embarrassed to be found in this condition,' the translator explained. And then it clicked. That's what the smile had been about. It was the feeble smile that goes with apology, the kind of smile you might give if you felt you had done something wrong.

Normally inured to stories of suffering, accustomed to the evidence of deprivation, I was unsettled by this one smile in a way I had never been before. There is an unwritten code between the journalist and his subjects in these situations. The journalist observes, the subject is observed. The journalist is active, the subject is passive. But this smile had turned the tables on that tacit agreement. Without uttering a single word, the man had posed a question that cut to the heart of the relationship between me and him, between us and them, between the rich world and the poor world. If he was embarrassed to be found weakened by hunger and ground down by conflict, how should I feel to be standing there so strong and confident?

I resolved there and then that I would write the story of Gufgaduud with all the power and purpose I could muster. It seemed at the time, and still does, the only adequate answer a reporter can give to the man's question.

I have one regret about that brief encounter in Gufgaduud. Having searched through my notes and studied the dispatch that the BBC broadcast, I see that I never found out what the man's name was. Yet meeting him was a seminal moment in the gradual collection of experiences we call context. Facts and figures are the easy part of journalism. Knowing where they sit in the great scheme of things is much harder. So, my nameless friend, if you are still alive, I owe you one.

I may be one of the BBC's specialists on Africa but, at the time of writing, I cannot be sure exactly who is in charge of Somalia. Or even who is supposed to be in charge of Somalia. I admit that I haven't been as diligent as I might since I left my beat in Africa, but the fact remains that Somalia has become an irrelevance.

There is a place called Somalia on the map, but by any other definition of statehood, the country has ceased to matter. Sure, if there is another famine we will, no doubt, report it and the aid agencies will, of course, do their bit. But as a state with which one could trade, a nation with which one might have diplomatic relations or a country one would want to visit, Somalia holds about as much interest as a patch of scrubland between Chad and Libya. Where's that? you might ask. My point precisely. Somalia has slipped off the radar screen of public consciousness and is not likely to return to it for some time yet. It's not the way I would want it, not the way it should be, simply the way it is.

It wasn't always like this. In the seventies and eighties, Somalia was a crucible of superpower interest. America and the Soviet Union fought over it, competing for a presence in the strategic Horn of Africa. Many of the weapons that tore apart the fabric of this once-thriving society were the legacy of a global rivalry that left the two main protagonists untouched while the objects of their deadly embrace almost always emerged tarnished and demoralised.

Somalia gained its independence in 1960, in the first wave of decolonisation. And for nine years it managed some semblance of parliamentary government. In 1969 President Ali Shirmarke – an

elected president, albeit by the national assembly – was assassinated and the country's political path took what was to become
for Africa an increasingly familiar turn. General Siad Barre
assumed control at the head of a military government. At the
time he was an ally of the Soviet Union. That relationship lasted
till 1977, when Somalia went to war with its northern neighbour,
Ethiopia, a client of the United States. The conflict prompted
what must surely count as the most bizarre event of Cold War
rivalry: the superpowers swapped clients. The USSR took
Ethiopia and America backed Barre. Its staunch support for him
continued throughout the eighties, despite his declaration of a
one-party state. So much for the US's commitment to democracy.

Predictably enough, the suppression of political opposition
served merely to provide a seeding ground for military opposition, and civil war ensued. By January 1991, Barre's forces had
been defeated and the opposition forces took control of the capital, Mogadishu. It was no more than a respite from the country's
agony. The opposition forces failed to agree on who would succeed
Barre as president and turned their guns on each other. They bat-
tled for control of the capital with even greater ruthlessness than
they had shown in fighting their common enemy.

It was at this stage that my year of living dangerously began as
I made my first journey to Somalia. This was the mayhem of
which I tried to make sense over the next twelve months.

Mayhem is, perhaps, the wrong word. It certainly felt chaotic
and it was, most definitely, dangerous, but the violence was never
quite as random as it appeared to the untrained eye.

Unlike most African countries, Somalia does not have distinct
ethnic groups with different languages, religions and social structures. It is a homogenous society organised through a number of
clans and sub-clans. Traditionally, clan elders wielded great
authority and influence over their people. Though their power
was dented and manipulated during the civil war, they retained a
measure of control over the militias. When, for example, our

video camera was stolen by an armed gang, it was the relevant clan elder to whom we turned, and the equipment was duly returned. The idea that Somalia was utterly devoid of authority, though it made for some sensational script lines, was misleading.

But that was something I would learn much later, when I had become what hacks call an 'old hand' on the Somalia story. On 31 December 1991, the day I landed in the country, all I knew was that I had arrived in what was then, by common consent, the most difficult place on earth for a journalist.

Mogadishu's air of casual menace hit me as soon as I set foot on the tarmac at the airport. Our plane, a charter out of the Kenyan coastal city of Mombasa, was surrounded by gunmen. At least, that is how I would describe them. They would beg to differ. Porters, airport security, immigration officers were the titles they flung at us. It didn't really matter which particular role they assigned themselves, the request was always the same: dollars. A request backed up by the nonchalant curl of a skinny finger on the rusted trigger of a hand-me-down Kalashnikov rifle.

We're not talking a $5 tip here and there, we're talking serious money. A $20 bill was the smallest I ever got away with. Fifty dollars was average, and $100 common enough. You could always tell the journalists who were arriving in Mog, as we called it, for the first time. They would have all their notes together, exposing their entire expense allowance to the sharp eyes of the airport reception committee. Those of us who were more experienced never kept more than a few notes in any one pocket. I became an expert in secreting cash in places I never knew I had. I once hid some $100 bills end to end in a roll of toilet paper.

Whether or not economists ever get round to creating a global currency is pretty irrelevant, because the dollar has already been serving that purpose for years. Even in countries that ostensibly detest the evil machinations of American imperialism, the dollar is king. Try paying a Kabul taxi driver in the local Afghanis, or suggesting you'll settle your room bill in Kisangani in Congolese francs. Sterling is not even in the running. Indeed, there are many places where they have never heard of it. The yen may be traded on the international money markets but it makes little impact in the streets and alleyways where the real business is done. The gunmen of Mogadishu and the child soldiers of Liberia, the Lebanese diamond-traders in Sierra Leone and the corrupt officials of Nigeria, the drug-traffickers of Central America and South African mercenaries in somebody else's war, all pay homage daily to the great and pervasive power of the greenback. I recoil from the notion of any form of global domination but that, I am afraid, is the way it is.

I had arranged to stay with the British Save the Children Fund aid agency. Its field director in Mog, David Shearer, was at the airport to see in some supplies that were being offloaded from the charter plane. He had his own negotiations to contend with, so our greetings could be only perfunctory. Shearer was a New Zealander who, in the way of antipodean types, had rambled over to Europe before landing what was the fund's most stressful assignment at that time. Not that you could tell that from his appearance, at least, not until you examined him a little more carefully. Then the puffiness under the closely set eyes betrayed the sleepless nights. Otherwise he was unmarked by the strains of living in a war zone. His broad forehead, sitting under a crop of curly brown hair, was not lined. I never saw him rush anywhere, though he had the kind of physique that looked like it could do an awful lot of rushing if it really had to. He wore a pair of baggy shorts and an outsize T-shirt in the easy way only people who've grown up in them can. His lips were that pale-pink colour you sometimes find in white people who have spent too long in the sun. My parents would have called them *avicha raal* – boiled prawn – lips.

Though Shearer was the man in charge, it was his right-hand man, Hussein Mursal, who made it all happen. All the aid-agency field directors relied on 'local hire' to guide them through the

bewildering clan loyalties that were both cause of and solution to
Somalia's internecine political strife. Mursal was the silent partner,
the one who never gets mentioned in dispatches but without whom
the whole show would come to a grinding halt. Shearer and Mursal
were like chalk and cheese. Shearer was tall and robust, Mursal
slight and wiry. Shearer sported a mop of hair, Mursal was balding.
Shearer invited familiarity from the start; with Mursal there was
always a reserve. Sometimes it felt like aloofness. In fact it was
simply that for a Somali the road from acquaintance to friendship
is longer and, they would say, deeper than it is for us in the West.

How many times did Mursal try to explain the difference
between the Hawadle and Habr Gedir clans, between the Abgal
and Marehan? How often did he gently warn me that, ferociously
as the clans fought each other, it was nothing to how they would
react if attacked by outsiders? He was the very antithesis of the
national stereotype. Somali men were supposed to be fierce and
ruthless. Mursal was peaceable and compassionate. Somalis were
meant to show allegiance to clan above all else. Mursal understood a greater notion of humanity.

David Shearer and his wife Nush, short for Anushka, shared a
house with several other SCF workers. That evening we began a
relationship that lasted, on and off, till Somalia dropped out of the
news bulletins.

Over the last twenty years – ever since aid agencies realised
that publicity was no bad thing and news editors woke up to the
idea that human suffering could make compelling television –
the links between journalists and aid workers have become a
defining feature of the way humanitarian disasters are reported. It
is a symbiotic relationship, each giving the other a little bit of
what they need. Aid agencies are now big-budget businesses using
sophisticated fund-raising techniques designed to ensure a steady
flow of cash. Their job, of course, is helped enormously if TV
reports make the public aware of the work they are doing on behalf
of the poor or hungry, usually both. For their part, journalists,

in these days of near-instant satellite communication, want to be able to transmit their reports as quickly as possible. The aid agency workers offer a ready-made network of contacts and a well-oiled support structure, not to mention a cold bottle of beer at the end of a hot and sometimes dangerous day.

Most of the time this relationship works to the good. What's wrong with charities getting some publicity in return for their assistance in uncovering the plight of people who deserve better? Occasionally, though, the association can turn sour. To err is human, and dealing with disasters is not a precise science, so things can and do go wrong with the relief agencies' operations. Then it is the duty of the journalist to expose the mistakes and the inclination of the aid agencies to cover them up.

I discovered this for myself some years later, in 1998, while on assignment in rebel-controlled southern Sudan. In the early part of that year there had been growing evidence of a shortage of food in this sparsely populated region. There is always hunger in southern Sudan and some of the major aid agencies – Oxfam, Médecins sans Frontières and Save the Children (UK) – were inclined to the view that 1998 was no worse than any other year. In short they refused to regard it as an emergency or countenance any sort of extra relief operation over and above what they were already doing.

When I visited the town of Tonj the locals themselves said things were worse than usual. That was good enough for me. In my dispatch I argued that to quibble about whether what was happening constituted a famine seemed irrelevant when people were dying. One or two aid agency staff told me that they agreed with my assessment but were prevented from saying so on camera. They had been ordered to toe the agency line.

The agencies went as far as to convene a meeting in Nairobi (where many had their regional headquarters) at which my report was discussed. Several options were discussed, including one that entailed an attempt to control my movements in southern Sudan.

Imagine that. A group of foreigners, sitting round a table, trying to decide who should enter a country over which they had no juris-diction. Two Sudanese priests who were sitting in on this meeting were apparently astonished. I know all this because an aid worker who sympathised with my predicament took careful notes which she passed to me.

As it turned out, a couple of weeks later the agencies did indeed accept the severity of the crisis. They called together the London-based Disaster Emergency Committee and agreed to launch an emergency appeal.

Back in 1991 in Mogadishu, none of these tensions were evi-dent as David, Nush, several of their colleagues, my TV crew – Steve Taylor and Matt Leiper – and I sat down for that cold bottle of beer and a bowl of pasta bolognese. I marvelled at their ability to ignore the horrific din of sporadic battle. 'Outgoing,' one of them would remark as our conversation was interrupted – and my appetite dulled – by the thunderous clap of another mortar being sent on its deadly trajectory. Eventually, I was able to fake the same nonchalance.

So indiscriminate was the targeting that the people of Mogadishu referred to the shells as 'to whom it may concern'. It was an example of the mordant humour I would often hear from people around Africa as they coped day by day with dire cir-cumstances.

Each volley was a reminder that this humanitarian crisis, though linked to years of drought, was exacerbated by war. Aid workers like David Shearer, determined to bring succour to the people of Somalia, had to run the gauntlet of factional rivalry to do so. To try to deliver aid was to venture into an intense and complicated web of clan alliances. You could negotiate and cajole your way through it, but the effort was all too often dispropor-tionate to the result. We spoke about this problem that evening.

'It was crazy the hard time they were giving you down at the airport this morning,' I said to David.

'It's pretty standard stuff,' he replied. 'In fact we got off lightly today.'

'But someone should have a go at these bastards,' I insisted with all the naïveté of the newly arrived reporter. 'I mean, you should talk about it, expose them; tell the world that while you're busy trying to save lives, they are destroying them and making a profit on the side.'

David's response was the response of an honest man trying to do his job in an environment where there was scant regard for truth or justice.

'Look, let's face it, we have a dilemma,' he explained with the weariness of one who has debated the issue a million times. 'If you tell the world about the level of diversion, you will end up putting people off helping the Somalis.'

It was the first time I'd heard the word 'diversion' used in this way. It would not be the last. It is a neutral word, carrying none of the moral repugnance of the activity it purports to describe, like 'rationalisation' in the mouths of managers talking about rationalisation on the factory floor when what they really mean is that they are going to sack someone.

All of us, journalists included, played our part in turning this diversion into an industry. The money siphoned off from aid agencies and reporters replaced the prewar economy of trading in goods and services. It also fuelled the conflict. And like all economies, Somalia's was susceptible to inflation. When I first arrived in Mogadishu that December of 1991, we were hiring vehicles for about $50 a day. They came complete with gunmen loyal to a particular clan 'warlord' – the term we ended up using to describe the men who led the various factions in the civil war. Many of them resented it, preferring to be described according to their political affiliation, as if the destruction over which they presided could somehow be justified in the name of ideological difference. And that's if you accept that ideological difference played any part at all in the conflict, which I don't.

The gunmen were ostensibly there to protect you, though I was never entirely confident of their commitment to that particular task. In reality their job was to ensure that the vehicle was returned to its owner in one piece, ready to be rented out to the next journalist to arrive in Mogadishu. You paid extra for the gunmen, of course. In those early days you could get away with about another $50 for a couple of stringy-sinewed youths carrying the ubiquitous Kalashnikovs.

A year later we were being charged $350. By then there was a separate charge for petrol, which was set at $70 a day. If we ended up out of town, we were expected to feed the gunmen, though not obliged to find them accommodation.

It's incredible how glibly I'm writing about hiring these gunmen, as if it were the most normal thing in the world. And I suppose that once I'd been to Mogadishu half a dozen times it did become as routine as renting a car from Avis. And therein lay a danger, for in Mogadishu what passed for routine was never more than a brief interlude between two violent bouts of factional fighting. Ignore that rule and you ignored your own safety.

On one occasion, towards the end of that first trip, I was lulled into just such a false sense of security. Although we had been the first British TV crew to go into Somalia, we were joined pretty quickly by ITN, and soon the race was on to get the first pictures out of the country.

I had chartered a plane from Nairobi to pick us up from Mogadishu. As it came in to land, the pilot realised he was being shot at. He aborted the manoeuvre and, sensibly enough (though I didn't think so at the time), headed straight back for Nairobi. Having heard that the ITN team had managed to get out, I succumbed to that most dangerous of occupational hazards, the competitive instinct.

I organised another charter, thanks to the wonders of satellite phones, but opted to try a different airstrip, one that had never actually been used by either journalists or aid workers. It had been a quiet few days, and I decided it was worth taking a chance. I'd heard about this airstrip because it was the one held in reserve by the aid agencies as an exit point of last resort. It was at an old air force base at Bale Dogle. For reasons that will become obvious, we nicknamed it Bloody Dodgy.

So there we were, the driver, a couple of gunmen, the cameraman, Steve Taylor, the soundman, Matt Leiper, and me, plus an extra passenger. He was English, and no one quite knew what he was doing in Somalia. He had the look of a man with an eye for the main chance, and I'd come across him in the most unlikely places. Let's just call him a trader. Anyway, the reason he was in the van with us was that he was sick, very sick. It was dengue fever, bad enough to need specialist care in Nairobi.

The drive out of the capital was utterly uneventful. We chatted about how peaceful it all looked, about how impossible it was to believe there was a civil war going on. We fantasised about how cool the beer in Nairobi would be, and about the size of the lobster we were going to order at the Tamarind Restaurant in the city centre. Our guard was down; we forgot we were in Somalia. After a couple of hours we turned off the road and on to the end of the Bale Dogle airstrip.

At the other end of the runway we could see a dark mass of something. It was difficult to make out exactly what it was at first, like having an ant's-eye view of hundreds of other ants far away. By the time we realised what the dark mass of something was, it was too late to go back. To have turned tail would have looked suspicious. It was a couple of hundred gunmen.

I got out of the van, exhibiting as much bonhomie as my frayed nerves would allow. It's one of the little tricks you learn on the road. I greeted each man with the kind of vigour you would normally reserve for a long-lost friend. The cigarettes that I never smoke but always carry came into their own. So far so good.

Things started to go wrong when Steve, the cameraman, tried to squeeze off a few frames while he thought no one was looking.

But they were looking. Guns were pointed, voices were raised, excuses were offered and apologies given. The mood changed. An air of malevolence descended over the airstrip. The gunmen were here for a purpose and we were about to find out what it was. We had been no more than a bit of light relief for them. Now we were in the way.

Suddenly, we heard the distant drone of a plane. But as we searched the sky for our twin-engined Kingair, we spotted not one plane, but half a dozen or more.

This airstrip, it turned out, was the main delivery point for *khat*, the mildly narcotic leaf most Somali men chew. You often see them sprawled out on cushions and rugs in the late evening, ruminating in a leisurely but deliberate manner into the early hours. I tried it once, but was defeated by both the taste and the inordinate amount of time it took to have any effect on my neural synapses. *Khat* is to Somalia what a pint of beer is to Britain: something nearly everyone likes and worth a small fortune if you're the one doing the selling.

The *khatlo*, the white-flowered, evergreen shrub from which the leaf comes, is not grown in Somalia itself, or at least, not in sufficient quantities. It flourishes only in parts of northern Kenya and Ethiopia. And since its effects are most potent when the leaves are freshly plucked, getting daily supplies of *khat* into the markets of Mogadishu and elsewhere is big business. He who supplies the freshest leaves quickest is going to make the most money. And in Somalia in those days, where money was at stake, violence wasn't far behind.

The planes taxied in and parked off the runway about twenty metres away from each other. The gunmen converged on them like bees in a swarm. There was no sign of our aircraft. I was sure of that because I'd been given its registration number. One by one, the pilots opened the doors of their planes and started kicking out hessian sacks of *khat* tied into manageable bundles. The gunmen pounced on them, shouting at each other. The whole scene became chaotic. Soon the gunmen that had been surrounding one plane merged with those besieging another. Every now and then you saw the glint of a knife as someone tried to cut open a bale or heard the clatter of a Kalashnikov as it hit the tarmac.

I remember the first shot. I remember it because it was the moment I realised we were in big trouble. There were a couple more. After that I lost count. Then I heard the rev of a car engine. It was our van: the driver had decided he had done his bit, and now he was off. Out on the runway, some of the gunmen who, just a few minutes before, had been happy to share our cigarettes threw dark glances at us. I knew what was going on in their heads: 'Perhaps there's more where those cigarettes came from.'

We talked through our options. There were only two. Let the planes take off and face the gunmen on our own, or try to persuade one of the pilots to fly us out. The first didn't bear thinking about. We decided to sort our luggage into two piles, stuff we could afford to leave and the things we had to take with us. The second pile was a small one. It included little more than our videotapes.

As I walked towards one group of planes there were more shots. Several people fell to the ground. I knew that if I stopped to look I would lose my nerve. The first pilot refused to help. 'We're not even supposed to be here!' he shouted over the engine noise of another plane that was already moving off. These flights were not really legal. It was a bit of money on the side for the pilots and the companies that owned the planes. Most had filed misleading flight plans.

The second pilot, a woman, also turned me down. I was running out of time. Another aircraft was picking up speed along the runway. I turned round. Perhaps I'd have better luck with the pilots at the other end of the airstrip. More shooting, more bodies writhing on the ground. Our trader friend, too, was lying on the earth, in a feverish daze.

I strode up to the nearest plane. The pilot was refuelling from jerry cans he'd brought with him.

'Can you get us out of here?'

'No way, man,' he said. 'This plane has to go back empty. Anyway I've got to get out now.'

'We're ready,' I pleaded.

'Look. Just look at these fuckwits,' he said, pointing to the commotion all around us. 'You think they're just going to let me fly you out of here?'

I was getting desperate. 'I've got hundreds of dollars on me,' I said. 'The crew has more. They're all yours if you get us out.'

It was that dollar thing again. It did the trick.

'OK. But move.'

I signalled to the crew as surreptitiously as I could. The last thing we needed was for the gunmen to get wind of our imminent departure. We clambered on board. I took the seat next to the pilot; the crew sat behind. Our patient lay down in the gangway.

The pilot was checking his instruments. 'For fuck's sake, let's get out of here.' I think that was Matt. Too late. First a gunman climbed on to one of the wings. Then some others joined him. They started shouting at the pilot. This wasn't a passenger airstrip, they were saying, though how the pilot understood them, God only knows. They wanted dollars, of course. Lots of them. I looked at the pilot. I knew what was coming.

'Look, I'm sorry, guys. You've got to get off. I know it could get messy out there, but I just can't afford to risk the plane. I'll phone the BBC when I get to Nairobi.'

By now one of the gunmen had managed to open the door and was pointing his rifle at us. We all had the same private thoughts, uttered the same private prayer: 'Please, God, get us out of this.'

What happened next was too ridiculous for words. We should never have got away, but we did.

Throughout this whole episode our English patient had been

virtually speechless. Finally, he broke his silence, and I will be eternally thankful that he chose that particular moment to do so.

'We have no money,' he said, straining to sit up. 'We had to give it all away in Mogadishu. But we can get some more in Nairobi. We will send some with the pilot tomorrow.'

The only logical reaction from the gunman should have been: 'Do you think I'm stupid or what?' But for some reason it wasn't. Instead he said 'OK', mumbled something to the pilot, and turned away.

Somebody slammed the door shut, the pilot pushed the throttle and we moved off. As we accelerated, I looked back. The other gunmen had turned on the one who'd let us go. They were beating him up. I could see a rifle butt thudding into his ribs. Somebody aimed a kick at his head as he fell to the ground. There but for the grace of God. A hundred thoughts raced through my mind, but one of them was more persistent than the rest: 'I never, ever want to go through that again.'

And in truth, I never really got used to Mogadishu though, as I said earlier, I managed to contrive an air of experienced disregard. The more I went there, the more frightened I became. Never so frightened that I couldn't go out and do my job, but scared enough to end each day with a nagging knot of tension between my shoulder blades. The cure, temporary though it was, in Mogadishu and elsewhere, has always been a slug of brandy and a pull on a cigar last thing at night under a star-studded African sky.

There are some war reporters who thrive on the danger. They keep going back not simply because the story is still there, but because they miss the thrill of journalism under fire. I am not that type. I have spent a great deal of my career in the middle of conflict, but my only reason has been that it was the only way to tell a story with any authority. There are TV correspondents who feel they have to prove to the audience (or perhaps to themselves) that they are flirting with danger. Some of them wait for the sound of gunfire before delivering their words to camera. They are mistaking drama for credibility.

Given what happened on that first trip, I suppose it's surprising I ever went back. My first impression of Mogadishu was as a vision of a post-holocaust society, a place where a social fabric built on tradition and kinship had been replaced by an almost precivilised regression to competition and violence. But this new primitivism had at its disposal the twentieth century's formidable array of killing machines. Everybody seemed to have a gun, and when everybody has a gun, no one has control.

The centre of town, the old stone quarter with its courtyards and alleys, was virtually empty. Everybody had fled. You might see the odd head peep out of a window, but these people were fugitives in their own homes. Every building bore the scars of battle. What plaster remained formed an intricate pattern between the pockmarks of a thousand bullets. In my mind I used to try to link the little plaster islands to form pictures. That group there looks a bit like a map of Sri Lanka, and those further up the wall make the shape of a flower.

Occasionally you would find an unexploded mortar embedded in a wall, like some exhibit in a gallery of modern art. The ground was strewn with rounds of used ammunition that tinkled underfoot like shingle on an English beach. I made a note of some of the types of shell casings that lay about. One of them was an 85mm artillery round made in the Soviet Union, dated 1945. The Somalis were fighting with weapons nobody else wanted any more.

They used to call this area, a no-man's-land between north and south Mogadishu, the Green Line – a backhanded tribute to that ferocious piece of real estate in Beirut. You had to pass through here to go from the south, territory controlled by Mohamed Farah Aideed, to the north, where Ali Mahdi Mohamed called himself president. In fact, he was in charge of no more than an enclave.

I remember peering out of a first-floor window one day to see a teenager weaving his way through a late-afternoon crowd, a rocket-propelled grenade-launcher slung over his shoulder, carrying it as casually as a suburban schoolboy might tote a rucksack full of homework. But even the grenade-launcher was a puny piece of equipment compared to the Mad Max vehicles that careered around the corners. These were four-wheel-drive Toyota Landcruisers, or more ponderous Land Rovers, that had been adapted to take an assortment of weapons on their open backs: machine-guns, anti-aircraft cannons and, in one case, a rocket-launcher which had originally belonged to a Somali Air Force plane. I later saw this vehicle again when Mohamed Farah Aideed proudly showed me round his weapons depot. He demonstrated how the rockets could be triggered by touching two wires attached to a truck battery.

We sometimes hired these vehicles for our forays out of Mogadishu, especially when heading into areas of particular tension. A team of gunmen would ride out in front on another of these killing machines, and we would follow at a discreet distance. You chose the gunmen according to the clan they belonged to. The Habr Gedir dominated the south of Mogadishu, which is where most journalists were based, but were not welcome in other parts of the country. If you couldn't get gunmen from the clan in charge of the area you were hoping to reach, the next best thing was to find someone from a neutral clan. The Hawadle was one such, and its gunmen were sought after by both journalists and aid agencies.

The vehicles were nicknamed 'technicals'. Many people claimed to have used the term first, and they all gave slightly different explanations for it. The one I favour is that it was an expression coined by an aid worker accounting for his expenses, who had listed the vehicles as 'technical support'. I was told, though it could be an apocryphal story, that the purchase of ammunition for agency gunmen was sometimes described in the ledgers as 'nuts and bolts'.

The public back home was never really told just how much the agencies paid in protection money, not to mention the fact that even then there was no guarantee that the food would get to those who needed it. To lose a third of any shipment to looters was common; often it was double that.

In October 1992 a boat chartered by the World Food Programme, the UN organisation that collects food or money from donor countries, made a delivery at the southern port of Kismayu. From there the supplies were due to be distributed to the aid agencies that were responsible for handing them out to the Somalis. The UN children's fund paid a transport contractor $160,000 to move the shipment to their feeding centres. This was on top of the $25,000 UNICEF was forking out for protection. The food never made it to the feeding centre. It was diverted – that word again – to sate the more pressing hunger of the Somali Liberation Army.

The man who told me all this and gave me those figures is dead now. His name was Sean Devereaux. Not long after I spoke to him, he was walking back to the UNICEF compound at the end of a hard day's work when he was jumped by a lone gunman. His death was not random. It was an assassination. He was a good man who thought a deal was a deal. He was brimful of optimism, eager to play his part in creating a better world. But that *joie de vivre* was misplaced in the cynical world in which the warlords were operating. They didn't like the way he talked, especially to journalists.

It is easy to mock the aid workers. They are always young and often naïve. Some are motivated by a thirst for adventure, others by a sense of duty. They are like the new missionaries, nowadays carrying their ideals instead of a Bible. The cassock and veil have given way to faded frocks and ragged jeans. They are putty in the hands of the warlords, the faction leaders, the extremists on whose terrain they have to work. It's not difficult to count the cost of their mistakes, but much harder to put a value on their quiet achievements.

What we, the journalists, were paying the various clans for

protection was just the icing on what had become an increasingly appetising cake. The warlords were making vast amounts of money. As the relief effort became more urgently needed, as hunger turned to famine, the greater the sums demanded became. The calculation made by the warlords and their benefactors was as simple and as amoral as that. Ton for ton, Somalia became the most expensive relief operation the world had ever seen.

Aid workers in Somalia were confronted with the age-old dilemma concerning ends and means. Was it OK to feed the greed of the warlords if, in the process, you were able to alleviate the suffering of hundreds of thousands of people? Every aid organisation I know came down on the side of the innocents caught up in the conflict.

Occasionally one organisation or another would try to make a stand. They might reduce costs for a while, but soon saw them rise again. I remember one such valiant, ultimately futile, attempt to buck the system. It was November 1992, and I was in the central Somali town of Bardera, which had borne the brunt of some heavy fighting. I was trying to check out the extent of the civilian casualties, but when I got to the clinic, everybody was on the move.

Mattresses were being rolled up, cartons of drugs piled one on top of the other and the patients were being put on to the back of an open truck. I watched as one man, a boy, really, tried to pull himself over the tailgate. His whole body quivered with the effort. His neck and shoulders were covered in bandages that failed to stem the blood trickling down his bony back. I learned later that he still had a bullet lodged in his shoulder. Up on the truck, another casualty tried to give what help he could.

In the middle of all this was Khalil Dale, a British citizen and Red Cross worker. He was virtually in tears as he told me that they were moving because the landlord had put up their rent. He wanted an extra $1,500 a month. The property was no more than a modest bungalow in a half-acre plot. The International Committee of the

Red Cross (ICRC) was already paying the Somali landlord $3,000 a month for the privilege of treating his own people. He was demanding a Mayfair rent for a war-zone property to which piped water was intermittent and electricity supply non-existent.

I shared Khalil's despondency but, privately, railed against his impotence. Khalil's forced evacuation of that clinic, the image of him standing there feebly as his patients were herded away, was a symbol of everything that was wrong with the Somali aid operation.

But this moral indignation – and it was felt by a majority of aid workers and journalists alike – was a dangerous sentiment. It was, more or less, the sentiment that propelled America into intervening in Somalia.

This was an intervention based on the notion that Somalia's ills could be solved if only you could sidestep the rapacious warlords and get food direct to the people who needed it. It was a bit like organising a soup kitchen for the homeless without stopping to work out why people are homeless in the first place. I call it the Hershey Bar intervention, because so many of the marines who came over that December believed that their task was going to be as easy as giving candy to a child.

Operation Restore Hope, a touchingly naïve codename, began a little after midnight on 9 December 1992. From the warm and tranquil waters of the Indian Ocean there emerged a posse of US Navy Sea, Air and Land troops (SEALs), as alien to this shoreline as a *dhow* full of Arab traders would be to Brighton beach. They were an advance guard, a crack unit trained to penetrate enemy territory and prepare the ground for the invasion force. They came dressed to kill but encountered nothing more threatening than the flashbulbs of the international press corps.

It was a moment of pure farce. The SEALs seemed more astonished than vigilant, and yet they must have known that the world's media had beaten them to Mogadishu. With their tarred faces and shocked eyes, they looked like the cast of a *Black and*

White Minstrel Show who'd discovered they'd been sent to the wrong theatre.

The entertainment analogies are not as gratuitous as you might think. The truth is that the whole production was stage-managed with TV audiences back home in mind. Americans were preparing to feel good about themselves. The timing was perfect for the prime-time news 'shows', as they call them. Why else send in an expeditionary force of SEALs with all their ridiculous military tackle under cover of darkness, when everyone knew there would be no counter-attack? Not even the most reckless Somali warlord would have been foolish enough to clash with the Yanks head-on. They would bide their time and pick the right moment. The day before I had seen one of the American commanders, General Frank Labuti, caught in a Mogadishu traffic jam with a gunman for protection. It must have been the most widely publicised surprise invasion in the annals of military history.

Yet for all its pantomime posturing, Operation Restore Hope was history in the making. It will be remembered as the first occasion on which the international community authorised military intervention for purely humanitarian means, an act sanctioned by UN Resolution 794. Unlike the interventions in Korea in the 1950s and Kuwait in 1991, troops had been deployed without the prior approval of the local government being sought. President George Bush (senior) had sent his men to foreign fields before. In Panama and Kuwait it had been in the service of America's strategic interests. But this was supposed to be different; here gum-chewing, flag-loyal American boys were putting themselves in harm's way for no other reason than to uphold our common humanitarian values. That, at any rate, was the theory.

The key words 'all necessary means' in the resolution meant that the marines could do whatever they thought fit in the pursuit of their goal, the saving of Somalia. Saving Somalia: it slips off the tongue so smoothly. It's as if the White House, too, had been so mesmerised by the prospect of doing good that it failed to understand, or chose to overlook, how easy it would be for the whole thing to turn sour.

Knowing the difference between good men and bad men, understanding the gulf that separates right from wrong – this is the stuff of moral certainty. This is the world in which America's celluloid heroes, the John Waynes and Gary Coopers, the two Toms, Hanks and Cruise, have fought the great fight. Alas for the Americans, moral certainty was a poor compass with which to navigate the internecine world of Somali politics. And Mogadishu was no Hollywood studio. It was always going to be difficult for the US to come in and play the sheriff as if it had had no hand in the problems Somalia was facing.

Indeed, the Americans failed to grasp that the break-up of Somalia was a political problem at all, as much a part of the fall-out from the Cold War as Bosnia was. In Bosnia, the warlords were treated with caution, if not respect. In Somalia, one had the impression that American planners were never really able to look beyond the apparently shambolic vision of men with rubber sandals and sarongs wielding worn-out weapons. Racial stereotyping may well have played its part in America's ultimately fatal under-estimation of the task at hand. They saw poverty but mistook it for weakness. Because they could not see any uniforms, they assumed there was no discipline. Because Somali gunmen did not salute, they believed there was no command and control. They were wrong every time. They failed to understand that even in these, the worst of all times, Somalis cherished a sense of national pride. After all, regardless of their clan affiliations, they speak the same language and worship the same God.

Nobody was asking the Americans to befriend the warlords, but neither did they have to turn them into outright enemies. Yet within hours of setting foot on the white sands of Mogadishu, the USA had managed to send out precisely the wrong message.

In the wake of those navy SEALs came waves of transport helicopters, heading for the airport. The crack of the rotor blades as they whipped the chill air could be heard from miles away. Set against the half light of an Indian Ocean dawn, they reminded me of a scene in the film *Apocalypse Now*. As it turned out, the comparison with that story of America's nightmare in Vietnam was not entirely inappropriate.

As each helicopter touched down on the tarmac, marines burst out of them like thoroughbreds released from the starting gate. They fanned out across the airport, sticking to a preordained battle plan. Even when they realised the place was full of gawking journalists, they were no more able to deviate from it than pre-programmed robots.

One group headed for the hangars, guns at the ready, safety catches off. As some of these lock-jawed marines took positions outside the hangar doors, the rest stormed in. Almost immediately there were shouts from inside. The men by the doors rushed in, too. You could sense from the look on the commanders' faces that something had gone wrong. Reinforcements were launched towards the hangar. It felt as if all hell might break loose.

But the climax never came. Instead, three or four Somalis emerged with their hands up. They seemed bemused rather than frightened. With their sarongs flapping around their ankles, they looked about as likely to take on the Americans as field mice cornered by a cat. No matter. The drill had to be played out. The Somalis were forced to lie face down on the tarmac. Shouting, 'Cover me! Cover me!', one of the marines used his massive, desert-issue boots to spreadeagle them. Now the Somalis' bemusement turned to anger. What had begun – let's give the marines the benefit of the doubt – as an honest mistake was developing into ritual humiliation. I said as much in my dispatch that day.

Several thoughts went through my mind as I watched all this, the most important of which was that the Americans had no idea how to deal with Somalis. The imagery was all wrong: the six-foot American with a Somali at his feet evoked domination, not co-operation. The marine was white, the Somali was black; the

American was big, the local was small; the soldier was oppressor, the civilian was oppressed. The men were at the airport because they worked there: they were guards. Not very good ones – they were said to have been asleep when the marines pounced on them – but that is beside the point.

The intervention was the most obvious outward sign of what George Bush had taken to calling a 'new world order'. Like many people who had watched Somalia's slide into lawlessness, I had believed that the use of disciplined soldiers in the pursuit of humanitarian goals was a good thing. If it worked in Somalia, it might provide a template for intervention in troublespots all over the world. But I think I knew then, as the Somalis were led away with their hands tied, that it was not going to work. What I was not certain about was whether soldiers, by definition, were ill suited to the task, or whether it was just these soldiers. Perhaps the Americans, with their oversimplified view of the world, were the wrong people for the job.

Even before the sun was up that day, it was beginning to look like America versus the Somalis. And if it was going to come to that, I was with the Somalis. In terms of both habit and intellect I had more in common with the liberal-minded policy-makers in Washington and New York who had conceived Operation Restore Hope, but in my guts, where it mattered, I felt an affinity with the Somalis. This was certainly not a case of sympathising with either the aims or methods of the war-lords. It was a visceral reaction to the sight of Africans being patronised by outsiders. Why, when the rich world intervenes, does it still have to do so in such an overbearing and insensitive way?

And it wasn't just me who thought that. It wasn't just the Somalis, who soon heard about what had happened at the airport that morning. The Americans, with their unthinking arrogance, also managed to alienate the UN troops who had already been in Somalia for some months and had borne the brunt of the conflict.

In Mogadishu the UN contingent was made up of Pakistani soldiers. Poorly equipped and heavily outnumbered, they had carried the can while diplomats in New York argued this way and that about what to do.

The Americans were the latecomers, but they strutted around as if they owned the place. Some of the most senior Pakistani officers told me they felt humiliated by the way their presence and advice was disregarded. The Pakistanis and, by implication, the United Nations were sidelined, relegated to the role of spectators, as the Americans set about doing things their way. From that moment, a UN mission that was already seriously flawed was undermined beyond redemption.

What the Pakistani officers would only tell me off the record, and would never have dared to mention in public, was that they felt they had been slighted because of who they were. In particular because they were not white. I believed them.

With this inauspicious beginning, the Americans began to lose the battle for hearts and minds long before they got anywhere near the hungry children of Somalia. In truth they appeared too late to do the job they'd set themselves. The debate will rage on, but there are many who believe that most of the people who were going to die of hunger and disease had already done so by the time the cavalry arrived. There is a Darwinian principle to famines: the weak (mostly children and the elderly) perish quite quickly and the rest survive, albeit in a weakened state. So if you don't intervene early, you might as well not bother. In a private briefing just two days before the beginning of Operation Restore Hope, Paul Mitchell, the World Food Programme's spokesman in Mogadishu, told me: 'What you have now are just pockets of famine.'

According to the United Nations' own figures, mortality rates had begun to drop well before the Americans set foot on Somali soil. I cited those figures in a documentary broadcast at the time, but they were never widely publicised. UN relief agencies were happy to go along with the notion that Operation Restore Hope was indeed saving Somalis. The UN could then argue that it was its lack of military muscle rather than negligence, inefficiency and political paralysis that prevented it from making an early impact on the crisis.

In the months that followed, the 25,000 or so US troops began to behave as if they were just another faction. In theory, they made up the most powerful force in the land, but power, as they would learn, was not enough.

In May 1993 they launched a manhunt for Mohamed Farah Aideed, the warlord who ran much of Mogadishu and the surrounding area. They even put up 'wanted' posters of the kind a sheriff might have nailed to the porch outside the saloon bar of a gold-prospecting town on the wild west frontier. Twenty-five thousand dollars was the asking price. It was a fatal miscalculation. Not only in the sense that it showed appalling judgement, but also because it would result in the deaths of eighteen fresh-faced American boys.

The manhunt served only to poison already deteriorating relations between the US military and the Somalis. It persuaded even those who did not support Aideed that the US was the real enemy. The notion that America – notwithstanding its Black Hawk attack helicopters, its TOW missiles and its army of well-paid informers, not to mention the most pampered troops on earth – could capture Aideed on his own turf was absurd.

And so it proved. On 3 October 1993, American troops launched yet another raid, this time on a location deep in Aideed's territory where they believed he would be present at a meeting. Some time in the afternoon, a crack team of US Delta Force commandos were dropped on to the site from helicopters. The plan was that they should make the arrests while the US Army rangers made the area safe. Both teams were then to return to base under the escort of a third team. But it all went disastrously wrong.

No sooner had the commandos made their arrests – and Aideed was nowhere to be seen – than they realised that they had been surrounded. The whole area was teeming with gunmen. It was as if every Somali man, every Somali teenager, became a fighter that day. In every alleyway lay an ambush; out of every window an AK47 spewed hot metal. Not only had the Americans lost any advantage they might have had on the ground, their air power was also severely dented. Two Black Hawk helicopters were downed, and one of the pilots was captured alive.

It was well into the night before the Americans were rescued. Hundreds of Somalis were wounded; how many were killed will never be known. What we do know is that eighteen American soldiers died: their highest number of fatalities in one battle since the Vietnam War.

The events of 3 October were recreated in Ridley Scott's film *Black Hawk Down*, which was shown in British cinemas in early 2002. I use the word 'recreated' loosely, in its Hollywood sense. Scott managed to reduce the whole sorry episode to a simple tale of good guys versus bad guys. Though British by birth, he contrived to Americanise the film, twisting it into a story of heroic Americans against nasty and evil Somalis. No mention was made of the so-called crack troops acting on flawed intelligence, or even of the fact that, when the surviving commandos were rescued that evening, Malaysian soldiers played a brave and crucial part.

I suppose none of this would matter – film producers need to put bums on cinema seats – if it were not for the fact that too many Americans get their world view from what Hollywood decides is the most saleable version of history. For Americans, it is a beguiling but ultimately dangerous and dishonest rendition of the way the world works. If they are constantly being told how benign their country's role in international affairs is, it is no surprise if they feel there is no need to change their ways. In the wake of September 11 that would be the worst of all possible

outcomes. No one in their right mind would seek to underesti-
mate the gravity of the attacks on the World Trade Center and
the Pentagon, but equally only a fool could maintain that
America has no lessons to learn from what happened. Simply to
carry on as before would be the real betrayal of the thousands of
good people who died that day.

The history of modern conflict is punctuated with images that
have come to define the wars they depict. Robert Capa's photograph, taken just as a bullet hits a loyalist soldier in the Spanish
civil war is one example. Another that comes to mind is Don
McCullin's picture of a dead North Vietnamese soldier surrounded
by scattered photos of his family and a bagful of spare bullets – the
symbols of peace and war.

   The strife in Somalia threw up its own arresting image
although, in keeping with the satellite age, it was broadcast on
America's CNN, reaching a much wider audience far faster. In the
days that followed, every paper and news magazine carried similar
photographs. They all showed the bound corpse of an American
soldier being dragged around the streets of Mogadishu. Somali
teenagers danced around the body. By this time the bulk of the
US forces had left Somalia, but there is no doubt that this
sickening illustration of the conflict precipitated America's
complete withdrawal from the country, led to its reluctance ever
to get involved in Africa again and left its people perplexed and
angry. 'Is this what we get for trying to save Somalia?' was the
inevitable cry from a million sitting rooms across the US.

   I can't remember exactly where I was when I saw those pictures.
But I do remember – and this is difficult to admit – how I felt
when I realised what happened. America, I thought to myself,
had only itself to blame. Don't get me wrong. I found the images
of Somali youth rejoicing over the battered and lifeless body of an
American soldier as repulsive as anyone else. I grieved with the
parents of that young man. I mourned with the families of all the

Paradise lost: we were not just leaving Ceylon, we were turning our backs on it.
Popperfoto

Moving up in the world: the Alagiahs in Ghana, proud owners of
a second-hand Mercedes.

Class photo, Christ the King School, in the mid-1960s (I'm the one in the striped shirt). Freedom's children: 'Be whatever you want to be, my child.'

Kwame Nkrumah, Ghana's first elected leader: Africa's time had come.
Marc Ribaud/Magnum Photos

Left: Boy soldiers in Liberia: children at play. Bang, bang you're dead. In Africa, it's for real.
Popperfoto/Reuters

Below: A year of living dangerously: in Somalia with Jim Thomson, Colin Blane, Mark McCauley and some technical help.

War and famine in Somalia: No rage, no whimpering – that simple, frictionless, motionless deliverance from a state of half-life to death itself.
James Nachtwey/Magnum Photos

America to the rescue: moral certainty was a poor compass with which
to navigate Somali politics.
Alexander Joe/Popperfoto

Saving Somalia: the marines thought it
would be as easy as giving candy to kids.
Wesley Bocxe/Network

The image that shocked America: Somalis
were rejoicing in the belittling of the USA's
power, not in the murder of one of its sons.
Popperfoto/Reuters

Above: Evacuation of Kigali, 1994: saving expatriates was more important than stopping the genocide.
Popperfoto

Left: The instruments of death: Hutus abandoned their machetes as they fled Rwanda.
Luc Delahaye/Magnum Photos

Save our souls: even the churches were no protection against genocide.
Jack Picone/Network

Left: Rwanda's Paul Kagame: 'We used communication and information warfare better than anyone.'
François Lenoir/Popperfoto/Reuters

Below: A nation within a nation: a million Rwandan Hutus fled to Goma, eastern Zaire, where the camps became a launch-pad for insurgency.
C. Steele-Perkins/Magnum Photos

Cholera strikes the Goma camps, 1994: you could smell death in the air.
Corinne Dufka/Poppertoto/Reuters

Thousands died in Goma every day: the corpses were left like rubbish
to be collected in the morning.
Panos Pictures

You laugh together, sometimes you cry together: at the border of Zaire and Rwanda with
Ngarambe Seth *(second left)*, my translator in Goma.
Bhasker Solanki, BBC

Zaire's Mobutu Sese Seko: government of one man, for one man – and his friends.
Abbas/Magnum Photos

The press conference aboard the Outeniqua: Mandela, the peacemaker, flanked by
Mobutu and Laurent Kabila – rogue and rebel.

Popperfoto

The seat of power: inside Mobutu's Kinshasa residence on the day he fled.
He had a palace and a throne, but he no longer had a country.

Gilles Peress/Magnum Photos

Expelled Ugandan Asians arrive in Britain in 1972: Idi Amin tapped into a distrust of Asians.
David Hurn/Magnum Photos

Uganda's Yoweri Museveni during the five-year bush war: 'Colonialism walked into an open house.'
Panos Pictures

Robert Mugabe: still ranting about the white man like a loser who claims
he never stood a chance.
EPA

Farmer's house, Zimbabwe: the land of the white people was another country.
Gideon Mendel/Network

South Africa's Nelson Mandela: not the first of a new order, but the last, and best, of the old.

Philippe Wojazer/Reuters

Mr Mandela with Betsie Verwoerd: forgiving your enemy does not cost a penny from the national coffers.

Juda Ngwenya/Popperfoto/Reuters

Frances with Khethiwe Badela and mother: on the other side of the wall of suspicion, fear, prejudice, culture and habit that still divided South Africa.

South Africa's double act: Nelson Mandela
and Archbishop Desmond Tutu, the freedom
fighter and the cleric.
EPA

Friends on the road: with BBC producer Milton Nkosi *(far left)*, Jerry 'Poncer' Chabane
and cameraman Glenn Middleton.

Dogon village, Mali: there are little victories in remote places.
Topham Picturepoint

With the village elders: they know they are much stronger working together than they would be if they set off on the lonely path of individualism.

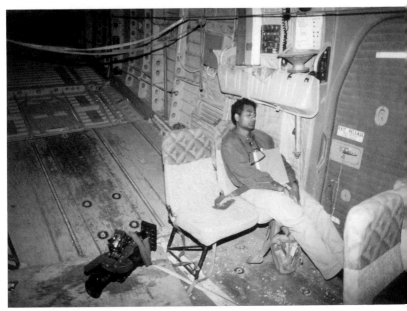

Journey's end: homeward bound on an aid plane.

If only the baobab tree could speak. They have seen it all: the best and the worst.

Panos Pictures

others who died that day, Somali and American. I have witnessed too many of the gory consequences of war to believe that any part of it, even victory, is a matter for jubilation. Relief, yes; jubilation, never.

And yet I felt I knew why Somalis had responded with unrestrained glee and merciless mockery. It was the celebration of the weak when the strong are brought down to size. They were rejoicing in the belittling of America's power, not in the murder of one of its sons.

And that, perhaps, is Somalia's true place in history. The country will be remembered not for the famine – there will be many more of them, some of them as severe – but for what its plight revealed about how rich countries deal with their counterparts in the poor world. When the historians review the crisis in Somalia, they will identify in it the false dawn of the new world order.

The question we should ask ourselves about Somalia is not the obvious one about why the famine happened, but whether it could have been avoided altogether. People went hungry because the failure of the rains in successive years was compounded by the effects of civil war. But the war itself might have been avoided if foreign-policy strategists in Washington, London and Paris had been as concerned about the effects of post-Cold War transition in Africa as they were about its repercussions in Europe. Huge amounts of money, some of it originally destined for Africa, were poured into Central and Eastern Europe in order to ease the passage from totalitarian rule to quasi-democracy.

The idea that Africa, the playground of the superpowers, might need extra financial help in its own journey out of Cold War rivalry was overlooked or forgotten. Basically, Africans didn't matter, or at least, not as much as Europeans. Proximity, not principle, has too often seemed to drive foreign policy in the rich world. The short-term deployment of troops, such as in Sierra Leone, is not the same as a long-term commitment of money.

So, while the carnage in Kosovo or the corruption in Moscow are put down to the inevitable teething troubles of the adjustment to a new world order, similar problems in Africa – and Somalia is but one example – are reckoned to be purely the product of Africa's apparently unique propensity for self-destruction.

As a result the problems are allowed to fester away till they become great, gaping wounds in its social fabric. When that happens there's always emergency money for Africa. Cash to fly in tents and bags of food. Plenty of aid workers happy to cradle the runt-like children of murdered parents. This is foreign policy of the sticking-plaster variety. It's dishonourable and, what's more, it doesn't work.

Sooner or later, we will have to confront these problems. If we fail to do all we can to prevent these disasters, they will land on our doorsteps anyway. It is no coincidence that over the last decade Somalis have accounted for one of the single largest groups of asylum-seekers in Britain.

Somalia did to the collective US psyche in the 1990s what Vietnam had done in the 1970s. Rejected and hurt, Americans vowed privately, though not explicitly, to stay away from this ungrateful and complicated world. After sustained and concerted pleas from their allies in Europe they reluctantly got involved in Bosnia, but when it came to Africa, no amount of pressure would persuade the White House to put its men in harm's way. So when the first whisperings of genocide in Rwanda reached American diplomats at the UN two years later they turned the other way. What's more, they pushed and cajoled till everyone else did the same. The UN pulled its peacekeepers out just when they were needed most. The international community literally just walked away.

7

Who to Bless, Who to Blame?

He's my friend; he's my enemy. He tells the truth; he's a liar. He's a victim; he's a perpetrator. He is innocent; he is guilty.

This is a story about a man I knew. It is also the story of his nation. His name is Ngarambe Seth and his country is Rwanda, the land of a thousand hills still soaked in the blood of genocide. It's about the two sides of humanity, good and evil. It's about how easy it is to identify the crime, but how difficult it is to accept and understand how a person came to commit it. It's about whether you can rebuild a nation when so many of its citizens are known to be killers.

There are two levels on which I came to understand the genocide in Rwanda and its aftermath. One was personal, the other professional. When I heard that my employee and friend Seth was in jail, accused of taking part in the genocide, I found myself caught between the two. My friendship with Seth pulled me in one direction while my instincts as a journalist dragged me in the other. Intimacy told me to trust the man I had come to know;

my reporter's training told me to give equal weight to the man who accused him.

It's not that I was ambivalent about what was right or wrong, or that I couldn't tell the difference between good and evil. There is no moral grey area between murderers and murdered. That wasn't the problem. It was that I could not fathom how to react, what to do, till a court decided whether or not Seth was guilty. Where would I place him in my mind? Among those with whom I sympathised or among those I despised? I had to put Seth into what I can only describe as a state of suspended animation, a kind of mental limbo, while Rwanda's painfully slow judicial system got round to his case.

I discovered that moral certainty, the ability to judge and proclaim who is just and who is unjust – the stock-in-trade of the foreign correspondent – deserted me when I was confronted with the dilemma in the person of Seth. It was no longer a decision to be made in the abstract. Suddenly, the verdict of a judge, whenever it came, mattered more than my intuition as a friend.

Like Somalia, as a nation, Rwanda is something of a rarity in Africa. Although there are two main ethnic groups, the Hutus and the Tutsis, they share a single language, culture and territory. So the sharp tribal or racial differences that feature elsewhere on the continent do not exist here. Apart from Somalia, I know of only two other countries in sub-Saharan Africa that share this distinction: Botswana and Burundi.

But if Rwanda is free of cultural differences, it does have other divisions that have been exploited by unscrupulous politicians, the media and the Church. These are largely to do with wealth and status. Traditionally, and this goes back hundreds of years, economic power has resided in the hands of the cattle-owners. They are the Tutsis, and they are in a minority. The majority of the population are farmers, known as Hutus. The disparities between the two groups are akin to the hierarchy of castes that prevails in India or Sri Lanka, but with one crucial difference:

some Hutus have moved into the Tutsi category as their fortunes rose, and intermarriage between the two groups is common.

Rwanda is the most densely populated country in Africa and consequently your neighbour's relative wealth is constantly in your face. There are various ways of dealing with the inevitable tensions to which this combination of caste and history gives rise. One of them is to blame the disparities on an ethnic conspiracy. This was the route chosen by some Hutu politicians in Rwanda, who portrayed the Tutsis as proponents of a master-race ideology designed to subjugate the Hutu. This message was pumped out for decades. So it was that careful planning and years of propaganda preceded what happened in 1994.

On 6 April, Rwanda was plunged into a nightmare from which it has yet to recover. It was the start of a hundred days of slaughter, a systematic attempt by Hutu politicians, the national army and their allies among the political militias to exterminate the Tutsis and anyone who supported or protected them – even if they happened to be Hutus themselves. It was, to put it bluntly, genocide. By the time the killing was brought to an end, about 800,000 Rwandans had been murdered, the vast majority of them Tutsis. Indeed, for every Tutsi who survived the slaughter, seven did not.

I first met Ngarambe Seth in July 1994 in the eastern Zairean town of Goma, just across the border with Rwanda. He was among a million or so Hutus who had fled into Zaire when the Rwanda Patriotic Front (RPF), a largely Tutsi-led military and political organisation, finally ended the genocide by defeating the national army and taking over the country. Those Hutus who had taken part in the mass murder had every reason to fear the wrath of the RPF. But some who had had no direct involvement in the killing also sought refuge in Zaire, convinced that the predominantly Tutsi army of the RPF would seek retribution without bothering to first establish who was guilty and who was innocent. The propagandists in the defeated Hutu government were sticking to their task to the very end.

To be in Goma at this time was like being transported back to a scene from the Old Testament. In less than a week, about a million people trudged across the border from Rwanda into Zaire. Boys and girls clutched their mothers' clothes with one hand, a plastic bottle of murky water in the other. Men staggered under the weight of the possessions they balanced on their shoulders. Every once in a while you would find a child on its own, buffeted like a piece of jetsam in this bursting river of humankind. When the exodus was over the aid agencies counted as many as 40,000 children who had come adrift from their families.

On the face of it, it was a story of exile, the all-too-familiar flight of a people driven from their homeland. It had happened during the Biafran war, it was still happening in parts of southern Sudan, and it would happen again in some other corner of this blighted continent. In fact, whatever the similarities with any previous refugee crisis, there had never been an exodus like this before – not in Africa, and perhaps not anywhere else. These were not refugees from a natural disaster or the innocent victims of a war. These were a people bound together by guilt, either of commission or by association. Tens of thousands had blood on their hands. Many had watched the butchers at work, egged them on from the sidelines. Some had simply let it continue, staying silent. There were nuns, priests, even children, who carried the burden of complicity and worse along with their belongings.

But you couldn't tell, by looking at them, who needed help and who deserved punishment; who to bless and who to blame. Perhaps there was one small outward sign of their inner turmoil, their attempt to exorcise the demons. In the first hours of the crossing, Zairean border guards ordered those entering Goma to abandon their weapons. They were not particularly strict with the Rwandan soldiers, most of whom were allowed to keep their weapons – the guns that had been responsible for much of the killing. The civilians were scrutinised more thoroughly. Soon a pile of machetes began to accumulate by the border gate. In the end people simply added to the collection without any prompting from the guards. For those civilians who had taken part in the genocide, the machete had been the weapon of choice. Tools designed to clear the ground and bring forth new life were instead used to do precisely the opposite. It was as if the Rwandans thought that by ridding themselves of their machetes they might also purge themselves of the sin.

Goma lies on the shores of Lake Kivu and in the shadow of the towering Nyiragongo crater, one of five volcanic mountains that dominate the landscape. When Nyiragongo, unexpectedly, became active – some say they saw an orange light above the crater – it added to the feeling that one was witnessing a scene of biblical retribution. The volcano did, in fact, erupt in January 2002, and as a result over a hundred people died and tens of thousands were left homeless.

Once, Goma had been a holiday resort, first for the colonials and then for the new masters of Zaire. In 1994 the whole area became one massive refugee camp. But to talk of anything as precise as a camp is to dignify it with a sense of order it did not have in those first days. Goma and its hinterland was simply the spot where the Rwandans stopped, too exhausted to carry on. There could not have been a more inhospitable sanctuary. The ground was harsh and jagged, a vast plain of black, broken lava, the legacy of Nyiragongo's previous eruptions. In the early morning, the thick smoke from thousands of fires would hang over the crowd like a huge, suffocating quilt. As it shifted this way and that in the breeze, it would reveal fleeting glimpses of squalor and hardship, death and disease.

As the first BBC journalist on the scene, it was down to me to find a translator, someone who could switch easily between English and Kinyarwanda. It was an unusual combination for the Rwandans, whose second language tended to be French, a hangover from Belgian colonialism. But I learned that there was a whole group of refugees who spoke English, all members of the Seventh Day Adventist Church who had fled the Rwandan capital, Kigali. They had taken shelter, appropriately enough, in a church compound in Goma.

I found them soon enough and, in my own fumbling French, put the word about that I was looking for someone who could translate for the BBC for a fee. Very soon I was surrounded by a group of men, each trying to push the others aside. One of them caught my eye. His English was more than adequate for the tasks I had in mind, but I was dubious about his physical fitness. Feeding the beast that is the newsroom on a headline story – which was what the Rwandan exodus had become – is an arduous business. We routinely worked eighteen-hour days in the toughest of conditions. Zaire is two hours ahead of London time, so when putting together something for the *Nine o'Clock News* you couldn't even think of taking a breather till eleven. At night we slept three to a room. Apart from me, there was the camera crew, Keith 'Chuck' Tayman and Nikki Millard. Somebody always ended up on the floor.

This man looked as if such a schedule might tip him over the edge of the exhaustion he was already clearly exhibiting into something much worse. He was sick – that was obvious. The eyes, sunk into a face that seemed to shrink from his prominent teeth, were yellow with fever. He coughed. It was the cough of a consumptive. His shabby clothes hung on him the way they might on a scarecrow.

'Look,' I said to him in a voice that pretended to be sympathetic but which, apparently, betrayed my impatience. 'The work we do is very tough. You'll be on the go from morning till night, and I just don't think you can manage.'

'Who are you to tell me I cannot manage?' he shot back, the sharpness of his tone at odds with his stooped and broken stature. 'I can do any work. I need the work. I have to find money for my family.'

I think it was the way he spoke of his commitment to his family that got to me. Unconsciously, I began to make assumptions about his history. Perhaps he was one of the innocents who fled because they believed the stories about the Tutsis' summary justice. I hired him.

'OK. What's your name? We have to start right now.'

'Ngarambe Seth, sir. And please can I take a few minutes to tell my children what is happening? They are resting inside the church.'

A moment later Seth was in our car, heading towards the couple of tents from which we worked. Ngarambe Seth, translator and newest recruit to the BBC team in Goma.

Reporting from Goma turned out to be the most challenging assignment I'd had. The crux of the matter was whether to treat the exodus as primarily a humanitarian or a political problem. Clearly, the fact that a million people were stranded on the shores of Lake Kivu with no clean water, food or shelter constituted an urgent humanitarian crisis. But many of those who were now victims had themselves inflicted great suffering and worse by playing some part, whether actively or indirectly, in the genocide. To report the story properly, to do justice to the victims of Rwanda, one had to reflect the reasons for the exodus as well as its consequences.

I began well enough. As the defeated soldiers of the Rwandan army came pouring into Goma, I recognised the instability their presence would create. 'Today's defeated soldiers may well turn out to be tomorrow's rebels,' I said in one report, foreshadowing much of the unrest that is still shaking the region. In another dispatch I showed how the exodus had created a people in exile, an army in exile and a political class in exile: the classic ingredients for continued warfare. And that, too, is precisely what happened. As aid agency millions flowed into them for months on end, the camps became a regrouping ground for the very forces that had planned and implemented the genocide in the first place.

Then, for a week or so, I lost the plot. Looking back through my notes, I can pinpoint the moment I lost my editorial bearings. It was 20 July, during a briefing by one Panos Moumtsis, a UN refugee official, when I wrote down: 'First case of cholera?' The question mark indicated that no one could be sure whether the case Panos was telling us about was the first to occur or merely the first to be reported to health workers. Whatever the truth, the significance of the discovery was not lost on anyone. Cholera, that most indiscriminate of killers, was about to be unleashed on a population of a million people who had no means of escape.

Within days you could smell death in the air. The disease swept through the population like a mediaeval plague. According to the French aid agency Médecins Sans Frontières, the infection was advancing in Goma three times faster than in any other comparable situation the agency's ten doctors on the ground had dealt with before.

Each morning we would drive up the road north of Lake Kivu, visiting the string of camps that ran along it to get our first pictures of the day. We saw the corpses, shrouded in straw mats, laid by the roadside, placed there by their families in much the same way as you or I would put the bins outside our front gates on the day rubbish is collected. The plight of the living had become so desperate that they had no time or energy to spare for the dead. The drive would take an hour, we'd spend an hour or so filming, and another hour getting back. Often the number of cadavers left for disposal would have doubled by the time we reached our tent.

At one point it was thought that 3,000 people a day were dying. As the gravediggers were overwhelmed, bulldozers were brought in to excavate massive trenches where once there had been banana groves. The bodies were disgorged into the pits by tip-up trucks. You could hear the stop-go, forward-reverse drone of their engines going all day. Sometimes the dead were swung into the pits one by one, like children being thrown into a swimming pool by their mates. They lay in the trenches in huge, inert piles, twisted and deformed in the ugly embrace of undignified death, a grisly echo of those black-and-white newsreels showing the Nazi concentration camps after the Second World War. Subliminally, the image added to the notion that these people were innocent victims rather than perpetrators of evil. Every now and then an arm or a leg would break free of its shroud, or a head would roll to face you. For a moment you wondered if someone had made a ghastly mistake, been too quick to pronounce death. That's when you looked away. That's when you felt chilled to the core, even if, on the outside, you were sweating from the heat and exhaustion.

The genocide was forgotten, and cholera became the story. That was all the newsroom wanted to know about. How were they treating it? How did it spread? What could Britain do to help? Could we follow a case from diagnosis to recovery – or death? I played my part. I fed the machine and, in the process, made my contribution to the idea back home that these people were primarily victims. I was linked up to London for live question-and-answer sessions with presenters such as Michael Buerk on the *Nine o'Clock News* and a radio debate with the human-rights activist Rakiya Omaar and Germaine Greer, and there were countless requests for newspaper and magazine articles. And I was not the only journalist who did this. For those few days I was following the herd instinct. Temporary though the lapse was, I regret it still.

With the twenty-twenty vision that returns with hindsight, many historians and quite a few journalists have castigated the aid agencies for giving succour to the perpetrators of genocide during the crisis. All I can say is that I was there in those early days of the Rwandan exodus, and it did not seem so clear at the time. Who was supposed to sit in summary judgement, deciding which stooped and hungry man was a killer, and which bent and thirsty woman was merely a bystander? Guilt is not worn on the outside like a badge for all to see; it lies hidden in the dark recesses of a troubled and traumatised mind.

Through all this I was getting to know Ngarambe Seth. At first I didn't ask him too many direct questions. Later I didn't have to: he talked to me unprompted. I sometimes think that my growing fondness for him may have affected my understanding of what I was witnessing. When the Hutu person I knew best, the man on whom I was depending more and more, told me how he had suffered, it began to seem plausible that many others might be in a similar predicament.

Seth recounted the story of how he had come to be in Goma. He was Hutu – no surprise there. He was educated and had had a clerical job in Kigali, the capital of Rwanda. His wife had been a Tutsi. This was not, as I said earlier, unusual, but it would certainly have made the family more vulnerable to attack by the militias who went on the rampage after 6 April. He told me how the Interahamwe – the stormtroopers of ethnic cleansing – prowled around Kigali, moving from house to house in search of Tutsis. The methods of the Hutu political militia were brutal, their determination unswerving. They roved around in gangs on the basis that there was strength in numbers – *interahamwe* means 'those who stand together'. They would arrive at one home with their machetes, clubs and clothes still dripping with the blood of those they had killed a few minutes earlier. Mostly they knew exactly who the Tutsis were; if they were unsure, they simply slaughtered on suspicion. Hutu fathers were ordered to kill their offspring for no other reason than that they looked like Tutsis. Tutsis tend to be lighter-skinned and to have longer faces – it's not an infallible rule, obviously, but a common enough means of identification.

Thousands of Tutsi women were raped. As if that were not enough, many are now dying of AIDS. Some gave birth to children nine months later, the progeny of hate. Who will dare tell these children, now at an age to ask about their fathers, how it was that they came into this world? And how will they feel about themselves when they come to know the ugly truth? Who will they bless, who will they blame?

Seth told me that he knew his wife would not escape the savagery, so the family decided to flee ahead of the killing gangs. But en route tragedy struck. Seth's wife was discovered and, he said, murdered by the Interahamwe. The family pushed on, cleansed of their Tutsi association but now motherless. Such was the rage of the gang that had set upon them that Seth felt he was lucky to get himself and his children away.

In the midst of the biggest news story for months, in the heat of the battle to meet another deadline, I tried to find words of consolation, though in my heart I couldn't see how any words could help.

I remember how the extent of Seth's distress was brought home to me. After days of incessant demand from the newsroom, we suddenly found ourselves knocked off the bulletin running orders. John Major had just announced a Cabinet reshuffle – or was it Tony Blair being made leader of the Labour Party? Both events happened around this time. Back in the newsroom, even the aftermath of genocide pales into insignificance when set against the fascination for a touch of political intrigue at home. To make the most of this respite, the BBC team, which had now expanded somewhat, decided to have a proper meal together. Incredibly, there were still one or two functioning restaurants in Goma. Menus were not exactly varied – chips with fish or meat – but it made a change from cans of meatballs and baked beans.

Someone produced a bottle of something; a few beers were ordered, then some more. There was plenty of laughter. Yes, we laughed even though from our table we could see and hear the presence of a million dislocated people. It is the way we stop ourselves from thinking about what is actually going on, the way we stay sane enough to churn out the next day's news.

But it was all too much for Seth. Towards the end of the meal, somebody noticed that he was crying. Embarrassed glances were exchanged, the bill was paid and we shuffled off. It was all rather awkward. Brenda Griffiths, one of our producers, took Seth in hand and the rest of us headed back to the airport that had, by then, become a sort of media village.

I asked Seth later that day what the matter had been. He said that our carefree banter had reminded him of how long it had been since his family had last been able to enjoy a meal together and of everything that had happened in between. He told me he wished it was he who had been killed. The guilt of the survivor was, it seemed, a heavy burden. We, the journalists, had learned how to shut out the fear and filth all around us and we had assumed that Seth could do the same. But of course he couldn't. That is the gulf that separates the observer from the observed.

So it was that, through these shared confidences, Seth became more than just another local employee. He was the person through whom I vicariously began to feel the personal, intimate effects of genocide. As for the big picture, the sheer scale and malevolence of what had happened, I had already had an inkling of that when I had first gone into Rwanda in May, some weeks after the genocide began.

It had started within hours of the death of Rwanda's president, Juvenal Habyarimana, on 6 April. He had been returning from a meeting aimed at bringing an end to the civil war with the Tutsi-dominated RPF when his plane was shot down in what can only be described as mysterious circumstances. What is certain is that many hardliners in his own party objected to his dealings with the Rwanda Patriotic Front and wanted him out of the way.

There can be no doubt that the killings were planned in advance. They had lists of those they had to exterminate. First they went after any Hutu moderates who might get in their way, then they turned on the Tutsis en masse. Hutu apologists have tried to portray the genocide as a sort of spontaneous uprising that, over three months or so, spread like a contagion from town to town, village to village. But that simply ignores the incitement to violence broadcast daily by Radio Milles Collines, a station with connections to the Hutu extremists, and by Radio Rwanda itself. Indeed, the national broadcaster, which, unlike Radio Milles Collines, could be heard throughout the country, helped to disperse the genocide from the capital outwards, from the cities deep into the rural areas. Always the message to Hutus was the same: either we kill them, or they will certainly kill us.

If the genocide was unpremeditated, why were the Interahamwe militias moved from place to place, especially to those areas where local government officials were a touch too fastidious about getting on with the job? There is plenty of evidence of the militias being used in these neighbourhoods as *agents provocateurs*.

From the beginning, the plan was to involve as many people in the genocide as possible. The extremist leaders wanted to ensure that when the killing was over the whole nation, or at least the Hutu part of it, would be tainted with the blood of the victims. It was a sort of insurance policy for those who masterminded the bloodbath. Who would point the finger of accusation if he, too, shared responsibility for it?

There were many Hutus who protected their Tutsi neighbours, who hid them and fed them even when the consequences of being found out were certain death. But they were the exception rather than the rule.

Picking out the Tutsis was easy enough. Since colonial times the information given on Rwandan identity cards had included a person's blood line, a practice started by the Belgians because it suited their divide-and-rule method of government. The Hutu gangs took this policy to its most extreme conclusion.

The killing was on an industrial scale. According to African Rights, the organisation that has produced one of the most

132

A Passage to Africa

comprehensive accounts of the genocide, on a single day in the parish of Karama in the southern city of Butare, 65,000 people were murdered between ten in the morning and three-thirty in the afternoon. That works out at about 13,000 an hour, over 200 a minute. Most died in a hail of bullets and grenades. Civilians were brought in later to finish off, with machetes, what the soldiers had begun. It was a pattern repeated over and over again across the country. In his book on Rwanda, *We Wish to Inform You That Tomorrow We Will Be Killed With Our Families*, Philip Gourevitch points out that this rate of carnage is three times that of the extermination of Jews in the Holocaust after the Nazis resorted to the gas chambers to speed things up.

The way in which people died – whether they were hit by bullets, or fell as grenades exploded in cramped church halls, or were hacked to death by machete-wielding mobs – is a crucial factor in determining culpability for the mass murder. Those who have portrayed it as a one-on-one struggle between neighbours inadvertently play into the hands of the apologists who still claim that the genocide was unplanned and, therefore, ultimately uncontrollable.

But if you accept the prime role of the military and the armed militias, then you also have to accept that there was a chain of command and control. Weapons were being stockpiled months beforehand. As early as January, the UN commander in Kigali, who was supposedly overseeing the fragile ceasefire between the government and the RPF rebels, was told by an informant of a weapons cache held by extremists. It is also said that there was an unusually large import of machetes in the months preceding the massacre.

If we're looking to point the finger of blame, we must address the awkward question of where the weapons came from. In his searing account of conflict in Africa, *Me Against My Brother*, Scott Peterson says that the French were supplying munitions to Rwanda in May and June 1994 – well after the genocide began. It comes as no surprise, then, that at the time the French authorities were enthusiastic supporters of the machete theory. Other countries with a history of arming the Kigali government were South Africa (under Apartheid), Bulgaria, Albania and Israel.

By the end of the hundred days, one in ten Rwandans had been exterminated. Even allowing for the fact that most of the large-scale massacres were carried out by soldiers with semi-automatic guns and grenades, to kill that many people in such a short space of time requires a huge number of assassins. No one will ever know exactly how many struck a blow for genocide. What is clear is that virtually every single person alive in Rwanda today either actively took part in the carnage or witnessed a killing and did nothing to stop it.

Leila Gupta, a health worker with UNICEF, helped to set up a programme to deal with post-genocide trauma. She told me that according to a survey carried out by her field workers, just under 80 per cent of the children questioned had seen someone being killed, one in five had witnessed a rape and nearly half reported seeing other children commit murder. Statistics like these begin to illustrate just how many people were culpable.

Here is how I try to visualise the scale of what happened. Look out of your window and count the houses outside. Imagine that, over the next few weeks, someone from every other house will be murdered. Then try to create in your mind all the noise, the screams you would hear if this many of your neighbours were being dragged on to the street, tortured, beaten, mutilated and then, finally, killed. Remember that many of the victims would be children. What do you do? You do nothing. In fact, you actually cheer on the killers. Just think how you would feel afterwards, first about yourself, secondly about your country for allowing this to happen.

Yet the response of the outside world was in inverse proportion to the magnitude of the crime perpetrated by the Hutu militia and their leaders, many of whom are still at large in Europe and elsewhere. At the time of the president's plane crash, there was a

UN force of around 2,500 Blue Berets on the ground, there to monitor the previous year's peace agreement between the government and the Rwanda Patriotic Front.

Ten Belgian peacekeepers were killed when they tried to rescue the prime minister, Agathe Uwilingiyamana, whose house had been surrounded by the Rwandan Army and its attendant militia. As a leading figure in a government that had negotiated the peace deal, she was viewed as a suspect by the extremists. Belgium's reaction to the murder of its servicemen was to withdraw the rest of its troops from active duty. By the third week of April, two weeks into the mass extermination of Tutsis, the UN Security Council decided to scale down the whole UN force by 90 per cent, leaving a paltry 270 troops in Rwanda. Their mandate was feeble and their power limited. Faced with one of the most staggering affronts to the principles on which the United Nations was built, the international community simply deserted its post.

The Americans, stung by their disastrous involvement in Somalia, from which they had only recently managed to extricate themselves, were loath to become embroiled in another African crisis. For weeks, the smooth-sounding, suit-wearing diplomats in New York found it hard even to utter the word 'genocide' lest it forced them into a moral duty to intervene: the Genocide Convention passed by the UN's General Assembly in 1946, a product of the 'never-again' sentiment that saturated international thinking in the aftermath of the Holocaust, imposed on member states a duty to prevent genocide wherever it threatened to occur. In this case it was a responsibility that the Security Council, led by the USA, was trying to avoid. One American diplomat even tried to draw a distinction between 'acts of genocide' and genocide itself.

Not only was the administration of Bill Clinton, who had succeeded George Bush senior as president, opposed to intervening on its own account, but it used all its diplomatic and economic might to persuade others to stay out as well. To its eternal shame,

Britain was among those countries to take part in this carefully orchestrated diplomatic inertia. Thus the ripples of culpability spread way beyond Rwanda.

The prime concern of the international community in those early days, apart from hiding its negligence under an avalanche of diplo-speak, was to evacuate Kigali of foreign nationals. So the few UN soldiers who were left in the Rwandan capital organised convoys of cars and trucks full, mainly, of white people, which drove through streets littered with the corpses of black people. Every mutilated body, every gaping wound was a rebuke, a reminder of the cost of betrayal.

It was May by the time I got to Kigali. The Rwanda Patriotic Front was well into its armed offensive, convinced that this was the only way to bring an end to the genocide. Kigali was a divided city, linked only by the night-time tracer bullets that criss-crossed the sky as the opposing forces fought for control of the capital.

I suppose a dozen or so of us, reporters and photographers, flew in together from Nairobi. Many of the journalists who ended up in Rwanda had, just a few weeks earlier, reported on the first free elections in South Africa. Although the genocide occurred first, it was the South African story that preoccupied most Western media. It was typical of the extremes this continent can throw at you. In the same month that Nelson Mandela held out the hand of reconciliation to his one-time oppressors, Rwandan leaders were urging their followers to commit the kind of crime that white supremacists, even in their worst incarnation, had balked at. Using, in many cases, weapons bought from Apartheid South Africa.

Our first priority when we finally arrived in Kigali was accommodation. The hotels had long since ceased functioning as such. Mostly they were full of people who had sought refuge from the militias. We ended up at the Meridien, literally on the front line dividing the two armies. My cameraman, Tom Samson, and I walked from floor to floor looking for somewhere to put our sleeping bags. I would poke my head round room after room, only to find it already packed with people. Others were living in the unlit corridors, and you had to be careful not to trample on anyone or knock over somebody's cooking pot in the dark. On one floor, I picked my way around a couple of goats. All the rooms that faced away from the fighting, the safer ones, were occupied. There was no alternative: we were going to have to camp out on the wrong side of the corridor. But which floor was the safest?

'I think as near the ground floor as we can get would be best,' said Tom. 'Just in case we have to make a run for it.'

'But that's just the height at which the stray bullets fly,' I pointed out. Several windows already bore telltale starburst cracks.

'Yeah, but go too high and you're a sucker for the mortars that fall short.'

The truth is that neither of us really knew exactly where the bullets were being fired from, or precisely what the trajectory of the mortars was likely to be. But on the road these are the kind of conversations you have. It's a way of sharing the anxiety, of admitting, in a convoluted sort of way, that you're quite frightened. In the end we settled for something in between and picked a room – Tom, myself and a freelance photographer, Mariella Furrer. The first thing we did was to prop up some mattresses against the full-length glass windows. They were of absolutely no use in practical terms, but the psychological reassurance was important. There was no water, so the toilet couldn't be flushed and the redundant shower was merely a reminder of more gracious times.

There was, however, one consolation to staying at the Meridien. One of the staff had stayed on and let it be known that she had found the keys to the hotel's wine cellar. So, that first night, and every other night of our time there, we washed down our Pot Noodle suppers with the finest French reds. They tasted all the sweeter for the heavy discounts Marie-Therese offered us.

While a part of the RPF army was locked into this fight for the capital, most of its troops were deployed in a great sweep across the country, starting from their rear bases in the north-east, passing through the central regions, then moving westwards and up towards the capital. The offensive was controversial. Though they themselves had decided against intervention in Rwanda, United Nations diplomats disapproved of the RPF manoeuvre, insisting that what the country needed was a ceasefire. The RPF argued, quite rightly, that a ceasefire would merely play into the hands of those guilty of genocide, giving them time to finish off the job.

The rich world's misreading – negligence would be a better word for it – of what was going on inside Rwanda was occasionally obvious from the line taken by some of the journalists. One question of staggering irrelevance was put by a French correspondent during a rare briefing by an RPF spokesman, Theogene Rudasirgwa, shortly after the RPF had captured Kigali Airport. When, the reporter asked, did the RPF intend to hold elections? Elections? The killing still hadn't finished, the RPF had yet to take control of the country, the extremists were still at large and here was someone talking about elections! The implication was that the RPF should deliver the vote to a people who had just proved, in the bloodiest terms possible, that they had no particular interest in the rule of law. Mr Rudasirgwa's answer, delivered with superhuman restraint, was simple: 'Elections are not a panacea for all the ills of our continent.'

After we had been in Kigali for a while we were told that the RPF had drawn up a list of journalists who would be allowed to accompany one of its convoys into the interior. Tom the cameraman and I were among them. The key word here was 'accompany'. The RPF, famous for its frugal but highly efficient marshalling of its scarce resources, was not going to provide food, water, shelter or, crucially, transport.

Kigali in those days was littered with vehicles that had been abandoned by their expatriate owners or discarded by looters when they ran out of petrol. Tom and I found what looked like an ideal vehicle for the cross-country drive ahead of us: a Mercedes-Benz four-wheel-drive. Its windscreen had been smashed and the battery was flat but, other than that, it appeared to be in good working order. We were in go mode.

It was time to do a bit of schmoozing. We needed jerry cans, plenty of petrol to put in them (we had no idea where we were going or how far), oil for the engine and someone to give the whole thing the once-over. I felt like the American in the *Colditz* film whose job it was to scrounge goodies for the escape committee.

Some days earlier, I had met a group of Ghanaian soldiers who were part of the rump of the UN force in Kigali. They knew Christ the King school in Accra, and were genuinely proud to learn that a former pupil was now a BBC correspondent. I remarked on how far all this was from the dream of African unity we had shared as children in post-independence Ghana. Lance-Corporal Jerry Jones-Awadey of 3 Battalion (Infantry), sitting on top of his armoured personnel-carrier, agreed. 'It's an African sick-ness,' he said. 'We have the same thing in West Africa. Look at Liberia. They are also behaving like animals.'

'The world will look at this mess and say Africans are to blame. It gives them an excuse to do nothing,' I replied. The camera was running and I was trying to stimulate a conversation, but I meant what I said. I believed there was a part of the international com-munity that was, by then, simply fed up with having to bail Africa out every couple of years.

'They can say that if they want to,' said Sergeant Emmanuel Owusu-Asante. 'But they know the truth. Many of these Western countries who are busy complaining now were the very ones sell-ing guns to these people. They have to take some of the blame.'

Before we left the Ghanaians, I had promised to go round to where they were billeted to talk some more about the good old days. Now that we needed help with our vehicle, I decided to pay them a visit. They were stationed at one end of the airport. When

I turned up in the newly acquired four-wheel-drive I was greeted like a long-lost friend. I suppose none of us really believed we would meet again. I explained my problem. A mechanic gave the vehicle a quick check and pronounced that all was well. They, too, were horribly short of fuel – UN troops are so often given a job to do without the logistical back-up to fulfil their mandates – but nevertheless our tank was filled and a couple of jerry cans of petrol were shoved in the back. 'Anything for an honorary Ghanaian,' one of them quipped.

We took three other journalists with us when we followed the RPF out of the capital, among them the photographer Luc Delahaye. Travelling in convoy on a dirt road with no windscreen is a bit like being force-fed with grit. Pretty soon we were covered with Rwanda's red earth, looking as if we had walked through a spray-paint machine.

Still, we made good progress till we reached the Akanyeru River, a tributary of the much bigger Kagera. Back in April, one of the first signs of the horrors that were happening inside Rwanda was the number of bodies that floated down the Kagera and into Lake Victoria. From one haunting image, filmed from the Rusumo Falls Bridge, of corpses stuck in a narrow ravine, it was apparent that many of the victims had had their hands and ankles bound.

Even now, in early June, we spied the odd bloated body in the Akanyeru. The bridge across the river had been blown up by the retreating government forces. The RPF commander told us that we could either turn back or do what they were going to do: row across in some canoes provided by the few people still around. We abandoned our vehicle, brought out what supplies we could carry and followed the RPF into the heart of the country.

In Somalia, in southern Sudan, in places where the ground is drought-hard and the landscape is bleached, it is natural, certainly understandable, to find that the people who lived there have moved on. But the emptiness of Rwanda's interior seemed all wrong. The earth was soft and fertile, the vegetation lush. It was the planting season, but there were no crops in the ground. Everywhere you looked, houses were empty. But the most telling feature of this abandoned landscape was the silence. A deathly silence. The sounds of Africa – women washing by a river, men arguing under the shade of an old tree, children crying – were chillingly absent.

I have travelled with several armies – everything from the super-served forces of NATO to the ragged rebel soldiers of the Sudan People's Liberation Front – in my experience, the RPF was unique. Unlike many guerrilla armies, its internal discipline was as stern, if not more so, than that of any formal force. If one of its soldiers was found guilty of a serious infringement of its rules, the punishment could be execution. And what it lacked in matériel it more than made up for in efficiency and ingenuity.

In 1994 its soldiers were ruthless in the pursuit of their goal, the liberation of Rwanda, and unwavering in their commitment to it. Unlike most soldiers, who are easy to engage, sometimes even flattered by press attention, these RPF troops were taciturn and aloof. You had the feeling that they would have preferred not to have anything to do with journalists at all but recognised us as a necessary tool in their political armoury. We had a 'minder' from the RPF's information department, but access to the rest of the troops was limited.

Only once did I manage to break through this studied reticence. Captain Peter Kwizera was typical of so many of the rebel soldiers, especially its officers. He was in his mid-twenties and had grown up in neighbouring Uganda, a child born in exile. His parents, both Tutsis, had fled Rwanda in 1959 when some 10,000 Tutsis were killed in the political upheavals that preceded independence from Belgium. A generation later, Peter had, he said, come back to claim his birthright, to reverse the injustices committed against his kith and kin.

In the 1994 massacre Hutu extremist leaders constantly reminded their supporters not to spare the children. 'That's what we did in 1959,' they said, 'and now they are back to cause trouble.' In one place we travelled through, Nyanza, I was told how the militias rounded up the children and hobbled them by slashing their ankle tendons so that they could not run. After dealing with the adults, the gangs would return to finish off the children. It was in Nyanza that the driver of one of the vehicles in our convoy discovered how his infant niece had been killed. Neighbours had seen a man pick up the tiny girl by her feet and swing her head against a brick wall.

Paul Kagame, the RPF's overall commander, was another man whose political instincts and military skills were honed in exile: he had also been a refugee in Uganda. Those who knew him well said he rarely expressed emotion, and certainly never in public. Everything was reduced to one calculation: does it help us to meet our goal? Kagame turned up one evening, unannounced, when we were with the convoy. He addressed his troops just as the sun was setting. I remember the blazing orange disc reflected in his wire-rimmed glasses. Later he spoke to us. The killing, he said, was still going on. The RPF would pursue the enemy to the shores of Lake Kivu. There they would have to surrender or face the consequences. In the event, most of them simply fled to the other side of the lake, into Zaire, which was where I would find them and, of course, Seth just a few weeks later.

Translator. That's all it says on the expense claim we hand in to the accountant at the end of an assignment. 'Translator @ $50.00 a day.' The fee varies according to the country, obviously. And in Rwanda $50 is a lot of money. Their names are rarely mentioned: the accountants are not interested in them as people, only in the service they provide and how much it costs. They take up a line in the claim somewhere between Transport and Donation, the euphemism for the inevitable bribe to a border guard or some such. The accountants back at head office are like rich men who know the price of everything and the value of nothing.

For how can you calculate the cost of all the other things these men and women do for us? If expense claims were meant to describe someone's value, you would start by writing down a name. I can remember some of them still: Rita in Kosovo, Clive in Kinshasa, Eric in Kigali, Hamid in Kabul, Majok in southern Sudan and, of course, Seth in Goma. Then all they have done for you. Try this for a list of duties: companion, guide, local historian, navigator, listener, organiser, fixer and friend. You break bread together, you share food, sometimes off the same plate. You sleep next to each other, sometimes on the same bed. You laugh together. Sometimes you cry together.

Except that one day you pack your bags and head for home, leaving them behind. It is a relationship forged in the media's fierce but fleeting gaze: all-consuming while it lasts, forgotten once it's over. You are like the lover who gets bored. You move on. You promise to come back, you make a pledge that you will both meet again, but mostly these are just words to cover your return to your other world, the world of mortgages, electricity bills and the odd night out at the theatre.

So when I left Goma I promised Seth that I would do what I could to ensure that the BBC continued to employ him, and that we would do whatever we could to help him return to his home in Kigali. The first part was easy. By then I was merely one of many fans Seth had among the BBC team, and on my departure he would work for the next reporter. As for Kigali, well, that was up to him. I did say that if and when he got there he would certainly be an asset to whichever BBC correspondent was in the city at the time. So we swapped addresses, hugged each other, shed a tear or two, and parted company. It had been a torrid three weeks, and I would not have survived them without Seth.

Just over a year later I went back to Kigali. By then I had been posted to the BBC's Africa Bureau in Johannesburg and, with my cameraman, Glenn Middleton, I planned to do a series of reports on how Rwanda was coping in the aftermath of genocide.

I had lost touch with Seth. I knew that he had managed to return to the capital, with a BBC team that had made the journey from the Zairean refugee camps. I had tried to contact him but hadn't got a reply, and frankly, I couldn't be sure that my letter had ever reached him. So when I arrived in Kigali I went to the address he'd given me. There I was told merely that Seth no longer lived in the house. I went to his old church. The minister could barely bring himself to acknowledge that he knew Seth. It wasn't till I found his son, who was working in a car mechanic's shop, that I realised something was wrong. The boy eventually told me what had happened: his father was in jail, accused of complicity in the genocide.

I remember a moment of gut-wrenching anxiety, a sense of shock but also a feeling of betrayal. My first instinct was to think, 'Christ, how could I have been taken in?' And then, when the implications of that question had sunk in, another question, this one prompted by loyalty to an old friend, replaced it. 'It can't be true,' I said out loud to Glenn. I had to get into the prison. I had to face Seth, look into his eyes. I told myself there would be no emotion, just the journalist at work.

At the time the Rwandan government admitted to detaining about 50,000 people in connection with the genocide. Conditions were worst at the jail in Gitarama, central Rwanda. Glenn and I had been the first journalists to get a TV camera into that prison. Our report told a story of Dantesque proportions.

At Gitarama some 7,000 people were crammed within walls built to hold less than a tenth of that number. We were let in through a metal gate and then left to our own devices – even the guards, and there were precious few of them as far as I could see, did not dare go inside. Their job was simply to ensure no one got out. I have, even at the best of times, a carefully suppressed fear of cramped spaces. In the prison I felt an incipient, rising panic as inquisitive, angry eyes stared at us. The din of a thousand voices.

The sickly-sweet stench of unwashed bodies. The air pungent with the choking smell of untreated excrement. My shirt was damp – my sweat, their sweat, I couldn't tell. The prodding and pushing of clammy hands. It was as if every step forward entailed another intimate brush with the filthy stain of genocide. There was room only to stand or squat.

In one corner some prisoners stirred great vats of gruel. The steam and smoke drifted across the compound to inmates too far away to stand a chance of a full bowl. They would have to do with the dregs. Those who had been strong and powerful on the outside held prime positions inside the prison, near the food, near the only covered space.

We pushed on towards the underground cells and the latrines. Some of the prisoners in this dank and fetid place had not seen the sun for days. They turned away from the sharp glare of our camera like nocturnal animals caught in the beam of a search-light. Their bodies glistened, their shoulders shivered in feverish spasms. Some just rocked to and fro in time with some maddening, mindless rhythm only they could hear.

The rains had come, and underfoot the ground was soft and squelchy. The prisoners' feet remained wet for days on end. They were literally rotting. Some of the inmates showed me how their toes had simply fallen off. Another disfigurement I noticed was the number of bulbous, deformed ears among the boys – many of the prisoners were no more than teenagers. A nurse who treated some of them told me that this was caused by a form of punishment meted out by the brutes who ran things on the inside. They would rub a victim's ear between their hands till the lobes filled with blood. Then, and they knew just when to do it, they would slap the ear, bursting the blood vessels.

If all this seemed an affront to our fastidious notions of justice, it barely raised an eyebrow among the many survivors of genocide.

Compared to what we had seen in Gitarama, conditions in the jail in Kigali where Seth was being held came as a relief. In the centre of the yard there was a sheltered area, where hundreds of people sat under vast sheets of green plastic. This was prized accommodation, available only to those who could afford to pay for the privilege – like every other jail in Rwanda at this time, Kigali Central Prison held many more people than it had been designed to take. Seth, I gathered, was here. It was too crowded for me to get in, so I had to wait till Seth found me.

One look at his face and my determination to show nothing but professional detachment just evaporated. He embraced me and I found myself reciprocating the gesture. We found a corner where we could talk without interruption, and I asked him for the truth.

He told me that his house had been taken over by squatters while he was in Goma. When he threatened to have them evicted on his return, the occupiers had gone to the police and accused him, quite falsely, of collaborating with the genocide. Both aspects of this story were common enough. Many houses had been taken over by Tutsis who had fled the countryside or returned from exile, and many Hutus did find themselves in jail on little more evidence than the pointed finger of accusation. Most were certainly guilty, many were probably innocent. Officials admitted that up to a third of them might have been arrested on dubious evidence. The problem was that the courts couldn't process the cases anywhere near fast enough: lawyers, most of them Tutsis, had been among the first victims of the genocide.

Once again convinced of Seth's innocence, I gave him some money for a few more nights under the plastic sheeting and promised to confront the person who had sent him to jail. It took a few hours, but Glenn and I eventually tracked down the man in the marketplace, where he had a stall. I expected aggression – I had already cast him as villain of the piece – and told our driver to be ready to pull off in a hurry. Glenn decided to shoot his pictures from the shoulder, dispensing with the luxury of a tripod, so sure were we that we would have only as long as it took for the man to turn on us. Eric Kabera, my fixer in Kigali, was primed to ask the right questions in Kiriyarwanda so that we didn't waste time waiting for him to translate.

But it wasn't anger or aggression that confronted us. It was relief. 'I know about you,' the man said. 'I know you are the journalist who befriended Seth in Goma. His story has burdened me for a long time and I want to tell you about it. I know you will not want to hear it, but I must tell you.' He was shaken, but not for any of the reasons I had foreseen. Tears welled up in his eyes.

Katabarwa Sortais looked like a decent man, as upstanding as Seth had seemed when I first got to know him. There was nothing about the way Katabarwa behaved that pointed to hidden motives or malicious intent. We took him to a quiet restaurant to record our interview. There were a couple of false starts. Every time the tape rolled and I asked the first question, Katabarwa would start sobbing, unable to utter a word.

Eventually, he began to talk. Here's his account of what happened. He was one of several young men who had rented a room in Seth's compound in the days before the genocide. They all knew that one of Seth's sons was involved in the Interahamwe in Kigali. Seth, too, was aware of this, and knew of the militias' plans. So the killings that began on 6 April 1994 were no surprise, Katabarwa said, to father or son. He recalled the day the militia turned up looking for Tutsis. We broadcast this part of the interview later that day.

'Seth told the man to take his wife. She was crying and screaming. Just think, this was the woman who bore his children. She was taken by force.'

'Do you know how serious an allegation that is?' I asked, in a final, desperate attempt to prick his conscience.

'Whenever I think about all this, about Seth, it hurts me. I sometimes think I would rather die,' he replied.

Those words again. 'I would rather die.' They echoed, precisely, what Seth had said to me when he had first told me his version of events. Then I had assumed he was trying to describe his sorrow. I wondered now whether subliminally he had been speaking of his guilt.

Guilty or not, the knowledge of genocide is enough in itself to haunt people. Katabarwa said he still woke up at night to hear the sound of a woman howling with fear. His story seemed credible. I could find no reason to doubt him.

But where did that leave Seth? Time was running out. I had a choice. I could go back to Kigali Prison to challenge Seth again in the light of what Katabarwa had told me, or I could leave things be. I chose the latter course. I told myself it was because Glenn and I now had other stories to unearth. But in my heart I knew it was because the fight had gone out of me. I was like a boxer who has been hit once too often. I wanted a comfort zone, a simpler tale to tell.

It was as if I'd never known Seth. So who was right and who was wrong? Who to bless and who to blame?

Seth was a man I had come to trust, someone I still wanted to believe in. I wanted to know the truth but feared its consequences. I spoke of justice but balked at its price. I hated the crime but I was not sure I wanted to know who the criminal was.

In May 2002, I got the answer I had been waiting for. It came not from Seth, but from Eric Kabera, who had helped me cover the story in the first place. Eric's e-mail said simply that Seth had been released. I asked him to arrange for Seth to contact me directly.

Within days I received an e-mail. 'Hello dear George!' it began. 'What a pleasure to be in contact with you again. I am out and free. God be blessed. It is true that a friend in need is a friend indeed. I cannot forget your kindness and sympathy when you came to visit me in prison.'

Seth was simply picking up where we had left off at our meeting inside Kigali Prison. His open and direct words were like a rebuke. I felt as if I had betrayed him merely by searching out the man who had accused him of aiding and abetting genocide. I have looked at Seth's message over and over again. It prompts as many questions as it gives answers. What about Katabarwa Sortais? Did he make the same accusation in court he had made when I interviewed him seven years earlier? If so, why was the court not moved as I had been? Was he the liar after all? Had I been too gullible? Who to bless, who to blame?

I ought to be overjoyed, but I am not. Of course I am pleased for Seth, but the seeds of doubt, sown in my mind all those years ago when I spoke to his accuser, seem to have taken root. I thought a judge's verdict would bring the closure I have craved, but instead it has left me with a sense of guilt – the truth is that, though I tried not to acknowledge it, I had come to doubt Seth. Now I must make my peace with him. I have to explain to him that I may not have been as faithful and loyal a friend as he thinks I have been. I am not looking forward to writing the letter, but write it I must.

All over Rwanda people are going through the same process. If it is hard for me, a mere observer, to come to terms with what happened to Seth, imagine what it must be like for those who actually survived the genocide. Many of them have had to learn to live side by side with people they hold accountable for the deaths of loved ones.

As for Seth, he must try to rebuild his life. His old house is now derelict and he hasn't the means to fix it. He used to earn a little extra money from a grinding mill he owned before the genocide but most of its parts have been stolen. Both his parents have died – his father while he was in jail, his mother shortly after he was released. 'Now I am at once widower and orphan. I accept the situation as it is,' he says in his e-mail.

Those who have studied the Rwandan case say only justice can lance the tumour of communal guilt. But how far down the hierarchy of murder would you have to go? How many Seths are out there? How many investigations can any nation bear before its very fabric is infected with the poison of accusation? Half the country might end up behind bars. There would be no end to the litigation, cases would be going to court for decades. Certainly the leaders have to be found and arrested. The trials set in motion by the International Tribunal sitting in Arusha, Tanzania must be allowed to reach their natural conclusion. But for the rest there has to be some other strategy. What countries such as Rwanda need is not so much legal redress as a spiritual renaissance.

Some Rwandans will try to accommodate their moral weakness, try to rebuild a new nation despite the part they played in destroying the old one. Others will remain in denial. They will argue that their only sin was the failure to complete their deadly mission. Indeed, as I left Rwanda in 1995, they were already planning their next assault. These were the people who would draw me back into the heart of Africa. Their actions would, in time, lead to the demise of Africa's last Cold War dictator, Mobutu Sese Seko of Zaire.

8

The Heart of the Beast

I saw President Mobutu of Zaire in the flesh only once. Or Mobutu Sese Seko Kuku Ngebendu Wa Za Banga, to give him his full title. It is not the name he was born with. The name his parents gave him, Joseph Desire Mobutu, was, it seems, far too simple a hook on which to hang his bloated ego. There are many versions of exactly what this self-styled sobriquet means. But the gist of them all is: 'the all-powerful warrior who, because of his strength and inflexible will to win, will go from victory to victory, leaving the earth burning behind him'.

On his return to Kinshasa, the Zairean capital, from France, where he'd been undergoing treatment for prostate cancer, Mobutu stood in front of the presidential residence – one of many – to address the world's media. It was in March 1997, just a couple of months before he was to flee the same palace. His electric blue, high-necked jacket glistened like the breast feathers of a peacock. He wore his trademark leopardskin hat and thick-rimmed black spectacles. The dark trousers hung loose; you could tell his legs were thin underneath. The whole ensemble ought to

have looked comical, but on him, somehow there was just the suspicion of elegance. The air of a matinée idol who had fallen on
bad times. He stood tall and spoke in the third person, in French.

'I am here not to defend Mobutu's interests or the fortunes of
Mobutu, but to defend the unity and integrity of the country.' It
was as if he himself was entirely unrelated to the chaos his nation
now faced. In fact, when he fled Zaire in May 1997 after thirty-
two years at the helm, he left behind him a nation in name only.
The one-time sergeant-major had amassed, and subsequently lost,
a fortune, bled his country dry and left his 45 million people in
penury. Zaire owed nearly £10 billion pounds. Mobutu's rapacious
reign had been as effective as any scorched-earth policy. In that,
at least, he was true to his name.

Zaire's Parliament – with 738 members, the biggest such gathering in the world – was a sham, and any laws it passed were
simply ignored by the rest of the country. There was no civil service to speak of, since the vast majority of its 600,000 employees
had not seen a regular pay cheque for years. The central bank was
empty and the notes it printed were virtually worthless.

Zaire's history is a distillation of Africa's dismal record since
independence some four decades ago. It is a study in freedom
denied, in opportunities lost. On a continent conspicuous for its
numerous corrupt and despotic leaders, Mobutu was the daddy of
them all. He stole more money from the national coffers than any
other president in Africa and, as I say, he was not short of competition. Some maintain he salted away $5 billion over the years,
others that it was more like $1 billion. Nobody really knows,
because only a paltry few millions have ever been traced.
Accurate book-keeping was never a desirable attribute in the
Zairean finance ministry. The ability to turn a blind eye was far
more important, and much safer for one's personal health. What
is beyond doubt is that Mobutu used the central bank as if it were
his personal account.

While huge amounts of money probably did pass through

Mobutu's myriad businesses and numbered accounts in Europe, there was little of it left in the end. A lot of it certainly went on keeping Mobutu's family in the luxury to which it very quickly became accustomed. There were a dozen palaces in the country and several villas and apartments in France, Belgium, Switzerland, Côte d'Ivoire and elsewhere. There were planes and boats and fleets of limousines. His home town, Gbadolite, a once insignificant place in the northern reaches of the country, was turned into a showcase city, boasting a runway that could take the heaviest of long-haul planes, though no international airline ever scheduled a flight there. It's said that the incessant, twenty-four-hour drone of the electricity generators drove all the monkeys from the area. Gbadolite simply leapfrogged the slow process of progress and development. Mobutu just took it from the Iron Age to the designer age without bothering with anything in between.

But most of the money was probably used to buy off opponents and pay courtiers for services rendered. The secret of Mobutu's political longevity was a system of patronage in which virtually everybody who was anybody ultimately depended on his largesse for their financial wellbeing. If they did not get their money directly from the big man himself, they knew that it was only under his system that they could fleece others less fortunate than themselves. There was a hierarchy of corruption in which everyone took something off the person just below. It was, to coin a phrase, a kleptocracy.

You were confronted with this system the minute you stepped into Zaire. The immigration officer at Ndjili Airport in Kinshasa would suggest *une petite consideration* simply for the privilege of having your passport stamped. *Un petit cadeau* would see you waved through customs. Arguing that you were not carrying any contraband items was to miss the point of the whole exercise. This was not about controlling the flow of illicit goods into the country, it was about paying the official's wages, feeding his family and sending his children to school.

As a system, it worked for all those who had some leverage over others: civil servants, who issued licences for everything from changing currency to driving a car; policemen, who had it in their power to make your life a misery; public utility managers, who could turn off your electricity; airline clerks, who could get you on to a full plane; shopkeepers, who could make sure you didn't have to queue for some scarce commodity as others had to do. They all played their part in turning corruption into a way of life. And yet, for all but the very highest officials in the land, this bribery was not a case of amassing untold wealth. It was simply what you had to do to get by. It was a massive informal economy based on market value, supply and demand. The more power you had over others, the richer you became.

It was an inverted version of the trickle-down economic theories favoured by some development economists: money rose from the bottom and went up. So in this method of wealth distribution the majority simply missed out. For the tens of millions who eked out a living as subsistence farmers, or as cleaners and cooks in other people's houses, or as workers in someone else's business, life was a downward spiral of poverty. For them, independence was a sick joke. They longed for the 'old days', perhaps even for the days of the ruthless Belgians, as they watched their children go hungry, knowing they could not afford the hospital charges if they ever got sick. Some managed to save enough to send them to school, but they knew in their hearts that their children were learning nothing that would be of any use in this blighted country. This was Zaire in 1997: an amorphous mass of humanity too weak to take action, too dispirited even to think about it.

By then the name Mobutu had become synonymous with all that is venal in Africa. In Zaire, more than anywhere else on the continent, government as a means of personal enrichment was turned into an art form. And if Zaire was a masterclass in corruption, then the maestro was Mobutu Sese Seko.

His beginnings were humble enough. Mobutu's mother was a

hotel chambermaid and his father, who died when Joseph was still young, was a cook, what the colonials would have called a houseboy. As so often happens, poverty was the spur to ruthless ambition. He was, by all accounts, a difficult child. Even the legendary disciplinary skills of Catholic missionaries were not enough to curb his delinquent tendencies. The fastidiousness of the priests who expelled him from their school was not a feature of the army, which he joined after a stint in prison. He rose rapidly, reaching the rank of sergeant-major. Zaireans could go no higher in what was, in those days, a white-led force.

After seven years in uniform, Mobutu moved into journalism. This was the beginning of his political education. Here, in the pre-independence capital, he made friends and began to influence people. He started to mix with a group of young *évolués* – black people deemed to have assimilated enough of the colonial habits of dress and education to be granted desk jobs – who would eventually lead the putative political movements in the Congo, as the country was called before Mobutu changed its name.

Ambitious and astute though he was, Mobutu may well have come to nothing had it not been for the CIA, America's Central Intelligence Agency. At the height of the Cold War, in the fifties and sixties, American foreign policy was driven as much by the not-so-secret agents of the CIA as by the diplomats in the State Department. In 1959 Mobutu met and became close to one of their number, a Lawrence Devlin.

Eventually he became personal assistant to Patrice Lumumba, the one-time postal worker who would become Zaire's first prime minister. In old black and white photographs taken during the talks that would lead to independence, you can see Mobutu on the fringes of the group photographs, waiting for his chance.

Like so many of his contemporaries who had fought colonialism, Lumumba was a socialist. Often this was not so much a matter of deep conviction as a reaction to capitalism as a handmaiden of colonialism, just as today, many of the young people who answer the rallying call of militant Islam are not necessarily those who are most deeply committed to the teachings of the Prophet Mohammed. Frequently they are simply the people most frustrated with what the West has had to offer. On the ground, the rich world's support for free enterprise can mean many things. Unfair trading practices, disregard for the local environment, poor working conditions and derisory wages. All of these traits and more are associated with the advance of Western multinationals across the globe. It may not be true of all companies, but it only takes a few to give the whole system a bad name.

Back in 1960, the CIA, of course, saw the world in much simpler terms. Lumumba was a 'commie bastard' and he had to be stopped. This was the message Lawrence Devlin relayed to his headquarters in Washington. Washington agreed.

Mobutu played his hand to perfection. To Lumumba he was a trusted adviser, the leader's right-hand man. So much so that Lumumba had sent him back to the army, this time as its chief. To the Americans, he was a reliable ally in a suspect government, someone on whom they could depend. This was an early display of the political dexterity that would become a hallmark of Mobutu's rule. The rest, as they say, is history. Lumumba was undermined, toppled and eventually murdered, a chain of events in which Mobutu, and his foreign backers, were heavily implicated.

What followed was a five-year period of political turbulence as volatile and violent as any in Africa (with the exception, perhaps, of the Nigerian civil war that was yet to come). But, as head of the army, Mobutu emerged a hero, saving the country, as many believed at the time, from almost certain disintegration. And he did bring a semblance of order, but that was all it was: a veneer of stability under which he began the most systematic plunder of any nation on the continent.

Nevertheless, for the next thirty years Mobutu enjoyed favoured status with the Americans, who lavished praise and money on their man in Africa. He was fêted at the White House.

In Britain the Queen entertained him on a state visit in 1973. He became an expert in playing the anti-communist card, twice calling on American help to put down uprisings in the 1970s. By the middle of the decade he was firmly in charge, the biggest of all big men in Africa.

When he was finally forced to flee, at dawn on 17 May 1997, Mobutu had been the longest-serving African leader. In his thirty-two years as president he had turned the old libertarian ideal – government of the people, for the people – on its head. His government was government by one man, for one man (and his friends).

To write about Zaire, as it was still called when I first went there, is to deal in superlatives. There is nothing ordinary, nothing prosaic one can say about it. Whether you are talking about the huge potential locked up in its vast natural resources or the criminal waste of that God-given abundance by a thieving élite, you are led to the extremes. There is no middle ground.

Zaire is the heart of Africa. It lies dead centre, bordering nine other countries, each of them affected by the political vicissitudes of the giant next door. No country on the continent has such a contiguous relationship with so many others. Political convulsions here spread through the region like the tremors of an earthquake.

It is the size of Western Europe. The Congo River, which arches across the north of Zaire, acts as a highway in a country that has none overland. If you took a river steamer from the inland port of Kisangani (Joseph Conrad's 'Inner Station' in *Heart of Darkness*) to the capital, Kinshasa, you would have travelled the distance between Moscow and Paris. At independence the Congo had 140,000 kilometres of roads. Today it has less than a tenth of that. There are some 200 different tribes in the country, each with its own distinctive language, and were it not for the river, the vast majority of people who live in the interior would be as isolated from the outside world and each other as they were 2,000 years ago, in the period just before the great Bantu migration to the south.

The river itself is the second largest in the world in terms of the amount of water it disgorges into the Atlantic Ocean. It crosses the Equator twice, the only river in the world to do so, as it progresses north from its source in eastern Zambia before curving west through a thick, dank, dense, lush rainforest, the largest in Africa. Further south, away from this life-force of vegetation, the land is blessed with the mineral deposits of primeval times. There's copper, zinc, diamonds, cobalt, uranium, gold, silver, tin, manganese and much more besides.

Zaire's people are among the most resourceful on the continent (you have to be to have survived under Mobutu Sese Seko). Their music is heard all over Africa and has influenced many an artist further afield. Call it Zaire, call it the Democratic Republic of Congo, as its current rulers prefer, the country still represents all that is possible in Africa and everything that is wrong about Africa. It is one of those pivotal states, like Nigeria in the west. If the DRC can be brought round, Africa will prosper. If it continues to sink into the quagmire of corruption and ethnically driven politics, there is little hope for the rest of the continent. It is the template, the anvil on which a new Africa has to be beaten into shape. Within its borders, it encapsulates all the talents and tribulations that afflict this continent.

If Africa is to work, it must work in Congo.

Zaire's physical splendour, its natural opulence, is matched only by the mythical status it has acquired among those foreign travellers who have visited it. Ever since Conrad used the Congo River to take his readers on a journey through man's capacity for moral corruption, the country has held a fascination for writers. V. S. Naipaul, Ronan Bennett and Barbara Kingsolver have all explored the human condition against the backdrop of an outrageously fecund Congo.

A hundred years ago Conrad wrote of it: 'The great wall of vegetation, an exuberant and entangled mass of trunks, branches, leaves, boughs, festoons, motionless in the moonlight, was like a rioting invasion of soundless life, a rolling wave of plants, piled up, crested, ready to topple over the creek, to sweep every little man of us out of his little existence'.

In *A Bend in the River*, V. S. Naipaul speaks of the 'land taking you back to something that was familiar, something you had known at some time but had forgotten or ignored, but which was always there. You felt the land taking you back to what was there a hundred years ago, to what had been there always.'

And here is Barbara Kingsolver, writing more recently in *The Poisonwood Bible*: 'The trees are columns of slick, brindled bark like muscular animals overgrown beyond all reason. Every space is filled with life: delicate, poisonous frogs war-painted like skeletons, clutched in copulation, secreting their precious eggs on to dripping leaves . . . behind the river, a rising rumple of dark green hills folded on each other like a great old tablecloth, receding to pale hazy blue. Looming like the judgement.'

All of these writers have recognised in Congo something pervasive and elemental, something so profligate, so powerful, that it might warp the senses and bend the human will. This raw and potent wealth was what seduced the white man to its interior over 150 years ago. It's also what corrupted him. Conrad understood the vulgar underside of the colonial project. 'To tear treasure out of the bowels of the land was their desire, with no more purpose at the back of it than there is in burglars breaking into a safe.'

But Congo's post-colonial years have been marked with even greater avarice than the Belgians ever exhibited. The big men who followed the imperial masters did not merely emulate the white men, they outdid them. And none more so than Mobutu the all-powerful.

'Yassus, man! Look at this! That's what I call being shit scared.' Glenn Middleton was pointing to the piles of disposable nappies on the floor of what had been the presidential living room. My cameraman, who was as much friend as workmate, often produced a flash of black humour when the going got a bit tense. Along with my producer, Hamilton Wende, we had sneaked into the presidential residence in Kinshasa, the first TV journalists to do so.

It was 17 May 1997, the day Mobutu fled. For me this moment was the culmination of a seven-month observation of the unravelling of Mobutu's power. I had predicted the dictator's imminent fall many times, but it wasn't till I had entered the lair of the beast that I understood just what a momentous event it was. If Mobutu could be driven out, if the vicious thugs he called his army could be made to take flight like rats from a fire, there was hope yet for Africa. That, at any rate, was what I thought at the time.

We were nervous as we picked our way from the entrance hall into the inner sanctum, the place where wicked plans had once been hatched and evil thoughts allowed to float free. Earlier in the day, when we had first tried to get pictures of the abandoned residence, we had been spotted by remnants of the presidential guard still in the compound and they had forbidden us to come back. They had been drunk and had waved their rifles at us.

The nappies to which Glenn had drawn our attention were strewn all over the thick-pile carpet like rubbish in a landfill. By the time Mobutu left Kinshasa for the last time that dawn, his prostate cancer had rendered him incontinent. Clearly he and his entourage had left in a hurry. It must have been a humiliating departure for the man who had ruled Zaire like a vast personal domain for thirty-two years. There had been a time when the city would have been brought to a standstill if he so much as moved from one of his many palaces to another. This time he had bolted, largely unnoticed, like a thief in the night.

This house, a modest one in comparison with his many other official residences dotted around the country, was on the northern edge of Camp Tsha Tshi, a heavily fortified military compound on a hill above Kinshasa. It was where he'd retreated with his family, his last refuge in the capital.

Down in the city slums, nearly 5 million people were having to survive without running water. Here the manicured lawns of thick-bladed buffalo grass glistened under a gentle but incessant covering of water droplets from a sprinkler system. The rhythmic hiss as the water escaped the nozzle was hypnotic. The president might have gone but nobody had bothered to turn off the taps. A sound halfway between a wail and scream indicated the presence of peacocks in the grounds, that almost obligatory accoutrement of presidential palaces across the continent.

Over to the west the sun was setting, its blood-orange tinge diluted in the churning waters of the Zaire River flowing past the presidential compound. In this part of Africa dusk is but a momentary hesitation between day and night. Darkness comes quickly, forgoing the more leisurely progress it reserves for northern climes.

We didn't turn on any lights as we entered the palace for fear of alerting the soldiers outside. We had only the artificial white illumination of the lamp attached to Glenn's camera. As he pointed his lens this way and that, shapes moved in and out of the shadows, giving the whole scene a surreal quality. It was like being at a peep show, surreptitiously watching something indecent. You would catch a glimpse of an object and then it would disappear, whetting your appetite for more.

We had been beaten to the palace by Mobutu's own presidential guard. By the time we got there anything of any immediate value, in other words, items that could be sold quickly for cash, had been looted. Like vultures feeding on a rotting carcass, they had rampaged through the building. The hi-fi system had gone; so, too, had some of the air-conditioning units. There wasn't a single TV set in the building, though you could see the satellite cable through which the 'all-powerful warrior' might have learned of his own imminent demise. I wondered if he had ever seen any of my dispatches.

The looters had left enough to suggest the man's expensive, if vulgar, tastes. No piece of furniture was unadorned. Everything was bigger than it needed to be. What I saw here reminded me of my colleague John Simpson's description of Nicolae Ceausescu's residence in Bucharest after the revolution there in 1989, and of the TV pictures from the Malacanang Palace once Ferdinand and Imelda Marcos had fled the Philippines. It was as if all these dictators shopped at the same impossibly ostentatious department store, or shared a roving interior decorator who specialised in homes for despots.

In the middle of the sitting room was a white throne. It was from this room that Mobutu had tried to cling on to his once-great empire, refusing to accept that he had already lost it. He had a throne, but he no longer had a country. The emperor had lost his clothes long before but it was not till the last day that any of his courtiers dared to tell him. According to an eyewitness I met some days later, he had sat in this oversized white chair, dumbfounded, as his generals told him the game was up. Whether it was the effect of the drugs he was taking to numb the cancerous pain, or simply the despot's inability to comprehend the idea of an end to his rule, as I heard it, Mobutu was in a daze, apparently incapable of making his final decision: to abandon the country.

Even as his wife, Bobi Ladawa, and other members of his entourage packed their most precious belongings, a rag-tag, wellington-booted army was advancing on the capital. Some walked along the road, others emerged from the bush. One group kept to the railway line; still more followed the great river, floating in on dugout canoes. So who were these boys, these unlikely conquerors who were about to drive Africa's most entrenched dictatorship into exile and history?

The seeds of Mobutu's demise had been sown over 1,000 miles to the east, on the distant shores of Lake Kivu, on the other side of the seemingly impenetrable rainforest that divides Congo.

Mobutu was but one victim of the political tidal wave that flooded the region in the aftermath of the Rwandan genocide. At first he had sought to profit from it, playing the honest broker as the world tried to work out what to do with the million Rwandan Hutus who had fled into his country. Ultimately, he was toppled by the instability they unleashed on the region.

Many people had predicted that the presence of the Rwandan Hutus on the Zairean side of the border would be profoundly destabilising. But no one, not even the most prescient of observers, could have foreseen that Kinshasa, the great city of bright lights and fast people on the other side of the continent, might be affected by events on this eastern fringe.

By the tail end of 1996, over two years after the Rwandan Hutus fled their country, the camps near the eastern Zairean town of Goma had begun to resemble permanent settlements. Where once there had been a sea of makeshift tents, more durable shacks had been built. Some of them even boasted second storeys. The Hutus had created a nation within a nation. When they had come over the border in 1994 they had stayed close to those they knew, replicating, in effect, the communes to which they had belonged at home. These were the very administrative structures through which Hutu extremists and the Interahamwe, their lynch mob, had organised the genocide, and those same extremists held sway in the camps. Before long, they began the business of insurgency, trying to undermine the new Tutsi-led government in Rwanda. The camps became the launch pad for raids across the border that threatened to undo what little progress the Rwandan leadership was making.

This activity was underpinned by the steady flow of food and medicines from the international aid agencies. One or two, most notably Médecins Sans Frontières, had seen the ludicrousness of the situation and had pulled out, but the vast majority stayed on. Many of the aid workers on the ground were, however, troubled by the implications of their presence in the camps. If a failure to distinguish between the innocent and the culpable had been excusable in those early, hectic days of the exodus, it was no longer acceptable now.

With every day that passed the camps were becoming more entrenched. I remember Vincent Nicot, a delegate of the International Committee of the Red Cross, telling me that the number of babies born in the camps was exceeding the number of people who were filtering back into Rwanda. In exile prospective parents were able to avail themselves of antenatal care and medical expertise that surpassed anything they might find in any African village. Attempts to persuade more people to go back to Rwanda were always thwarted by the extremists, who were well aware that the continuing presence of the refugees was their best guarantee of evading capture and being held accountable for what they had done. The problem was getting bigger, not smaller.

Dismantling the camps had now become a major preoccupation of the Rwandan government. Its hope of putting the leaders of the genocide on trial and trying to rehabilitate those who had followed their orders was impossible while the refugees remained in Zaire. Paul Kagame, the Rwandan vice-president and its chief strategist, knew his country would have to act on its own. He had long since given up any hope of help from the United Nations. On the contrary, after its negligence when faced with the genocide two years earlier, Kagame saw the UN as an obstacle rather than an ally.

In the end, the Hutu extremists themselves inadvertently set in motion a sequence of events that would lead first to the break-up of the camps and culminate in the fall of President Mobutu.

Soon after they had arrived in Goma, the Hutu leaders had begun to spread their poisonous prejudices in Zaire. Their target was the 300,000-strong Zairean Tutsi population, the Banyamulenge. Given the arbitrary way national borders had been drawn during the scramble for Africa, it was common enough to find people of a common ethnic or cultural stock separated in this way. The Tutsi peoples had been split in three, the majority finding themselves in Rwanda or Burundi, the rest in Congo. Lines marked up on a map in the drawing rooms of nineteenth-century Berlin bore scant relevance to life on the ground in Africa.

The relative success of the Banyamulenge population in eastern Zaire made them easy prey to the politics of envy. Seizing the chance to score some cheap political points, the governor of Kivu province ordered the expulsion of the Banyamulenge. 'Go back home' was the gist of his message, the rallying cry of ethnic cleansers everywhere.

This now-forgotten governor could never have imagined the seismic effect his decree would have on his own country. All he was looking for was a little local kudos, something that would keep him in office, and bribes, just a little bit longer. Instead the expulsion order triggered a Banyamulenge uprising, which was eagerly aided and abetted by a grateful Paul Kagame in Rwanda. Here was the proxy army with which he could prise open the camps.

With the help of some Rwandan troops (my colleague Allan Little spotted some on one of several incursions into Zairean territory) and some carefully aimed mortars, the Banyamulenge managed to disband the camps, and by November 1996 the refugees were racing back across the border into Rwanda. It was like a reverse action replay of the exodus of 1994. What UN negotiation and persuasion had failed to achieve in two and a half years, Rwandan military strategists and their Banyamulenge partners had managed in a number of days. A hardcore group of extremists fled further into Zaire, but the rest of the refugee population was back in Rwanda at last.

What happened next was a surprise to everyone, perhaps even to the meticulous and calculating Kagame. The Banyamulenge threw away the script and started making up their lines as they went along. What had started as a local uprising began to look more and more like a national rebellion. It even got a new name, in keeping with its more ambitious goals: the Alliance of the Democratic Forces for the Liberation of Congo-Zaire.

Its leader was one Laurent Desire Kabila, a man unknown to

most of the journalists covering the crisis, although he had been in opposition to Mobutu more or less from the time the president seized power. The few who had heard of him said he'd been something of a fellow traveller, a political opportunist, a servant to many causes, not least of which was self-enrichment. But no one could argue with what he had achieved in this latest incarnation. Most of eastern Zaire was now, nominally, under his control. Cometh the moment, cometh the man.

At the end of 1996 Kabila told us, the journalists, that he looked forward to inviting us to his next press conference. It would, he added, be in Kinshasa the following June. There was *sotto voce* derision in the sitting room of the lakeside villa in which he made his remarks. June was just six months away, and between him and Kinshasa lay a thousand miles of African bush, much of it thick rainforest. There was also the small matter of the Zairean army – not famed for its tactical ingenuity, it must be said, but notorious for its viciousness – and the white mercenaries who were known to be helping the soldiers. And then there was Mobutu Sese Seko himself, the master of survival. We trooped out of the press conference. 'See you in Kinshasa!' we shouted to each other. We thought it was a joke. It wasn't.

Every war, every crisis has its press centre. There's nothing formal about it, it's just the place, usually a hotel, where most of the journalists gather. In Saigon there was the Caravelle, Beirut had the Commodore, in Mogadishu it had been the Sahafee. In Kinshasa in 1997 it was the Memling, where the majority of the journalists were staying.

The Memling had a long history of entertaining foreign correspondents. In *Banana Sunday*, his irreverent but telling look at journalists in Africa, Chris Munnion writes about how the hotel became the base for reporters covering the Katanga secession at the time of Congo's independence in 1960. This was the crisis in which several white nuns and wives of Belgian officials were raped. Munnion claims that it was in the bar of the Memling that the now legendary line 'Has anyone here been raped and speaks English?' was first uttered by a reporter.

Nearly forty years later, having been shut down for a long period, the Memling bar was once again doing a brisk trade with the international media. Such was the speed with which the rebel forces were sweeping across the country that many of the journalists who had scoffed at Kabila's boast were actually in the capital by March. I checked into Room 425 on the 19th, and the following evening I filed my first report, opening with the words: 'Kinshasa is a city in waiting.' The people of Kinshasa knew little about Kabila. He was a man of the east, a faraway place on the other side of the forest. Yet they waited to greet him, called out his name and chanted his slogan: 'Change.'

Over the next two months I watched the great edifice of power that Mobutu had built over three decades crumble and disintegrate. Or perhaps implode would be a better word, because it collapsed from the inside, like those high-rise blocks that are demolished to make way for new housing. By the time Mobutu left, most of his henchmen had already jumped ship, and the great conflagration so many of us had predicted never happened. Mobutu's troops were no more steadfast than an addict in search of a fix. They were his so long as he could satisfy their craving for booze and booty. When he could no longer guarantee that, they just melted away.

Towards the end our greatest fear was not the crossfire of raging battle but the ugly vengeance of Mobutu's drunk and defeated army. From every place to which they retreated there were tales of looting and gratuitous violence. Too cowardly to defend the regime that had once served them so well, they vented their spleen on those who had gained nothing from Mobutu's corruption. Like back-alley bullies they compensated for their shrivelled status by beating up those too weak to defend themselves.

We, the foreigners, were not immune from their anger, but it was the locals who suffered most. Anyone who travels the wilder side of Africa should be aware of this order of vulnerability. To be a black man in Africa is bad news indeed. Your skin, though it symbolises your oneness with the land, also advertises your expendability. You are an African – who cares if you get roughed up? Who is going to defend you? Where are the laws that will protect you?

Next in line for a beating is the Asian. You have the protection that comes with money. You are a trader and you can buy friends when the going gets tough. But once your pockets are empty, then you, too, are vulnerable. And they will punish you with relish. When they strike the African, it is an act of brutality; when they strike the Asian it's an act of revenge for all the times they have paid over the odds for scarce goods.

Then there is the white man. In the back of too many African minds, even in those who spout the language of independence, there is a residual respect, a vestigial fear of the power of the white man. The rich countries may ignore Africa when its needs are greatest, but they will send an army to protect the precious skin of their citizens. The message is clear: mess with a white man and you are asking for trouble.

My fixer in Kinshasa, Clyde Salumu Sharady, was a black man. So when the soldiers turned on us one day in May 1997, it was Clyde who got the beating. We had gone to the airport to do some filming. No sooner had Glenn rested the camera on his shoulder than we were surrounded by a pack of them. They screamed at us, stared at us, pushed me, shoved Glenn – but it was Clyde they hit. There was a sickening thud as one of the men landed a blow on his shoulder with the butt of his rifle. Then another soldier whipped Clyde's legs away with one powerful kick. That was the signal for the rest of them. About four or five climbed on to Clyde as he curled himself up. We pleaded, we begged – they just smiled. Then they dragged him away, along with our driver, a man in his sixties.

As for Glenn and me, there was a little more shouting, a little more shoving, but no violence. They were more interested in our wallets, my pocket radio and my camera. They took them all. We were released only after the intervention – bribe would be more accurate – of an airline official we had got to know quite well. Clyde was bruised, bloody and shaking as we got into the car. Our driver had footprints on his white shirt. The soldiers had stood on their heads and chests. The same day, Clyde moved out of the room he rented in town. The soldiers had said they knew he was getting paid in dollars, and that they would find him to get their share.

Everywhere you looked there was evidence of the moral decay and crumbling infrastructure that were the hallmarks of Mobutu's three decades in power. Kinshasa was bad enough, but outside the capital in the great interior, it was as if time had stood still since independence.

I remember a trip to the village of Bolobo on the edge of the forest. This was the place where, nearly a hundred years earlier, Roger Casement, the British consul to the Congo Free State and latterday reformer, had begun his investigation into the atrocities committed in the name of King Leopold's civilising mission. It was here that he began to corroborate the rumours of slave labour, of workers who had had their hands chopped off for not producing enough rubber. I was retracing his first steps, my mission virtually the same: to uncover the crimes of another man who ruled the country with little care for the plight of its people.

I went there with a colleague, Roger Hearing, on a plane hired by the Baptist Missionary Society. We were accompanying Owen Clark, a British citizen who had worked in Zaire since 1961, the latest in a long line of missionaries who had been coming to Bolobo since 1888. His predecessors at the turn of the century had been reluctant to expose the unparalleled cruelty of soldiers under Belgian command. Perhaps he was making amends by taking us with him now.

Bolobo was just under 300 kilometres from the capital if you took a boat upstream from Kinshasa. It was even further over

land, but that option was academic: the road had long since disappeared under the prolific African bush. The village sits on a
bend in the Zaire River, its lifeline to the outside world and to
produce from the hinterland. In better times, the people of Bolobo
had bartered with the traders who plied these waters, but the war
had stopped all that. They told me it had been weeks since they
had seen any of the steamers that normally moved up and down
the river like floating markets. Nothing came now except the
great, rubbery, knotted clots of hyacinth that bobbed downstream
like green water monsters on the move. Those and cholera.
Soldiers retreating from the front had brought the sickness with
them. There were some 400 cases of it in the village, and thirty
people had already died from what is the simplest of diseases to
cure. Clean water and some salt is all it takes, but in Bolobo in
1997 that was too much to ask.

There was a clinic in Bolobo. That didn't mean a dispensary, or
clean sheets and vaccinations. It was just the name of the place
where the sick gathered to wait for a man like Owen to turn up
with a boxful of drugs. I asked if all this was the war's doing. No,
no, they said, it had been like this for as long as anyone could
remember. In a system built on the trading of favours and patronage, Bolobo had nothing to offer. It was one of the forgotten
communities of Mobutu's Zaire.

And just as Mobutu's modern Africa had rejected them so they,
too, had begun to turn away from his failed promises, seeking out
the potions and skills of those who had ministered to them long
before the white man had ever come here. Talika was three years
old. Her eyes were puffy and immobile, her abdomen horribly
swollen. Her parents had started their search for a cure with a traditional healer, but he had waited too long before pronouncing his
inability to find out what was wrong. Now it was too late. Talika
had a tumour on her liver; it was now too large to be operable. But
even if an operation had been possible, her parents, peasant farmers, could never have afforded to take Talika to Kinshasa, the

nearest place where such surgery might have been performed. In Mobutu's Zaire there were a thousand Talikas in a thousand villages: lives cut short before they had even begun.

It was not so different in Kinshasa itself. The vast majority of the city's 5 million inhabitants lived in the *cité*, a sprawling slum of shacks built between a network of muddy tracks and open sewers. Here children died from the diseases of poverty. According to the UN's figures, there were 300,000 clinically malnourished children in the capital alone.

And amid all this Mobutu's henchmen were still talking up his chances of survival. Zaire needs him, they would say when they came round to the Memling. The country will fall apart. He is the one who has kept it together all these years. They were clutching at straws. Zaire had already started to fall apart. The challenge facing whoever took over from Mobutu was to put it back together.

Part of the reason that Zaire was on the verge of disintegration was that Mobutu was happy to have it that way. His theory of government was that when the periphery is weak, the centre is strong. The fact that there were no roads linking the Zairean provinces to the capital, or to one another, for that matter, reduced the chances of any individual provincial commander or politician moving against the capital. Underdevelopment and poverty were part of the grand plan, too: no institution or province would then grow strong enough to rise against Mobutu.

There were no fewer than six different arms to his security forces: the Presidential Guard, the Force Publique, the Zairean Armed Forces, the Civil Guard, the intelligence service, and the police. No single unit was powerful enough to mount a coup on its own, and by making them compete against each other for resources, Mobutu ensured that any concerted action was unlikely. It was a classic example of the old divide-and-rule strategy. It also meant, though, that when the time came to defend the regime against the advancing rebels, each unit passed the buck to another.

One part of the country, Eastern Kasai province, had already followed this Zairean version of separate development through to its logical conclusion. I visited Mbuji-Mayi, Zaire's diamond capital, in the days before the rebels took Kinshasa. We had left Kinshasa before breakfast and, when we arrived, I tried to buy bread at the market. My offer of Zairean currency was greeted with howls of derision from stallholders and shoppers alike.

'Prostate! Prostate!' they shouted. It was the nickname they had given to the central bank's money.

'It's Mobutu's money. It is sick money. It is no good,' one of them added, relishing the acid humour with which so many Africans cope with the poor hand fate has dealt them.

I learned that Eastern Kasai had printed its own money and, in effect, ran its own mini-economy. The sale of diamonds was thought to account for about a third of Zaire's overall revenue. In Mbuji-Mayi, the gems were traded openly in the marketplace, which turned over about $500,000 a day. How much of it actually ended up in the national coffers was a moot point. The head of the Zairean diamond marketing organisation told me that about $100 million of diamond revenues had been lost to corruption the previous year alone.

In 1960, just after independence, Eastern Kasai had, along with the neighbouring Shaba province, been involved in a secessionist movement. It seemed inconceivable that such action was not once again on the agenda. 'Look, we went down that road once,' said Monsignor Tharcice Tshibangu Tshishiku, the Catholic bishop of Mbuji-Mayi. 'It didn't work then, and it will not work now. It is not what the people want. They know there is a greatness in us as a united people. It is not Zaire they hate, it is the man who runs it.'

This was the reason Laurent Kabila's boy soldiers were able to make it to the outskirts of the capital so quickly. In every village they passed on their long march to the capital, they were greeted by people who wanted change. This enthusiasm wasn't about politics or policies, it was about deliverance.

Even as Laurent Kabila was proving on the ground that he was the new master of Zaire – or Congo, as he had already begun to call the country, reverting to the name it had before Mobutu changed it – foreign diplomats were still trying to contain the situation to ensure some form of orderly transfer. A 'dignified exit for Mobutu, and a soft landing for the rebels', as some put it. The Americans were there, of course, picking up the pieces of their past folly. While they did most of their work behind the scenes, South Africa, and Nelson Mandela in particular, played a more public role.

Before the Zairean crisis, South Africa, keen to show that it was a collective player on the continent's diplomatic scene, had been careful not to throw its weight about. A previous foreign-policy intervention, made when the Nigerian dictator Sani Abacha condemned the human-rights activist Ken Saro Wiwa to death, had left Mr Mandela with a great deal of egg on his face. On that occasion Mr Mandela had shunned the advice of several prominent Nigerian activists, who told him that the Nigerian dictator would only understand tough action, and opted instead for quiet, behind-the-scenes diplomacy. Sani Abacha returned the favour by hanging Ken Saro Wiwa in circumstances designed to maximise Mr Mandela's humiliation. He was attending a Commonwealth conference in New Zealand at the time.

Mr Mandela should have learned his lesson. The emollient charm that had worked such wonders with his people in South Africa – especially the whites – carried little weight in the much rougher trade of African politics. But he stuck to his tactics nonetheless.

On 6 May, the South Africans managed to get both Kabila and Mobutu on to one of their naval ships, the *Outeniqua*, which was moored off Pointe-Noire on the coast of Congo-Brazzaville. Negotiations work when both sides have something to gain from getting round a table rather than fighting it out on the battlefield. This, however, was a very one-sided affair. The physical stature of the two protagonists was an accurate reflection of the unequal struggle in which they were now engaged. At the final press conference, Mobutu and Kabila sat on either side of Nelson Mandela. Mobutu was pale, thin and sickly. His eyes darted from side to side, as if searching for a friendly face. Kabila, on the other hand, sat there looking round and shiny. His neck was thick, his presence powerful. He had the air of someone who had better things to do, as indeed he had. His eyes betrayed a sense of boredom – and, we were given to understand, the effects of the liquor he had consumed the night before. At some points in the proceedings it seemed as if he might even have nodded off.

And there was Nelson Mandela trying to sell a deal that was already obsolete. Mobutu Sese Seko had agreed to step down, and only the how and when were still unclear. But surely that was the whole point of the exercise.

In South Africa Mr Mandela had used the language of reconciliation to bind black and white in a new nation. He had reminded his people that they all shared a common past: they were all Africans. He returned to another version of that theme on the *Outeniqua* that day. In his opening remarks, he described both men as 'two of the greatest sons of Africa'.

After the press conference, I discussed his comment with Ofeibea Quist-Arcton, of the BBC's World Service, one of the most respected journalists in Africa. 'How dare he!' she said. 'That kind of nonsense might have worked in South Africa, but it is an insult to tell Zaireans that the man who has ruined their lives is a great son of Africa.' Clyde Salumu Sharady, my Zairean fixer, just shook his head in disbelief. I looked at Nelson Mandela a little differently that day. I described him as 'hapless' in my report of the talks. I was told that South African Foreign Ministry officials didn't like it, but, in truth, it was the kindest adjective I could think of.

Back on shore, it was business as usual. The rebel advance continued. The soldiers were by now about a hundred miles from the capital. Information was difficult to come by. As far as I know, no journalist actually made it to the front. We all depended on the grapevine, that mix of rumour, sensible conjecture and reliable sources that forms the basis of a reporter's copy. As it happened, I had one of the most reliable sources of all: a local businessman. He wishes to remain anonymous.

This man's family had been in Zaire since the 1920s. They had built up a little empire of businesses that traded in everything from foodstuffs to steel. You wouldn't have guessed it from the modest office he used, but it didn't do to flaunt your wealth. He once told me that he set aside about 20 per cent of his profits to 'oil the system'. The family had survived because they knew how to play the Zairean game. When you cannot depend on the rule of law, when the institutions of state do not function, it is who and how much you know that counts. It is a delicate balance. You need just enough information to give you some leverage; find out too much and you put yourself in danger.

As the formal sources of information dried up and it became more and more difficult to establish the facts, my friend's network of contacts across the country became an invaluable conduit for bulletins on what was really happening. When CNN reported that Matadi, the port on the Atlantic through which Kinshasa's supplies had to pass, had fallen to the rebels, he told me otherwise. When news reached us of heavy fighting in Kikwit, he assured me that the town was empty. The Zairean troops had looted it and moved on, retreating towards the capital.

And when Mobutu's closest officials were telling us that they still had faith in the president, my source gave me a list of all those who had already fled. It was like a *Who's Who* of Mobutu's regime, complete with times and locations. On 14 May a General Kalume had crossed the Zaire River to Brazzaville at 11 pm. General Baramoto Kpama, head of the Civil Guard, had left, bound for South Africa, about a week earlier. Much of his ill-gotten wealth had preceded him, apparently carried out in suitcases by relatives.

Nendaka Bika Victor and Bomboko Justin Marie, men who had helped Mobutu to power all those years ago, had unsuccessfully attempted to leave on 6 May. They would try again.

And so it went on. I never asked him exactly how he got hold of all this information, only if it was reliable. To my knowledge, he did not once let me down.

There was a surreal quality to these final days of the Mobutu era. The restaurants stayed open till the very last gasp, their expatriate owners fretting about whether they could still get oysters flown in fresh from Europe. If it was bizarre that the professionals at the tennis club were still ready to take bookings for lessons, it was even more incredible that anyone should be worried about the state of their backhand when the state of the nation was in doubt. But old habits die hard, and routine becomes a refuge. Everyone knew the end was coming but no one could be sure when or how it would happen. You could go indoors, close the shutters and pray, or you could hit the town and make the most of the time that was left. For Kinshasa's élite, the latter option came much more naturally. This was a city that knew how to party, and if you were rich, you did little else.

The Intercontinental Hotel held a fashion show, the playboys still churned the waters of the Zaire River on their jet-skis and the nightclubs stayed open till the last man left. Their customers ordered Johnnie Walker Black Label by the bottle and smoked Cohibas by the boxful. They danced till they dropped and then got up to do some more. The whores who hung around the nightclubs and bars had never had it so good, and their clients had never had it so often.

And then morning came, and reality forced itself on even the most committed reveller. The glory days were over and it was time to think about leaving. The airline offices were full and the queues at the airport grew longer. The great escape had begun. The expats wore something sensible for the journey; the Zaireans wore something expensive.

Those closest to Mobutu stuck to their lines even though the set was collapsing around them. The show had to go on. Late one evening, just a couple of days before the rebels walked into the city, word went round that someone from the president's office had summoned all the journalists to the lobby of the Memling Hotel. We gathered there, certain that the round-up meant one of two things: either the president had capitulated, or we were all going to be thrown out. Both dénouements were plausible, but neither took account of the bubble of unreality that surrounded Mobutu and his entourage. There is no one so cut off from the world around him as the dictator who has had his way for too long. Those who have enjoyed absolute power are always the last to realise that it is seeping away from them. So it was with Mobutu and the small band of hangers-on, relatives and misfits who stuck it out till the bitter end.

'Get your cameras, gentlemen and, of course, the ladies. We are going to take you to the front,' the official said. 'We are going to show you that all your talk of rebels coming to Kinshasa is propaganda.'

The convoy was led by Kongulu, one of Mobutu's two sons. The brothers were very different characters. It was as if the split personality of the father had been neatly divided between them. Nzanga was the urbane one. Whenever he visited the Memling it was in jacket and tie. He had inherited the father's capacity to charm. Kongulu, on the other hand, had inherited the side of the father that came alive when the charm didn't work. On the streets they used to call him Saddam Hussein.

On that day Kongulu looked like an extra from a low-budget African version of a Rambo film. He wore black boots and combat fatigues with a T-shirt cut away at the shoulders to accentuate his impressive biceps. Crossed bandoliers and a beret finished off the costume. He strutted in front of a tank that was in such poor shape it had difficulty keeping up with him. The soldiers who followed in its belching wake seemed as bemused as we were. A

Jeep or two and a couple of trucks made up the procession.

The attention to safety that had preoccupied the journalists for all of a couple of seconds soon gave way to disbelief and then mirth. It dawned on us that we were extras in a farce. As TV crews broke ranks and raced ahead to get their shots, the unseemly mêlée that is a feature of cameramen and photographers at work reached comical proportions.

'Put your fucking head in my shot once more and I'll knock it off, you arsehole,' shouted the man from AP TV as a snapper got in his way.

'Yeah? You and whose fucking army?' the photographer retorted.

TV reporters trying to do their 'stand-ups', the commentaries direct to camera, spluttered ineffectually as they choked on the diesel fumes. The newspaper correspondents and wire service reporters looked on in a superior sort of way, as if wondering who were the more ridiculous, the TV crews or the soldiers they were attempting to capture on tape.

Throughout all this, Kongulu carried on unperturbed, lost in the make-believe world where tyrants never get beaten. He might have convinced himself that all was well, but if he had hoped to win us over, he failed miserably. He simply couldn't see what was obvious to us: that if this was the best he could muster, Mobutu was a goner.

The whole exercise petered out at a petrol station where one of the Jeeps had to make a fuel stop. So much for being battle-ready. The convoy hadn't even reached the outskirts of the airport, which would have been the rebels' first target.

We raced each other back to the hotel, generating more heat and dust than anything that was happening on Kongulu's imaginary front line.

Those who hung around Kongulu were either too stupid or too brainwashed to work out that the game was up. Even as these people were playing at fighting the rebels, the man who actually had that task was making a much more realistic appraisal of Kinshasa's fate. The defence of the city, if that is what it came to, fell to one General Donat Lieko Mahele, commander of the army.

I doubt that anyone who held any position of power in Mobutu's system could have escaped the corruption that spread through it like a virus, but Mahele stood out as being not as bad as the others. He was as close as you got to a professional soldier in Zaire. He was a moderate, whatever that meant in this context, and a commander of some intelligence. He was also – to his cost – a man with a too highly developed conscience for the dog-eat-dog world of Mobutu's regime as it faced the abyss.

Other service chiefs had, as I say, already deserted the capital, taking with them as much as they could carry of what they had looted over the years. In the end only Mahele was left, and it was down to him to decide Kinshasa's fate. When he'd made up his mind, he chose the BBC to broadcast the news.

The summons from the Ministry of Defence mentioned me by name. General Mahele, I was told, wanted to convey an important message. It was the day after Kongulu's pantomime, 16 May 1997, early in the afternoon. We knew by now that the rebels had reached the outskirts of the capital. I asked my trusted colleague Ofeibea Quist-Arcton and Howard French of the *New York Times* to come with me.

At the ministry we were ushered into a long room and asked to sit on one side of a conference table. The room was remarkable for what it lacked. There was no phone, and the map on the wall was no more detailed than the kind of thing you pick up at the market. When a line of officials filed in, General Mahele, too, was conspicuous by his absence. There was no sign of any general, or anyone in any sort of uniform at all. 'We've been had,' I heard Howard whisper to Ofeibea. There was just one consolation: sitting down directly opposite me was the most implausibly beautiful woman one could imagine.

'My name is Colette Tshomba,' she said in an accent that

mingled African roots with a touch of Francophone Europe. I was smitten. So was Howard, despite his understandable scepticism. Thank God for Ofeibea.

'Will the general be joining us?' she inquired.

'No. He is busy. There is a lot to do,' Colette explained.

'It's just that we were told he had a message for us,' I said, partially recovering my equilibrium.

'Oh yes, we have a message. We want to help you. You see, some of the things that have been written are not correct.'

So that's what the call was all about. It was nothing more than a slightly subtler version of what Kongulu had tried to do the night before. But then, when even I was about to lose faith and patience in Colette, she uttered the words that every journalist wants to hear.

'There are things we can tell you. For your information, I mean. Not for you to go and say, "So-and-so told me this thing."' From this point onwards, the words 'background, off the record' are underlined in my notebook. We waited for her to continue.

'You see, there is no point in a war for war's sake. If war came to Kinshasa we can only imagine what that would be like.'

'Are you saying you don't want to fight?' I can't remember which of us asked the question.

'Of course we can fight. We have the power. You have seen the troop movements. General Mahele is preparing to keep the city secure.'

There had to be a 'but'. It came soon enough.

'But General Mahele does not want to sacrifice a people and a city over a battle for the future of one man. That sort of thing is past.'

There it was. The message. The general had decided to dump his one-time master. I could see now why he had decided not to address us himself. This was dynamite. It was a surrender, and we were being asked to fly the white flag on his behalf.

On the way back to the Memling we checked and cross-checked our notes. All three of us had the same wording and, more important, interpreted it in the same way. I didn't have a TV bulletin for a few hours so I gave the story to Richard Downes, a colleague from our Johannesburg bureau, who was filing for radio that day. It was a good story, an exclusive of sorts, but broadcasting it put us in danger. Outraged by the message, Mobutu hard-liners wanted to shoot the messengers.

At least, that's what Howard French was told when he cross-checked the story with his own contacts within the regime. Some people were 'after the BBC', he was warned. Soldiers were said to be making for the hotel. The information was corroborated by our fixer, Clyde. His sources in the military had told him it would be a bad day for the BBC, and he'd been advised to stay away.

The next couple of hours were terrifying at the time but, in retrospect, our fear owed more to the feverish, rumour-laden atmosphere of those last days than to any cast-iron cause for panic. There was a hurried meeting of the BBC team. We decided to lie low for a while, dispersing ourselves among the rooms of colleagues from other organisations. About half a dozen of us crowded into the room used by Jennifer Glasse, the correspondent of the *Christian Science Monitor*. It was a choice that revealed a subliminal but utterly unjustified faith in the protection afforded by an organisation with religious roots, however distant.

My colleague Allan Little kept notes of the day's events for his report. We sat there, paranoid and silent, waiting for a knock on the door. Then the phone rang. A cameraman filming from the roof had been shot at. So they had arrived at the Memling. The phone rang again. This time we were told that European ambassadors had agreed an evacuation plan. Belgian paratroopers were going to secure the area around the hotel. And then someone said: 'Never in my life did I imagine I could be overjoyed to hear the words "the Belgians are coming"'. We laughed and, as Allan put it, the 'whole absurd edifice of rumour and paranoia' fell away.

When, later that day, I told my friend the businessman about Mahele's message, he confirmed everything. The general had already been in contact with the rebels by satellite phone. In fact, many of them had already infiltrated the capital, ready to take up their positions when the word was given. 'But take care,' he cautioned me. 'These are going to be the most dangerous twenty-four hours we've ever had. Mobutu's people could start fighting each other, and that will be a lot worse than if they fought the rebels. Mahele is playing a dangerous game.'

It was a long night. The bar at the Memling was as full as ever, but there was one crucial difference in the air. It was the difference between the anticipation of an event and the certain knowledge that it is about to occur. Nonchalance gives way to expectancy, and expectancy, in turn, to anxiety.

It was after two in the morning when I went up to my room. I was tired but not sleepy; a day's worth of adrenaline still coursed through my body, a sensation I can liken only to being at the wrong end of a perpetual wake-up call. I turned off the lights and lay down, my ears tuned in for the gunshots that I thought were inevitable. But all I could hear was my own pulse. Sleep, as it always does, must have crept up on me, because I was suddenly woken by the nerve-jangling ring of my bedside telephone.

'I hope you were not sleeping.' It took me a couple of seconds to recognise my businessman friend's voice.

'Christ, no. Who could sleep on a night like this?' I lied. It was not yet four.

'Mahele is dead.'

Mahele . . . Mahele . . . what the hell was he talking about? My mind was still struggling into consciousness. I knew what he was telling me was important, but I couldn't fit all the pieces together. It felt like the hiatus between turning on your computer and seeing it whizzing and whirring into life. And then my mental computer screen appeared and everything clicked into place.

'Are you sure?' I remembered his warning of barely twelve hours earlier. Was this it? Was this the internecine struggle he'd feared?

'I'm absolutely positive. I've had it checked.'

'When did it happen?'

'During the night. He was ambushed at Camp Tsha Tshi. Now they've surrounded his house in town. It's looking ugly.'

'Where is Mahele's house?' My mind was turning to the possibility of pictures. It would be getting light within the hour.

'Don't even think about going anywhere near it. These bastards want revenge before they get out of town. I'll talk to you later.'

I think it was only when I put down the phone and started to digest our conversation that I realised just what it meant to talk about the 'end of an era'. It was a phrase that had flown effortlessly from my lips in so many reports back to London, along with the other clichés we had all indulged in. 'The demise of a despot' was one of my favourites – the alliteration was pleasing – and occasionally, in my more colourful moments, I had spoken of the 'long night of Mobutuism' coming to an end.

But nothing ever comes to an end just like that, least of all dictatorships. They have to be brought down. There is a price to pay, a cost to be extracted. General Mahele had paid that price.

I had never met General Mahele. I didn't really know if he had been a good man or a bad man. Yet I was struck by a profound sadness at his death. I felt connected to him in a way that surprised me. I had carried his message. The words were not important now; the man was. He had, like the prodigal son, returned to his senses. He had forsaken the system that had served him so well and found his place among the people. I started wondering about the children he might have, the wife who, even now, would be coping with her grief somewhere quite close by.

Sitting there on my bed, the room still dark, I felt the tears pricking my eyes. I knew that if I turned on the lights my vision of the room would be a blur, so instead of reaching for the switch I waited for the control to reassert itself; for the professionalism of the reporter to smother the responses of the man, as it had done on so many other occasions in so many other places. I put this little chink in my emotional armour down to tiredness. It had been a long and exhausting couple of months. I phoned Allan. I phoned Steve Scott, my counterpart from ITN, and told him to be careful. Then I got dressed. This was the day we had been waiting for.

The progress of the rebel forces through the interior had been as remorseless as the march of soldier ants in an African drought. Has any conquering army ever claimed its prize so quietly? There was no shouting, no singing, no shooting into the sky. As the last remnants of Mobutu's troops shed their uniforms and melted into the townships, the Alliance of the Democratic Forces for the Liberation of Congo-Zaire simply walked into Kinshasa. Tired feet that had trodden the rich earth of Africa's forest now marched along the barren and rutted roads of the capital.

They were boys who had done men's work. They were people of the countryside who now found themselves in the city, strangers in this place they now ruled. They looked bemused by the joyous welcome they received from the citizens of Kinshasa. It was as if they instinctively shrank from the massive weight of expectation that bore down on their shoulders. The people of Kinshasa, too, acknowledged that their liberators were outsiders. They shouted 'Jambo! Jambo!' in Swahili, the language of the east.

From the moment Mobutu's demise seemed plausible it had begun to acquire an extraordinary, even mythical, status in the minds of all those who wanted change in Africa. It would, many thought, mark a turning point not only for the country but also for the continent on which it occupied such a central position.

But it was not to be. Laurent Kabila's government squandered the goodwill with which so many received it. On the face of it, his Democratic Republic of Congo was no different from Mobutu Sese Seko's Zaire. Mr Kabila's failure to ignite the energy of his own people or to meet the great expectations of other countries in the region is both depressing and unnerving. Worse, it is grist to the mill for all those who revel in ridiculing Africa.

In a parody of the transformation of so many of Africa's one-time revolutionaries into despots, Kabila banned political parties, vested vast powers in his home-province cronies, placed the army under the command of his inexperienced thirty-one-year-old son and raided what little was left in the national coffers. Pretty soon it all became so familiar that some of Mobutu's greediest lieutenants returned to Kinshasa and simply picked up where they had left off. Mobutu was gone, but his legacy lived on.

In a measure of staggering cynicism and appalling judgement, Kabila even made common cause with the extremist Rwandan forces against whom he had launched his military campaign just two years earlier. Banyamulenge ministers in his government abandoned him and fled back to Goma, ready to start yet another march across the country. So it was that, within a year and a half of deposing the old dictator, Kabila was himself facing a rebellion.

The war sucked in the rest of the region. Angola, Zimbabwe and Namibia came to Mr Kabila's side; Rwanda and Uganda backed the new rebels. For the first time since independence, Africa faced a regional war. If it began for political reasons, it soon degenerated into a scramble for Congo's vast and plentiful natural resources. In a sense all wars are about enrichment, but the conflict in Congo took the hunt for booty to a level hitherto unknown in Africa. There has been a systematic and sustained exploitation that is only possible if some very senior people are involved, and the peace accord signed in Lusaka in 1999 (but not fully implemented) and more recent attempts in South Africa have made little difference to the plunder.

It is surely no coincidence that the foreign troops are most concentrated in the areas rich in gold, diamonds, copper, timber and coltan. According to a report published by Oxfam (UK) in January 2002, Zimbabwean troops have been deployed in Kasais and Katanga, Rwandan troops in Kivu and Maniema and the Ugandan army in Ituri and northern Kivu. Oxfam's conclusion was straightforward: 'Wealth from natural resources is sustaining the war.'

In January 2001 Laurent Kabila was struck down by an assassin's bullet. His son Joseph is the new head of state. So much for the winds of change. And yet Mobutu's fall did mark a turning point of sorts. It is not something you can plot on a graph, but it is significant all the same. All over Africa little people took heart from the fact that a man who had once been deemed unassailable could be brought down. In their minds they can now see that real change is possible, that it will come. And after Mobutu, big men up and down the continent look over their shoulders more often than they ever did before. It may not be the seismic shift that so many wanted, but the pendulum of power is swinging slowly from the rulers towards the ruled.

What's more, it is happening in an entirely African context. A generation ago, change in Africa was impossible without the involvement of the superpowers or the old colonial masters. And when it came, it was often orchestrated from outside. Patrice Lumumba, Congo's first elected leader, was ousted and murdered because his vision of a free country did not suit the big mining companies and their political masters in Washington. Mobutu, on the other hand, was deposed because the Africans themselves didn't like what he had done to the country he renamed Zaire. This time the kingmakers were in Kampala and Kigali. Kabila's rebellion was sustained from within. This was a first for Africa, and a sign of how much the continent had changed.

This shift is part of a process of realignment within Africa and in the continent's relations with the outside world. A century after the first scramble for Africa, there is a new one. This time Africans are rearranging the political architecture of the continent on their own terms. Sometimes it is an ugly business. But as perverse as it may sound, it is a victory of sorts. One man could reasonably lay claim to have epitomised, if not organised, this process. His name is Yoweri Museveni, and he was the man who defeated another African tyrant, Idi Amin Dada of Uganda.

9

Hope for the Future

I couldn't take my eyes off Hope's long, ebony-brown, silver-ringed fingers. Elegant hands. I like hands. Waved about or clasped together, open and expressive or closed and inert, they tell you a lot about a person. It wasn't just the way Hope's skin set off the burnished jewellery, it was the assurance with which these adorned hands held the steering wheel of the powerful four-wheel-drive vehicle we were travelling in. Her hands spoke of the city, of sophistication; the vehicle and terrain around it spoke of a more rugged, rural world. Yet Hope seemed to straddle the two with ease and confidence. I watched her right hand as she lifted it off the wheel and pointed into the bush.

'I grew up in an area just like this,' she said, as if to remind me that she was a woman rooted in Africa's soil; as if she had sensed my temptation to box her into the world of apartment blocks and urban privilege. 'I used to walk to school. Barefoot, of course.'

'And here you are taking a BBC reporter to an interview with the president of your country which will be beamed all over the world.'

'Education has moved us from one century to the next. Without education we would be stuck in the past.'

Hope Kivingere: a life of contrasts, a product of a new Africa. A girl who grew up in traditional bucolic simplicity; a woman playing her part in the crucible of change that is contemporary Uganda. An activist in the armed movement which fought to liberate her country; a graduate of the Sorbonne who speaks French fluently. She respects Africa's customs, but she knows which of them are holding her people back. You cannot stick a label on her. She is the sum of her parts. She doesn't make the headlines, yet much depends on her and her kind, the new generation of Africans determined to reconstruct the continent. They are people who want to rebuild Africa's infrastructure, but who know that first you have to repair the shattered image Africans have of themselves. Hope Kivingere is personal assistant to Yoweri Kaguta Museveni, the president of Uganda and considered by many to be the most influential leader of recent times. His is a new vision of Africa, and it is people like Hope who are making it work on the ground. If there is an African renaissance, as some have suggested, then it is they who are bringing it about.

Museveni came to power in 1986, putting an end to nearly a quarter of a century of death and destruction in this Central African state. He led a five-year bush war that is unique on a continent boasting bush wars by the dozen. Museveni began his military campaign in 1981, when Cold War rivalry was fuelling several conflicts across Africa, but managed to steer clear of its warped priorities. Though he did have some outside help, notably from the Libyans, his was a largely home-grown operation based on the support of his own people.

I first met Mr Museveni in the first year of his presidency, when I was still learning my trade as a reporter, just after his forces had marched into Kampala. At the time all he had proved was that he could lead a successful rebellion. By the time I met him next, in October 1997, I was the BBC's Africa correspondent, based in South Africa, and he was running what was arguably Africa's greatest success story. Here was a man who, unlike so many other rebels, had proved to be as good at ruling as he had been at fighting; a man who turned the aspirations of rebellion into the policies of government.

We were both at a conference in the Zimbabwean capital, Harare. Museveni had seen my dispatches from Zaire, and when he heard I was in town, he sent word that he wanted to discuss some of the issues I had raised. I wanted an interview with him for the report I was preparing on the conference, so I did a deal with his press office. I got my interview, but in the end there wasn't any time left to discuss the Zairean crisis. 'Come and spend some time with me,' he said. 'Talk to my people, they will arrange it.'

His 'people' turned out to be Hope Kivingere. I was impressed by Hope long before I met her. When I spoke to her on the phone she told me that Mr Museveni's invitation was serious. 'He doesn't just say things like that. He means it. When can you come?' It is not a question you hear very often in Africa, and certainly not from the office of a president. Swimming through treacle is the image that comes to mind when I think of the efforts I have made to secure interviews with other heads of government. The second surprise was that Museveni wasn't just talking about a quick in-and-out at his office in Entebbe. Hope explained that I was being invited to Mr Museveni's farm, about three hours' drive west of the capital.

Dates were fixed, hotels booked, transport arranged, and Hope met me at the appointed time in the lobby of the Sheraton Hotel in Kampala. This, I thought to myself, is an unusual woman. Everything went like clockwork. She even offered to drive me to the president's farm herself, which was how I came to be sitting next to her in a Toyota Landcruiser. It was a powerful antidote to the stereotypical image of Africans as indolent and disorganised.

In his book *My African Journey*, Winston Churchill described Uganda, or the area that is now the Republic of Uganda, as the 'pearl' of Africa. The book is a panegyric to colonialism, and I would normally issue a stern health warning to anyone tempted to explore Mr Churchill's views on Africa, but in this case he happens to have been spot on.

It is a beautiful country, endowed with some of the most fertile land anywhere on the continent. In the rainy season the undulating hills in the south are lush and verdant beyond comparison. In the west are the Ruwenzori Mountains, or the Mountains of the Moon, as they are sometimes called. Further south this range spills over into Burundi. It is in these volcanic outcrops that you will find the great silverback gorilla colonies made famous by the late Dian Fossey in *Gorillas in the Mist*. They are part of a range that forms a sort of backbone dividing East and West Africa. On one side is Congo and the dense, and still largely untouched, equatorial rainforest; on the other is Uganda, where the land has been intensively cultivated and slopes away in softer folds. Keep going eastwards, through neighbouring Kenya, and you eventually reach the balmy shores of the Indian Ocean 1,000 kilometres away.

The beauty of the land belies the violence that has been done to its people. Indeed, it is the killing and maiming that most people remember, not nature's gifts of a gentle climate and rich soil. For this is the land of Idi Amin. It is also the country of Milton Obote, who ruled the country twice, before and after Amin. Between them they were responsible for the politically motivated murder of hundreds of thousands of Ugandans between 1962 and 1985. Obote was dictatorial; Amin was a tyrant. Their regimes differed only in the methods they used and the number of people they had killed. Otherwise, they shared a common goal: control.

Milton Obote was Uganda's first elected leader, and took the country to independence in October 1962 as its prime minister. By the end of the decade he had sacked the titular president, banned opposition parties, outlawed the traditional kings and kingdoms of southern Uganda and declared a republic. The jails were full of political detainees and the number of unexplained murders began to increase.

In 1971 Obote was attending a Commonwealth summit in Singapore when Idi Amin, his army commander, seized control of the country. (Given that so many coups d'état occurred during summits, it's a wonder these meetings ever managed a quorum.) Such was Obote's unpopularity that Amin's takeover was greeted with jubilation on the streets of Kampala. There was quiet satisfaction in Western capitals, especially in London's Whitehall. Obote had been busy nationalising British and other foreign companies. It has been claimed that the British secret service helped engineer the coup. Whatever the case, it almost certainly knew about it in advance.

Amin had served in the colonial army as a sergeant-major in the King's African Rifles and, at six foot four, had been an awesome Ugandan heavyweight boxing champion. Though a bit slow on the uptake, he was regarded as an amiable and obliging soldier. Just the sort of fellow the colonial masters used to like – not so bright that they might get fancy ideas. 'A tremendous chap to have around,' in the words of one British officer.

Once in power, Amin took the elimination of opposition to hitherto unscaled heights. One way or another, over the next eight years, he was responsible for the deaths of some 300,000 people. And they were not quick deaths, either: the bodies that turned up in the mortuaries often showed signs of abuse. But most corpses never made it to the mortuaries. So many people were executed that Amin's security forces, spearheaded by the innocuously named State Research Bureau, took to dumping them into the River Nile, which wells up just fifty miles to the west of Kampala. Three sites were used: one just above the Owen

Falls Dam, another at Bujagali Falls and the third at Karuma Falls. It is said that during the worst years, the superintendent of the Owen Falls Dam employed a full-time boatman just to remove the bloated bodies from the river.

At one of the killing grounds, the headquarters of the equally misnamed Public Safety Unit in the Kampala suburb of Naguru, prisoners were made to kill each other using a hammer. Each prisoner would, in turn, be offered freedom in return for the murder of another.

This reign of terror on the political front was matched by the destruction of what had been, at independence, the region's most promising economy. The single most devastating blow of this assault was the decision in 1972 to expel the country's 'Asian' population and to expropriate their businesses without compensation. This ethnic group are described as Asians all over Africa, although most of them are, in fact, the descendants of immigrants from one country: India.

The first Asians had been brought to East Africa by the British in the late nineteenth century to help build a railway from the Kenyan port of Mombasa to their landlocked protectorate in Uganda. The railway was finished at the turn of the twentieth century, by which time many Indian families had begun to trade. The railway took their influence deep into the hinterland, and by independence they controlled Ugandan commerce.

Given the economic fashion of the time, that fact alone might have explained the takeover of Asian businesses. All over Africa governments had been nationalising companies. Amin's motives, however, were political rather than economic. First, he wanted to reward his henchmen, most of whom hailed from the hitherto underprivileged West Nile province in the north. But he also understood that nothing serves politics or politicians so well as a bogeyman, an outsider on whom all ills can be blamed. He knew, too, that expulsion would tap into the visceral distrust of Asians shared by many indigenous Ugandans.

On one level, the Indian in Uganda suffered the kind of victim-isation experienced by successful minorities everywhere – the same victimisation that had driven us, the Alagiah family, out of Ceylon all those years ago. In America there have been a number of violent clashes between African-Americans and Korean shopkeepers, who they have accused of exploiting the inner-city poor. It is only relatively recently that Jewish people have come to be regarded as influential and powerful. For most of their history, they have been the despised minority, subjected to a hatred that ultimately resulted in the genocide perpetrated by the Third Reich. And indigenous Africans are no more immune to seizing upon a convenient scape-goat, whether it be Tutsis in Rwanda or Indians in Uganda. But there is much more than persecution to the Asian experience in Africa, and in Uganda in particular. The Asians were Ugandan citizens but they behaved as a race apart. And that is what Amin exploited. Asians were, and many still are, socially élitist – even racist – and economically exploitative. It's as simple as that.

Asians will deny this in public, but in private we all know it to be true. In Ghana, as a child, I heard Tamil friends of my parents refer to their African colleagues as *kuranghe* – monkeys. Asian families rarely, if ever, mixed with their African counterparts. Often the only social contact between them was the offer and acceptance of a bribe. In a community obsessed with status and caste, the worst misfortune that could befall a family was that a daughter might get mixed up with an African man – a theme that has been explored in film by Meera Syal and Gurinder Chada *Bhaji on the Beach* and in *Mississippi Masala*, directed by Mira Nair. Such a relationship was the great fear: it was rarely, if ever, realised, because any sort of amorous contact was simply forbidden.

Asians stick together. I remember afternoons on Labadi Beach in Accra in the sixties. As many as a dozen Sri Lankan families would gather together, a mass of billowing saris, multicoloured rugs and spicy piles of *lumprai*, rice and curry wrapped in broad green banana leaves.

A generation later, in the eighties, I saw Asians gather at another beach, this time on the east coast of Africa. At weekends, you could have been forgiven for mistaking Oyster Bay in Dar es Salaam for coastal Maharashtra or Gujarat in India. Here the merchant class of Tanzania would come to take the air, perhaps to look out across the sea to where they came from, to where their souls belonged. The women were pale and covered, untouched by Africa's sons or sun. And the men stuck together, talking quietly, conspiratorially, about how they had managed to sneak some money out of the country, sidestepping the currency-exchange controls.

Separateness has been the key to the survival of the Asian in Africa. It has also been his undoing. In his book *North of South*, Shiva Naipaul, who also witnessed the clannish gathering at Oyster Bay, described the Asian predicament like this: 'In East Africa as in India, a Patel is a Patel before he is anything else. The caste-bound Asian is not so much a racist as communalist.' Whatever name you give it, the result is the same: exclusivity.

Typically, Asian businessmen would operate an informal cartel, debarring outsiders from a chain that stretched from suppliers in Europe or the Far East through shipping agents to retailers in some far-flung corner of Africa. They could fix prices and often kept them artificially high. It goes on even now.

I met one businessman who boasted that he was selling Cadbury's chocolate milk at a 400 per cent mark-up. He argued that the huge profits compensated for the corruption and the sheer uncertainty of doing business in Africa. I can vouch for the corruption, I can attest to the uncertainty, but I also know a rip-off when I see one. All over London Asian men are driving Mercedes-Benzes and BMWs, their wives are shopping in Knightsbridge, and their children are being educated at private schools – and it's all being paid for by the unfortunate people who fork out four times the price you and I pay for a jar of hot chocolate.

The fact that you can get away with something doesn't mean the people around you are not aware of what's happening. They are just waiting for the right moment to act. In the meantime, they harbour a brooding sense of injustice and a determination to even the score. That is how it was in Uganda, and how it still is in other parts of Africa.

Asians often feel aggrieved by this state of affairs, pointing out that their exploitation is a mere trifle compared to the rape of Africa by Europeans. And of course, not all Asian businessmen are of the fat-cat variety. Many make a far more straightforward and modest living. For example, all over East and Central Africa, sometimes in the remotest towns and villages, you will find the *duka-wallahs*, traders who sell everything from talcum powder to a fanbelt for a truck. It was not these people who were the targets, nor those, like the Goans, who had gone into the professions. It was the shiny, glass-fronted emporiums of downtown Kampala on which Amin and his friends had their greedy eyes.

Asian properties and businesses were handed out by Amin's henchmen to cronies and contacts who had no proven record of running anything. There are numerous stories of the incompetence of those who gave away the properties and the ineptitude of those who were granted them. In his book *A State of Blood*, Henry Kyemba, who was a Cabinet minister under Amin for five years, tells of a furniture store that was allocated to one man, while its warehouse went to somebody else. Or there's the case of the man who ended up with a clothes shop. He mistook the collar size on a shirt for the price, and sold it for 15 Ugandan shillings to a surprised but delighted customer who had been expecting to fork out a lot more.

Asian businesses weren't the only victims of Amin's arbitrary management of the nation's wealth. The great sugar and tea plantations, many owned by Western multinationals, were also expropriated around this time. The cotton industry, which was largely based on smallholdings, collapsed with the demolition of

the Asian buying networks and ginneries, and foreign exchange
earnings plummeted.

I remember being shown round a tea estate that was, in theory,
being run by the government's Uganda Tea Authority. In the seventies it had been a huge and profitable concern with over 1,400
hectares under cultivation. When I saw it, only 45 hectares produced anything saleable. As for the rest of the land, you could
hardly tell that it had once been a tea estate. Some of the bushes
had been allowed to grow into trees twenty feet high, good for
nothing but shade.

Amin's plunder of the economy and persecution of people
might have gone on for many more years had it not been for a
ludicrous military adventure. In 1978, he ordered the invasion of
neighbouring Tanzania after a territorial dispute. His forces were
not only driven back, but the following year Tanzanian troops
pushed their way to the Ugandan capital. It was the first and only
occasion on which one African country has invaded and conquered another.

The Tanzanian invasion force was assisted by several exiled
groups, one of which was led by a young Yoweri Museveni.
Through a political dispensation worked out under the auspices of
the Tanzanians, who retained a military presence in Uganda,
Milton Obote was once again elected as president in December
1980. The election, in spite of the attendance of Commonwealth
observers, was widely regarded to have been rigged, and several
political organisations took up arms in protest.

Of these, Museveni's National Resistance Movement (NRM)
was the most important. Over the next five years of civil war, it
emerged victorious, and the National Resistance Army (NRA),
took Kampala on 26 January 1986. Museveni had hoped to proclaim a government straight away, but the announcement had to
be postponed for three days while the NRA's engineers rigged up
the necessary equipment. Kampala itself had no working tele-
phones, the electricity supply had been cut and the national radio

station was off air. The swearing-in of Yoweri Kaguta Museveni was eventually broadcast over a transmitter that had been used to sow the seeds of revolution among the population. That day's broadcast was like a flowering of those seeds. The five-year bush war was over and Uganda began the long road to recovery. It is by no means over yet.

So there we were, Hope and me, heading towards the village of Rwakitura, a route that literally cuts across the Equator. Behind us, in another vehicle, was my TV crew. Philip Darley, one of two cameramen, was an impressionable and eager white South African, a young man who was still discovering the continent he was born in but from which he had been separated by the folly of his parents' generation. The other cameraman, Nikki Millard, an implausibly lanky Australian, was from another continent but seemed to find an instant affinity with Africa's easy rhythms. I had persuaded Hope to organise another formal interview before we got down to the African equivalent of a fireside chat.

When urban Europeans talk about spending time in the country, they are often talking about a leisure activity. To many of them the countryside is a pretend place, somewhere they can make believe that they are a part of nature. They can pop into this fantasy world for a few days in the knowledge that their real home is the city.

In Africa there is still a generation who live in the city but for whom the countryside is a calling; people for whom the rural areas are the reality and the city a necessary aberration. Tens of millions of people still know the little village from which they set forth into the brave, new world of independent Africa, and are tugged back to it by the bonds of kinship. So it is with Yoweri Museveni. The area around Rwakitura is where he is from. This straightforward statement of fact also encompasses a claim to a place of spiritual wellbeing, of natural connection. It is to do with memory and a sense of belonging.

All of which seems to sit ill at ease with the thoroughly modern house he has built on his farm. Its white walls stand out from the gently rolling grassland like an ugly geological eruption. The harsh corners and tiled roof owe nothing to the age-old skills of the rural artisans Museveni champions. Its angular, engineered presence is as incongruous in Rwakitura as a mud hut would be in the Sussex countryside.

But what may be an architectural aberration to European eyes is a matter of pride to the people of Rwakitura. Africans who return to their villages have to exhibit to the extended family proof that they have conquered the city, made it work for them; to bring something home from the city. A big house on the hill is just one way of doing that.

We sat in the shade of a huge, thick-leafed *mukoma* tree, one of those trees that branches out into multiple trunks almost as soon as it emerges from the ground. You have a sense of going into it rather than under it, as if you were entering a large, cool tent.

Museveni is not a good-looking man, but he is a handsome one – the difference between an image that works in photographs and a face that works in life. His features are neat, his complexion light brown. His eyes reveal an energy that has not been dulled by age or office. I remember looking at him and thinking that the best way to describe his face was to say that it was everything Idi Amin's was not. Amin's head was large and fleshy, giving an impression of a man of vast and vulgar appetite. Museveni, I would guess, is someone of more restrained habits. He exudes a sense of self-belief; he is comfortable in his own skin.

When lunch was served, the three of us sat at one table while Museveni ate off another one placed a few feet away. We were given a heavy beef stew. The president had something much simpler. But apart from this contrived separation, the next few hours were quite different from anything I have experienced with any other African president. There were none of the flunkies who usually attend these occasions. Even Hope Kivingere disappeared.

The afternoon had an atmosphere of informality and openness. So much so that Nikki Millard, sitting to my left, fell asleep. What many other presidents might have considered a snub was casually dismissed by Museveni. 'Let him rest. He has eaten well.'

Museveni is indeed different. His political development has been framed not by the struggle against white colonialism, but by the battle against black exploitation. He has refused to define his life, and that of his people, in terms of a reaction to what outsiders have done. It is the part black people have played in the injustices of the past and the failures of the present that interest him. There are no sacred cows, no taboos that limit his vision of what has gone wrong and how it can be corrected. Mr Museveni's demons are not white men with a Bible in one hand and a gun in the other, to borrow a phrase from Archbishop Desmond Tutu, but black men with a Mercedes-Benz in the garage and a bank account in Switzerland.

We spoke about slavery and the colonial order that followed. Museveni, in common with just about everyone else who has studied the 500-year trade in humans, understands the debilitating effect slavery had on Africa. The loss of over 20 million (in his book *Sowing the Mustard Seed*, he puts the number at 50 million) of the fittest and most able people skewed the continent's progress and undermined its growth. Although only northern Uganda suffered slave raids (for the Arab market rather than the Atlantic one), the trauma of forced removal is a psychological burden on the whole continent that is impossible to calculate, but no less valid for that. But alongside all this is the sinful shadow of complicity. The slave trade could not have grown in the way it did had it not been for the active participation of Africans – often the chiefs – in the chain of events that began with capture in the interior and ended with a voyage in a dark, cramped, sickly vessel headed for the Americas.

For Museveni, today's leaders are not so different from those headmen who sold their best people for the shining baubles of European civilisation.

'While two to five hundred years ago, African slaves were being exchanged for beads and trinkets by the African chiefs of the day, today African coffee, cotton, gold, oil and uranium are being exchanged for toys, wigs, perfumes, whisky and Mercedes-Benzes,' he said.

'A lot of people would be angry to hear you say that sort of thing,' I suggested.

'Let them be angry. That is not my problem. It is the truth.'

'What, that black people were accomplices in the process of exploitation?'

'You can't talk about colonialism without talking about African chiefs. Colonialism walked into an open house. Like the robber coming to a house and somebody opening the door for him.'

Mr Museveni has tried to shut that door. It's not about race; it's not about revenge. It's about having the right to choose who your friends are. He still lets white people come through the door, but only on his terms. And the irony is that they love him for it. He decided long ago that he would run his country his way. For example, virtually the first thing he did on coming to power was to reject that shibboleth of Western foreign policy, multiparty elections. Yet Mr Museveni is courted by Western diplomats with an assiduousness that is the envy of the continent. 'We live for ourselves now. If I work with you it is because there is a mutual advantage to be gained. Not because I am your agent and you are a parasite on me.'

Hordes of economic consultants, thousands of aid workers, scores of development experts have all been desperate to find an African success story. Most of them rather conveniently ignore the fact that the progress they acclaim in Uganda has been achieved by a government that has sought to define its own path. Many of the tough decisions, especially those relating to economic management, simply wouldn't have been possible if they had been subject to the veto of democracy. And for well over a decade, Uganda has boasted one of the fastest economic growth rates not just in Africa, but in the world. It averages about 8 per cent a year. True, when you are starting from zero and your population is growing by about 3 per cent a year 8 per cent growth is not much, but it is still enough to be noticed by people in their everyday lives.

Despite misgivings in many quarters, Yoweri Museveni encouraged Asian businessmen to return to Uganda and gave them back the properties confiscated by Idi Amin. This was not just a grand gesture of reconciliation but a sensible act of self-interest, too. Mr Museveni has not asked the returning Asians what's in their hearts, what he wants is the money in their pockets and their proven business acumen. I told him how, even in the new, supposedly non-racial South Africa, there were people who muttered bitterly about the advances being made by Asians. 'Those people are stupid,' he said. 'I like my Asians. They work hard. All the time they are working. And me, once a year I collect my tax. That's all. They make some profit, I collect my tax.' That's the deal. Abide by the law, pay your way and nobody's going to ask you where your allegiances lie.

Part of the explanation for Mr Museveni's attitudes is his comparative youth. At the time he was becoming politically aware, Africans had already taken charge all over the continent. So not for him an education in the liberal institutions of the west – the common denominator that linked virtually all the men who went on to form the first generation of African leaders. He is a home-grown product, graduating in 1970 from the University of Dar es Salaam, then a hotbed of radical thinking.

What he and his colleagues in Dar saw was Africa's continued dependency on the very countries they had so recently fought against. It was a relationship that didn't make sense, because it assumed that those who had been responsible for exploiting Africa under colonialism would suddenly become its impartial benefactors. In fact, post-independence relations between Africa and the former colonial masters were as lopsided as they had always been. Museveni says that the only difference he could see was that after independence it was Africans rather than colonials who were drafted in to do the dirty work. From then on, self-reliance became his guiding principle.

Little wonder, then, that Museveni is treated with a degree of suspicion in state houses all over the continent. He once described the Organisation of African Unity, which holds an annual summit of leaders, as a 'gang of criminals'. For decades the conference halls of Africa have reverberated with pious speeches about the iniquitous interference of foreign powers; speeches made by men who, even as they stood at the lectern, were heading governments that had reduced their countries to the status of paupers on the world scene. The chairman of the OAU in 1975, for example, was Idi Amin, whose murderous ways were obvious to anyone who cared to look.

After our long, though alcohol-free lunch, Yoweri Museveni took me on a tour of his farm. I sat in his Range Rover, never entirely convinced that he was in total control as we ploughed our way across country to where his beloved longhorn cattle were grazing that day. He wore a wide-brimmed hat and carried a six-foot long cattle prod. As we walked through the herd he called out to his animals by name – he said he knew them all. It was getting late, and the resting sun shed its dappled light over him. At one point I caught him in silhouette. Stripped of his features, standing alone among the cattle, he might have been any farmer at the end of a day's toil.

It was difficult to imagine that this was the man who, even then, was seen as a model leader in what some were calling an African Renaissance, though I'm not sure I ever heard him use the phrase himself. 'There is a new order,' was the way he put it. 'A patriotic order. Uganda is a new place. We still have links with the old colonial powers, still have pressures from Europe, but they are pressures on a healthy body, not a sick body or a sycophantic body.'

The term 'African Renaissance' was first used by Nelson Mandela in a speech in June 1994, the year he led South Africa to freedom. Speaking at that year's OAU summit, Mandela described a continent on the threshold of change. The expression struck a chord because it was uttered by a man of towering moral authority. And after the miracle of South Africa's peaceful transition to democratic government, the whole world was willing to dream a little. Even, it seemed, to set aside the horrendous events that were unfolding in Rwanda at the time.

Mandela was not specific about what he meant. 'Africa,' he said, 'cries out for a new birth. We must say that there is no obstacle big enough to stop us from bringing about an African renaissance.' Over the years, he has returned to the theme again and again.

Thabo Mbeki, South Africa's current president, also often speaks of an African Renaissance. Indeed, some have said it was his idea in the first place. In his 'I am an African' speech, perhaps the most eloquent he has yet given, Mbeki eulogised Africa's prospects. It was the day in 1996 when South Africa adopted its new constitution. 'This thing that we have done today, in this small corner of a great continent that has contributed so decisively to the evolution of humanity, says that Africa reaffirms that she is continuing her rise from the ashes.'

But repetition and erudition do not make the concept any clearer or, indeed, any more credible. It might be argued that it is merely a reworking of an old tune. Decolonisation itself had been heralded as a rebirth. Over forty years ago, Kwame Nkrumah of Ghana evoked a similar resurgence when he talked of a new, assertive continent making its voice heard in international affairs.

So what is the African Renaissance? To the liberal establishment in the West, and its acolytes in Africa itself, it came to mean a flowering of democratic government and respect for human rights. They took something Africans had been talking about as an aspiration and turned it into a checklist for promotion to their world of moral certainty and social democracy. They appropriated the concept and gave it their own spin.

And when Africa failed to deliver on their terms, when the liberals could not place their ticks next to the relevant columns headed 'Democracy', 'Human Rights' and the like, they turned away in dejection. They gave Africa a low score and pushed her to the back of the class. You would hear people say things like 'It was all too good to be true,' or 'What did you expect?'

But what if the African Renaissance meant something entirely different? To men like Yoweri Museveni, if he subscribes to the idea of an African Renaissance at all, it means simply an assertion of whatever Africans think is in their best interests. And that, as Mr Museveni has shown, may not always include a commitment to the way we, in the rich world, happen to interpret political, economic or social progress.

It is, above all, an attitude of mind rather than a set of principles that can be written down and examined. It can mean different things at different times. It can involve both close cooperation with Western countries when that is useful and ignoring Western overtures when they are deemed unnecessary. It is a repudiation of the notion that because something has worked for the industrial world of adversarial politics and social competition, it must also work in the same way for Africans whose roots lie in the soil of collective endeavour and consensus. It is a rejection of the old idea that Africa can be broken up according to which rich country's 'sphere of influence' a particular part of it is deemed to fall into, this bit anglophone, the next francophone and so on.

'There were never any anglophones here,' Museveni told me that afternoon. 'There were never any francophones. There was just a bunch of people, traitors, who would go to London and Paris and tell them that the people of Congo were francophone and those in Uganda were anglophone. The traitors would say this even though ninety per cent of the people in our countries do not speak those languages. I speak the same language as the people in

Congo. I share the same dialect as the people of Tanzania and Kenya. My people in the north of Uganda speak the same language as they do in southern Sudan. These are the "phones" we should be talking about, these are the real affinities. Forget about this concept of the invaders who came here for some decades and thought that we all wanted to be European like them.'

Museveni is not alone. There are others who might be described as members of a vanguard in this new order. They are all young (in their late forties and early fifties) and have a common distrust of the advice given to Africans by outsiders. Meles Zenawi and Issaias Aferwerki, for example, fought and beat the totalitarian regime led by Mengistu Haile Mariam, and about a decade ago they became leaders of Ethiopia and Eritrea respectively. Although their subsequent two-year border war (which flared up in 1998 over a piece of apparently useless territory) has dented their credibility, it cannot entirely rob them of their place in Africa's new political class.

Paul Kagame, the president of Rwanda, is closest to Museveni in intellect, outlook and chiefly in the singleminded pursuit of what he thinks is best for his country – though the two have had a spectacular falling-out involving battles in Congo. A dry, ascetic man, at least in public, Kagame has been savage in his criticism of the way the aid agencies and the United Nations dealt with Rwanda's genocide and its aftermath. They have variously described him as prickly, arrogant and downright unhelpful. His supporters say that's because Kagame refused to slot into the role of beggar with a bowl.

I was at a conference in London in May 1998 on the reporting of humanitarian emergencies – 'Dispatches from Disaster Zones' was its catchy name. It brought together some of the most influential foreign correspondents and their counterparts in the aid agencies. One session was devoted to the uprising in eastern Zaire in 1996 (see Chapter 8) and the extent to which the Ugandan and Rwandan authorities were linked to those events. Neither government was in a position entirely to control the Zairean rebellion, but both certainly gave material and diplomatic support to it. Each had an interest in ensuring a friendly presence on the border separating their countries from Zaire.

One of the keynote speakers bemoaned the way the flow of information to reporters trying to cover the uprising was controlled by Mr Kagame. The Rwandans were trying to hide the level of support they were giving to what was then still only a fledgling rebellion with few resources of its own. The journalist in me rallied to the speaker's side, but the honorary African in me couldn't help but applaud the fact that one of the continent's leaders had, at last, managed to assert his agenda over the media that have, by and large, reported on the continent from an entirely Western perspective. More than one delegate described the Rwandan government's action as 'sinister'.

But in employing what that speaker called a 'new, undeclared doctrine of information control', the Rwandans had merely caught up with the age-old tactics of American and European governments in times of war. When, for instance, NATO set up a slick and expensive media operation to control and influence the coverage of its bombing of Serbia in 1999, the majority of reporters turned up to the daily briefings like pilgrims queuing up for a blessing. With few exceptions, they seemed to accept NATO as a reliable source. But it wasn't. It was a combatant with a vested interest, just like the Rwandans in eastern Zaire.

Broadcasters and newspapers dutifully trotted out NATO's figures for the number of ethnic Albanians who were supposed to have been killed by Serbian paramilitaries and the army. The total climbed from 10,000 to 100,000. British foreign secretary Robin Cook spoke of 'rape camps', though it has never been substantiated that anything of the sort existed. And we now know that the number of people murdered by Serb forces was probably nearer 3,000. We also know that the British and American press officers were happy to use the most exaggerated figures because it served their purpose to do so, even though, at the time, they could not have proved their veracity. NATO also claimed that its aerial bombing was highly successful and accurate. It has now come to light that many bombs missed their targets.

NATO's officials, who had at their disposal the slickest video techniques and huge public-relations budgets, were playing hide-and-seek, concealing the facts and putting the onus on journalists to seek the truth. Rwanda has none of those resources, but it is trying to do much the same thing: to protect and defend its policies. Its tactics are very different from the art of partial disclosure and clever evasion perfected by press officers in the rich world. I deplore them, but no more or less than I object to what NATO did.

The efficient management and manipulation of information is, whether we like it or not, also part of the African Renaissance. 'We have found a new way of doing things,' is how Paul Kagame has summed up his media management. 'We used communication and information warfare better than anyone.'

So the African Renaissance is not necessarily a pretty thing. It is not yet the era of enlightenment and creativity evoked by the word 'Renaissance' in Western minds schooled in the artistic and intellectual advances of Europe in the fifteenth century. Africa might be on a similar path, but the business of reaching its destination may involve yet more violence and conflict. As the Zaireans discovered, the old order will not be vanquished without a fight. And in many countries battle has yet to commence.

The African Renaissance is not so much a victory of any particular set of political values as a period in which the continent is searching for its own voice, free of the distortions of colonialism or the Cold War. And if, like me, you have watched Africans as they have tried for decades to fit into a mould shaped in another man's image, you will understand what a huge achievement it is simply to be able to say no. It takes courage, because there is nothing so challenging as taking responsibility for your own welfare.

No other continent on earth has been interfered with as much as Africa. First there was slavery, then there was colonialism, and after that came the disguised and insidious captivity of development. Africans have been subjected to every passing fad to emerge out of the think tanks and financial institutions of the West: trickle-down, structural adjustment, poverty focus, bottom-up, and so on, and so on. They have swallowed every half-baked nostrum, only to be told there is a better one around the corner. The number of development consultants running around Africa now far outstrips the number of white civil servants it took to run the place even in the heyday of colonialism.

In the early part of the twentieth century, it was the colonial governor, or merchant kings like Cecil Rhodes, who ran the show. By the end of it, the accountants and economists of the World Bank or International Monetary Fund were calling the shots. An African minister of finance might make a speech in the legislature, but the policies he or she urges on a reluctant nation are hatched in Washington. Ask any reporter to whom he talks when he wants the latest on a country's economic status. Almost all of them will say that they make a courtesy call to the relevant ministry of finance before getting down to the real business at the offices of the World Bank and IMF.

So many Africans are beginning to believe that there has been a kind of recolonisation at work. They see that the rich world has got richer while Africa has got poorer, a continuation of the lopsided trading relations established on the day 500 years ago when a Portuguese sailor set foot on the continent and admired its bounty. In 1980 the average Westerner was fifteen times better off than the average African. Twenty years later, the ratio had climbed to a staggering fifty to one.

The old way of dealing with such a stark disjunction of wealth and opportunity was to blame the white man in one sentence and then ask for his help in the next. It was a risible and humiliating position to be in, but one that typified Africa's relations with the rich world. Africans became dependent on aid, like paupers waiting for alms.

Yoweri Museveni has begun to change that, but his is a work in progress. It's not clear whether there is a system in place that will survive him. He won another five-year term as president in 2001 but, while there were no claims of out-and-out vote-rigging, many inside and outside the country deemed the electoral process flawed. Museveni was almost certainly the most popular candidate, but the prominent use of the military during the polls set an unpalatable precedent.

His is not a perfect society. He is fighting his own rebels in the north and supporting Congo's rebels in the west. There are many Ugandans who will tell you that corruption is creeping back like an ugly stain spreading across a sheet. Museveni is nonetheless trying to lay the ghost of the white bogeyman to rest, and to drag Africa out of its maudlin self-pity over the injustices of colonialism. There are some who hear his message but cringe from its meaning. These are the people who prefer the easy posturing of the old Africa. Robert Mugabe is one of them, still ranting about the white man like a loser who claims he never stood a chance.

10

The White Man's Burden

There was a time when Robert Mugabe, the president of Zimbabwe, was something of a political celebrity. When he came to power in 1980, after one of the most brutal and bitter wars of independence in Africa, even those who recoiled from his radical background respected his determination and consistency. He was courted by leaders in rich countries: they would make space in their crowded schedules to meet him. You wouldn't believe it now, but even a decade ago Robert Mugabe's Zimbabwe represented new hope for Africa.

Mr Mugabe seemed to hold the key to a problem that preoccupied many people outside the continent and quite a few inside it: the future of white people in Africa, as in did they have a future at all?

On independence in 1980, he had spoken of forgiveness and reconciliation, using the kind of language Mandela would echo much later to dispel any notion that his victory at the ballot box – a victory that most whites within the country, with the help of Britain, had tried to prevent – would be a licence to seek revenge. 'If yesterday I fought you as an enemy, today you have become a friend. If yesterday you hated me, today you cannot avoid the love that binds you to me and me to you.' All round the country, white civil servants and farmers who had filled their petrol tanks and packed their bags for a hurried getaway breathed a sigh of relief. They didn't 'take the gap', as they used to say. They decided to stay and to try to make a go of it. And indeed it looked as if Mugabe would preside over the prototype multiracial society. If black and white could live in harmony in Zimbabwe, then there was hope for whites across the Limpopo in South Africa.

But twenty-odd years later, as Africa's century of decolonisation was left behind, all that had been forgotten. Mugabe was a diminished and discredited figure. The spare, intellectual demeanour that had once led Africa-watchers to dub him the Black Robespierre was now the stuff of caricature and ridicule. Instead what people remembered was that he had just 'won' two elections – parliamentary in 2000 and presidential in 2002 – in which politically motivated violence and murder played a key role. Above all, they saw and heard the way he had encouraged thugs to go around the Zimbabwean countryside intimidating, maiming and sometimes killing supporters of the opposition party, the fledgling Movement for Democratic Change led by the one-time trade unionist Morgan Tsvangirai. Farms owned by white Zimbabweans were the battlegrounds on which this desperate political war was fought. Very occasionally this was because some white farmers had a reputation for being racist; often it was because white farmers were supporters of the MDC.

Mugabe created the fiction that these thugs were war veterans in search of the land for which they had once fought. In fact, they were little more than political stormtroopers, a rent-a-mob with malice on their minds. Foreign journalists tended to concentrate on the white farmers who were murdered but many more black people were killed. Teachers, nurses, black farmworkers and community leaders of any kind were subjected to a systematic and violent campaign of 're-education' by gangs that had, in effect, become a ruling-party militia.

Robert Mugabe accepted no responsibility for any of this. Like an unfulfilled adult who lays his failures at the door of a loveless childhood, he continued to point an accusing finger at the white man – even after he had himself been running the country for twenty years. It is easier to blame everything on the way you were brought up. It is a form of dependence. Whenever and wherever he got the chance, he would return to his theme. As the rest of the world moved into a twenty-first century in which corporate power was the new menace, he was stuck in the time warp of the battle against colonialism. He had become an expert in the politics of blame, the last refuge of a man who has nowhere else to go.

At the UN's New York summit in September 2000 he spoke of Africa's problems 'dating back to the days of slavery and colonialism'. He urged the poor world 'to stand up and say, "Not again."' But nobody of any consequence was listening. People had moved on – in some cases, literally.

As if searching for a more appreciative audience, yearning for the acclamation that was once his due, Mugabe left the confines of the UN Plaza on First Avenue and addressed a gathering in Harlem, a rallying point for America's black community. Here he spoke of the iniquities he was fighting back home in Zimbabwe. He told the crowd that 70 per cent of the best land was still in the hands of a white minority comprising less than 1 per cent of the population. He told them he was going to get it back, and that he didn't care what the old colonial masters thought about it. The cheers may have lifted his spirits, but he achieved little else. Some in the hall barely knew where Zimbabwe was, and those who did were hardly in a position to influence events there.

What Mugabe did not tell that crowd was that nearly three quarters of the farms owned by white people in Zimbabwe had been bought by them during his presidency The properties are held legally under the laws of Zimbabwe, not those of the country's previous incarnation, Rhodesia. Neither did he tell the Harlem faithful that many of the farms his government did procure ended up in the hands of his cronies rather than with the landless poor he claims to represent. He failed to mention the many government-owned farms across Zimbabwe lying idle. The fact that without the income generated by the white farmers, his country would have been in even worse shape than it was already also seemed to slip his mind.

Mr Mugabe may have mesmerised the people of Harlem, but he doesn't fool anybody back home, where he presides over a failing economy and a deeply unhappy people. The charge against him is not that he is wrong about the continent's afflictions, but that he has blown his chances of solving them. True, he inherited a country disfigured by the unfair distribution of land along racial lines, but he is no longer the man who can put things right. He has the power, as he has shown, to take land away from white people, but it is a pyrrhic victory. Idi Amin's confiscation of Asian-owned property in Uganda in 1973 may have been popular but it was economically disastrous. In Zimbabwe, even those people, white progressives and black nationalists alike, who hoped Mugabe would cut the Gordian Knot of the land issue have now abandoned him.

It is a measure of his ineptitude that most people outside the country, and a good many inside it, now believe that it is the white landowners who are being treated unfairly. Mugabe has given credence to even the most selfish white farmers, the ones who still long for the old ways. He has forsaken the moral high ground and allowed charlatans to occupy it in his stead. He has taken a just cause and sullied it, blurred the lines between what is good and bad, legal and criminal, right and wrong.

It is some achievement, considering that, not so long ago, the claim staked by white Zimbabweans on as much land as they wanted was, to most people, as morally repugnant as it was socially untenable. The case for land reform was blindingly obvious.

*

It was the season of bleached grass and hard, dry earth, a season when the dawn air is as sharp as cold steel and the white noon sun has the endless blue sky to itself. August. Winter in the Tropic of Capricorn.

It was the time of year when the dams start to run dry, when the water retreats from the edges of manmade lakes. The mud on the banks begins to bake and crack, creating a pattern like the scaly skin of a snake.

It was the time of year when the farmers, the black farmers, who do not have vast irrigation schemes, begin to worry about whether the rains will come soon enough.

Frances, my wife, and I were heading south, away from Harare, on the Masvingo road, where the cultivated landscape around the capital, with its exotic jacarandas and flame trees, gives way to the grasslands of the high veld. It was 1985. We were going to see an old friend from our college days in Durham. Tom Skitt, an Englishman, had first fallen under Africa's spell during a stint as a voluntary worker in Gambia after we all left university. He had recently come out to the Mhondoro Communal Land in Zimbabwe to do some research for his MSc and to develop skills that would lead to a career on the continent in water supply. He is the kind of white man no one notices, the kind who fits in. The kind who never gets rich in Africa, but leaves Africa all the richer for his passage through it.

I was driving. We peeled off the tarred highway. The Rhodesians had built roads that would last decades, but they led only to the kinds of places white people might want to go to. Mhondoro was definitely not one of those. Under a loose, stony surface, the track was hard. Driving on these dirt roads requires a certain dexterity and a touch of nerve. Go too slowly and you will be subjected to the bone-shuddering vibrations caused by the corrugations created when they harden after the summer rains. If you pick the right speed you can match the ribbed surface of the road with the rhythmic bounce of the tyres so that they cancel each other out.

It's a different speed with every car. For our Volkswagen, about eighty kilometres per hour was just about right.

At least it was until I took a gentle corner and hit a sandbed. It might as well have been sludge for all the control I could muster. I braked, then changed my mind. Stupid. I accelerated, then changed my mind. Even worse. In the end, as the view through the windscreen jerked from side to side like a video game in the hands of a hyperactive child, I just stopped doing anything. The car veered off the track, seemed to gain speed, climbed the bank on the left-hand side and ploughed through the scrub. The noise of broken bushes scraping the undercarriage was like the rasp of a fingernail on a blackboard. Whip-like branches bounced off the windscreen and lashed us through the open windows. Frances shouted out – not words, just a noise. I held grimly on to the steering wheel, even though I had abandoned any attempt to use it. We hit a tree.

Suddenly, it was utterly silent. We clambered out. The dust still floated in the air. We didn't speak. We were alone. There was nothing on the bush track save the telltale signs of our chaotic crossing of the reddish sand. It took us a while to realise that we would have to go for help, because it wasn't going to come to us.

Winter is a time of contrasts. A pale landscape against a rich blue sky. Frosty nights and searing days. By now it was noon, and the sun was hot on our backs. We knew there was nothing for many kilometres the way we'd come. So, hand in hand, we set off on foot in the other direction.

Twenty minutes, half an hour? I can't remember exactly. The *kraal* was set back from the track. Three huts, a stockade for livestock. The place looked deserted. '*Mangwanani!*' we called out. It was the Shona greeting for the morning but, like many foreigners, we tended to use it well into the day. Our Zimbabwean friends tolerated this abuse of their language. At least we were trying, they used to say.

An old man emerged, eyeing us with care but not suspicion. I was wearing khaki trousers and a T-shirt; Frances a simple, loose, cotton frock. Yet, standing there in front of him, we felt over-dressed. His frayed trousers were puckered round his waist, where he'd tied them round his slim frame. His shirt had reached the stage where it would never look any older or more soiled.

Beyond the rituals of greeting, our Shona was virtually non-existent. We tried to explain what had happened. In the end it came down to sign language and sound effects. We weren't sure if he'd understood, but he started out in the direction from which we'd appeared and asked us to follow him.

At first he kept to the track. He didn't look as if he was hurry-ing, but we struggled to keep up. His was the pace of rural people all over Africa. They don't start fast and end slow. They don't rush, but they don't dawdle, either. It is the pace at which you walk if you are used to moving with your livestock, the steady, determined pace of people for whom walking is a way of life and not something they do of a weekend for a bit of exercise.

After a while he headed off into the tall, ivory-coloured grass. He was following a path. The soil underfoot was hot and tired. Ahead of us, all we could see was woodland – the indigenous msasa and munondo trees which, over millennia, have learned to survive the ravages of overgrazing and inclement weather. We began to wonder if he had, after all, misunderstood us. Who, out here, would be in a position to help us? We needed a phone, not a trek through the bush. Still, we walked on. This was his coun-try, and we were in his hands.

The conical thatched roofs came into view as we rounded a corner. Here the earth was beaten hard and compact by a thou-sand bare feet. The children came running towards us; their parents just watched. We smiled; they looked unsure.

Beyond this little hamlet we could see a tall wire fence. Its dull, metallic glint was incongruous amid the warm, earthy tones of an African village. It rose from the ground, snaked round in a huge arc and divided the landscape, an iron curtain. Invasive. Different.

We peered through its silvery mesh. On the other side the gin-bottle green grass, perfect, trim and spread out like a carpet, glistened under the constant spray of irrigated water. Here nature had been cheated. Whitewashed walls set off the exotic, imported beauty of bougainvillaea and hibiscus. A toddler chased a playful dog. It was another country: the land of the white people. We were at the border, the dividing line, between Africa and settler country.

The gardener was summoned. He would escort us through the frontier. We thanked our old man and left him in Africa. As we walked over to the farmstead, we crossed the great fault line that divides Zimbabwe. It was like stepping through the looking glass into a world of make-believe.

It was, and remains, the dream of the settler to tame Africa, to turn a patch of it into an imitation of the 'mother country'. When David Livingstone wrote about the 'open sore' that is Africa, when Cecil Rhodes fantasised about a map of the continent painted pink, this is what they meant: the recasting of Africa as a country garden in England, the only concession to geography being the inclusion of tropical flora alongside the obligatory rosebushes.

Yet the greatest deceit of all is not the attempt to transform Africa but the embellished, picture-perfect image of the mother country that settlers hanker after. Very few of them could ever have enjoyed this horticultural splendour in their native country. The home they tried to recreate was not the one they had left, with its terraced houses and smoke-stack factories, but the one to which they had aspired. In Africa they could live out a life that was merely the stuff of dreams there. That is what pulled so many of them to the continent, not the spirit of Africa or its people.

What followed that afternoon was as surreal as it was unnerving. Just a couple of hours after an accident in the African bush that had shaken us to the core, Frances and I found ourselves round a table eating fresh poached river trout washed down with a white wine chilled to perfection. We had no appetite and our minds were numb, but we managed some small talk. Later, as a maid prepared coffee, we watched a tape of highlights from the Wimbledon tennis championships sent out by someone 'back home'. That was the surreal part.

It was unnerving because it was a confrontation with a way of life that lay at the heart of nearly a century of oppression and years of bitter civil war. Yet we were beholden to our hosts, whose care and attention was freely given. At table, the conversation ran something like this:

'I wonder if I could use your telephone? I really think I ought to sort out the car. There must be a breakdown service in Harare.'

'Ah, relax man! We'll sort you out.'

'Well, it's just that I think I should get something done before it gets dark.' It was about three in the afternoon.

'We'll have you out of there quick, quick. I'll get some of the boys to come round with the tractor.' The 'boys' were the farm labourers, the fathers we had seen on our way in. 'It'll do them a bit of good. They're just sitting around drinking *chibuku*.' He thought he was being funny. We smiled. We wanted to chide him; instead, we thanked him.

And so there we were, out on the track: the farmer, his wife, their child, the family dog and, of course, the 'boys'. The farmer issued the instructions, the 'boys' scurried around the wreck of our Volkswagen, tying on chains and freeing the wheels. I was surplus to requirements, so I just watched.

The toddler had got hold of a screwdriver and was crawling towards the sleeping hulk of the pet Rhodesian Ridgeback. They are big dogs, bred for their size and ferocity, a favourite on the farm. The child prodded the dog with the handle of the screwdriver. The Ridgeback lifted one lazy eyelid, grunted and changed position. The child laughed. We all made indulgent, cooing noises, so the child did it again, this time just a bit harder. The dog got to its feet, towering over the child, and found another spot.

'Now there's a patient dog,' Frances said. 'It's obviously very good with kids.'

'Oh, it would never harm the children. It's got such a sweet temperament.'

'It looks terribly fierce.'

'No, it's very friendly really. It knows who's who.'

A moment or two later, about fifty yards down the road, I saw a solitary figure coming towards us. The dog noticed the man, too. Its ears pricked up. I could see that the man was nervous. He was watching the dog as he approached us on the other side of the road. As he drew level with us, the dog sat up and growled. The man's pace quickened. He mumbled a greeting and hurried past. When the man was some distance past us, the dog turned away from the road, lumbered over to the child and licked its pink, plump arm.

In Zimbabwe even the dogs knew the difference between black men and white men. They knew that white men were the masters of the land; that the black men mostly worked on it. It had been that way for nearly a century.

From the moment on 12 September 1890 when a group of adventurers and mercenaries paid by Cecil Rhodes, the 'pioneers', stuck a pole into the ground on a hill in Mashonaland and tied the Union Jack to it, land became the source of white power and black grievance in Rhodesia.

In later years, confronted with their history of oppression, Rhodesians would say that the land had been there for the taking. They would gloss over the fact that the indigenous people had been sufficiently enraged by their dispossession to mount a revolt just six years after the so-called Pioneer Column had set foot in Mashonaland. In fact, whites implicitly recognised that force lay at the heart of their presence on the land. Right up to the 1960s, they celebrated 12 September as Occupation Day. After that they came up with Pioneer Day, which had a more neutral, though less honest, ring to it.

In his book *Kandaya*, Angus Shaw writes about how his grandfather 'pegged out his good land at the turn of the century and it became his for the price of a sixpenny revenue stamp from the British South Africa Company'. The BSAC ran Rhodesia till 1923. What white settlers grabbed in those first years – 16 million acres by as early as 1900 – they legitimised once they became a self-governing colony. In 1931 the division of land on racial grounds was formalised in the Land Apportionment Act, one of those 'heads I win, tails you lose' laws that settlers were so fond of. The white people, a minority, got the best of it, while black people were restricted to marginal land which quickly deteriorated due to the high density of population. The act sanctioned the forced removal of black people, and in the first ten years after it came into being, 50,000 of them were evicted from their ancestral lands and taken to 'reserves' called the Tribal Trust Lands.

By 1965, when Rhodesia declared unilateral independence from Britain under Ian Smith, the country was an Apartheid state in all but name. Smith was a white supremacist, revered by a small-minded and sullen white population. 'Not in a thousand years,' boasted the butcher's son from rural Selukwe, when asked about the possibility of majority rule. And he enacted legislation to prove his point.

His 1969 constitution was a study in racial politics. Black representatives were given just over a third of the seats in Parliament with a promise of more in the future depending on, among other things, the black population's contribution to tax revenues. Under this complicated, not to say unfair, system of franchise qualification, it was reckoned that it would take black people about 460 years to achieve any increase at all in their parliamentary numbers and another 520 to gain parity with white representation. Hence the thousand years, I suppose.

Smith amended the land laws, too. He made it even harder, that is to say virtually impossible, for a black person to acquire land, and thereby condemned many black people to the status of temporary residents in their own country.

Three years later, in 1972, a group of guerrillas attacked Altena Farm in the Centenary district, about forty miles from the Mozambiquan border. It was, in effect, the start of a bitter civil war that would eventually account for 20,000 lives. The choice of a farm was both tactical and symbolic. An isolated farm was an easier option than clashing with the Rhodesian forces head on. But the farm attack also sent a political message: 'This is our land.'

Thus it was that when black nationalists, including Robert Mugabe, sat round the negotiating table at Lancaster House in London in 1979, land remained the key issue. The Lancaster House Agreement's clauses on land distribution, which were later written into the independence constitution, are worth reading if only to understand why Mugabe reserves some of his most vitriolic verbal assaults for the British who, as the one-time colonial power, presided over the conference. The clause made it extremely difficult for Zimbabwe's democratically elected government to procure land, even land that was unused. The legal hoops through which a government would have to jump to do so were designed to ensure that it would rarely, if ever, happen.

Take just one aspect: the question of payment for unused land. Having first proved in court that the land was unused, that it was needed for the public benefit and that 'adequate' compensation was being offered, the government would have to fork out the asking price not in Zimbabwean dollars, but in a foreign currency of the vendor's choosing. It's a bit like being required to pay a thief to leave your house and letting him decide when and where the money should be deposited. In *The Road to Zimbabwe*, the historian Anthony Verrier had no doubt as to where to assign the blame: 'Whitehall's draftsmen had, indeed, displayed their skill, not in precision of language but in a combination of restrictive provisions and vague phrases.'

So Zimbabwe was effectively hobbled at birth. The negotiated settlement, blessed by a Tory government in Britain, ensured that the most crucial question of all would be left largely unresolved, hanging over the country like a thunderous rainy-season cloud, eclipsing any other progress it might make in its social and political life.

That was the challenge that faced Robert Mugabe as he stood on the podium in the middle of Rufaro Stadium with Prince Charles and Lord Soames, the last imperial governor in Africa, at midnight on 17 April 1980, watching the Union Jack being hauled down to mark the end of one era and the beginning of another. It was a challenge to which he seemed uniquely suited. His unyielding pressure during the independence negotiations, his apparent readiness to return to the bush war and his subsequent victory at the polls had earned him unrivalled authority over the black population and a grudging respect among whites.

Zimbabwe was unique in that on independence it inherited what was in 1980 the most entrenched settler community in Africa (freedom in South Africa was still a long way off). The story of Robert Mugabe's presidency cannot be separated from that one fact of history. Zimbabwe's fitful journey is, without question, attributable to his mistakes and misdemeanours, but it also raises questions about whether the white man has been willing to pick up his burden in post-colonial Africa.

At first things went well. The extension of technical support to black farmers paid dividends almost immediately, and their output of maize and cotton grew. In education, Mugabe's government overturned decades of discriminatory practice. Schools started to 'hot-seat', teaching children in shifts, with one group replacing the last while the chairs were still warm. But Mugabe was never as strong as he seemed. As we've seen, the Lancaster House Constitution ensured that on the question of land use and reform – the raison d'être of the war between 1972 and 1979 – the government would have to move at the pace of the most recalcitrant white farmer.

This constitutional brake on land reform distorted Zimbabwe's politics. It meant that Mr Mugabe was susceptible to the charge of failing to deliver on his promises from those – and they ranged from ideological radicals to the churches – who wanted genuine transformation. Unable to retain the support of this wider constituency, Mugabe began to rely ever more heavily on the pretend radicals in his Cabinet, the inner circle of the ruling party. During the mid-1980s, the genuine radicals or progressives, those who worked in the nascent civic sector, found themselves marginalised. In an early demonstration of his capacity for manipulation and cynicism, Mugabe grew ever closer to white businessmen, some of whom had been the most enthusiastic supporters of the old Smith regime. There were quite a few sanctions-busters among the new-found friends of the prime minister (he hadn't made himself president yet). In effect, there was an accommodation between white business and black politics which squeezed out the liberals in the middle.

Mugabe shored up his power base within the party, the Zimbabwe African National Union (ZANU), by ignoring, some would say encouraging, their excesses, leaving the door to corruption wide open. Some of the richest men in the country, and almost all of those who got rich quickly, came from within the ZANU fold. They grabbed all the usual trappings: the Mercedes-Benz cars, the big properties on which they could never keep up the repayments, the import-export deals, the wine, women and song. Who you knew mattered more than what you achieved.

No country can survive long on that basis – that much had been proven elsewhere in Africa – and the president was caught in a vicious circle. The worse the economy fared, the less money he had to spend on land reform. The lack of land reform, in turn, meant he had to find some other way to prove his radical credentials. As each election (there were three parliamentary polls before the last one in 2000) drew near, he would roll out the land issue. Each time it worked. In the rural countryside, where the pressure on good farming land is most acutely felt, a majority always voted for Mugabe.

But by the time he prepared for the parliamentary election in June 2000, Mr Mugabe had used up his quota of promises and excuses. Even in the countryside people began to lose faith in him. That's when the president decided he would go for the jugular. In his quest for power the white farmers themselves had become the last tradeable commodity he had left. Robert Mugabe turned on them with unprecedented ferocity. He sanctioned the forced occupation of white-owned properties, unleashed the thugs and turned a blind eye when murder was used as a political weapon. Land acquisition was no longer an end in itself. It became the means to a different end: the winning of an election.

So, many years after that earlier, accidental lesson in the inequality of land distribution on the road to the Mhondoro Communal Land, I found myself back on another pristine farm. This time I was a BBC reporter, not a man in need of a favour, but I had changed in a far more profound way than that. By March 2000, it was the plight of the white farmer that troubled me.

Anthony Wells is a short man, though not a slight one. He might have made a good scrum-half: agile enough to switch the play from one side to the other, but strong enough not to get run over in the process. He wears the white farmers' uniform of comically meagre navy blue shorts and a khaki shirt open to the third button. He says 'Yah man' a lot, which is also par for the course. He has the demeanour of a man who spends more time in the sun than is good for him. His nose looks permanently sunburned; so, too, does the back of his neck. Born here, in the Karoi region, about 200 kilometres north of Harare, he's a country boy, the kind that would fidget with his collar if you put him in a suit and tie.

Dawn, his wife, is different. She grew up in the big city, in Harare, a background that is immediately apparent. Her skin is pale, and she takes care of herself. She is the perfect complement to her husband. You look at Ant, as she calls him, and you think beer and *boerwors*. You look at Dawn and you think fresh salad and iced tea. They have a son and just over a thousand hectares of prime agricultural land.

Anthony's father had started farming in these parts in 1958. Having fought the 'terrs', white slang for terrorists, Anthony had every reason to fear for his future but, like many thousands of white people on that March evening in 1980 when Mugabe addressed the nation after an astounding election victory, he was won over. 'If you must migrate, why do you have to go overseas?' the president asked them. 'Stay with us. Migrate from Rhodesia to Zimbabwe.' Buying Maunga Farm in Karoi was Anthony's vote of confidence in the future. Instead of 'taking the gap' and heading off to South Africa or wherever, he took up Mugabe's invitation.

And the future did indeed, look bright. As black people, with the help of government schemes, were beginning to produce the old staples, maize, cotton and tobacco, Anthony, like many other young farmers, decided to diversify into more specialist, exotic, cash crops. The paprika that was ripening nicely when I met him, for example, would be sold by an agent to a company making natural dyes. In the evenings, after the maid had got their little boy ready for bed, Dawn and Anthony would sit on the *stoep* and watch the kudu and nyala walk past the bottom of the garden. Maunga Farm was beginning to feel like a dream come true.

And then, one weekend in March 2000, it turned into a nightmare. As land invasions swept the country, the Karoi region was particularly badly hit. About thirty or forty 'war veterans' turned up outside the ubiquitous fence, that social fault line Frances and I had stepped over all those years ago. They demanded to be let in. Whatever they called themselves, they were no war veterans. Any man who had fought in the *chimurenga*, the struggle against the settler government, even as a teenager, would have been in his thirties or forties by then. The average age of those who raked the fence with their metal rods and makeshift weapons was about twenty. They were in fact the unemployed youth, the legacy of Mr Mugabe's teetering economy.

Anthony Wells' first thought was to make sure Dawn and their child were taken to safety. The farm manager drove them out through a rarely used gate at the back of the property. There was no question of trying to tough it out. He had a gun, of course, but even to display it would have been to court the wrath of the crowd. Their mood was ugly enough as it was.

He tried not to show it, but inside Anthony was panicking. Perhaps he thought back to the war, to all those times when he and his kind had trampled on the rights of others and abused their dignity. Ceasefires can end a conflict, but they cannot blank out the memories of it. Both oppressor and oppressed have to live with those. Those memories form history and folklore, handed down and embellished according to who is telling the story. Each side has its own interpretation of what happened, of what it regards as the truth, and of its consequences. If they had been fit to think, this half-crazed gang would have justified their presence at the gates of Maunga Farm as a claim to their ancestral rights. Anthony, as he peered at the leering faces through the gunmetal mesh fence, clung to the notion of legal rights. The stand-off was a symbol of history versus the law. But the youth had the supreme comfort of knowing that their version of the past had prevailed. That thought perhaps gnawed away at Anthony's mind as he pondered what to do. When it came to it, the barrier, the physical manifestation of property law, afforded no protection in the face of the tectonic power of history. Eventually he slid back the bolts, and let Africa march across the threshold, reversing the occupation of the Pioneer Column.

The youngsters, it seemed, were as interested in humiliation as in land reform. One of them grabbed Anthony by the nose and paraded him about the compound. He was slapped about a bit. The others laughed – it was quite a joke, a white man being pulled around by the nose like an animal being taken to slaughter. When they tired of that, the ringleaders walked on to the *stoep*, sat down in the comfortable chairs and asked Anthony to bring a map of the farm. He couldn't think where he might have one so instead he pulled down an aerial photograph of the property. One of the men drew a finger across the glass that covered it. 'This side, we will take it,' he said. Anthony agreed to the division. He wrote as much on a piece of scrap paper and signed it.

It was done. Land reform, Mugabe-style. No lawyers, no surveyors, just a greasy fingermark on a sheet of glass.

Similar scenes were enacted all over the country. In all, over 500 farms were occupied in this way before that election. Anthony Wells had been lucky. Elsewhere, many farmers were seriously hurt; some were killed. The seizures would continue right up to and beyond the presidential election in March 2002.

The president could have stopped it but he didn't even try. For many inside and outside the country, this put Mr Mugabe beyond the pale. It was the last straw even for those who had tolerated previous abuses of power. And there had been plenty of other violations of the rule of law, some of them gross. The deployment of the murderous, North Korean-trained 5 Brigade in Matabeleland in the mid-eighties was one of them. This region was the stronghold of Joshua Nkomo, Mugabe's great rival in the struggle for independence. The government's response to an insurgency there which began about two years after independence was extreme and illegal. Innocent civilians were tortured, raped and killed in their hundreds.

But times had been less certain then. South Africa was trying to destabilise its newly independent neighbour, and there had been sabotage and assassination attempts. Joshua Nkomo, the nationalist favoured as leader by both London and the Rhodesians, as well as by South Africa, had never quite reconciled himself to his crushing defeat in the 1980 election, and was himself by no means an innocent bystander in those early years.

But by the late eighties, Nkomo's party and its insurgents were finished both politically and militarily. A humbled Nkomo had joined forces with the ruling ZANU party in what was a buy-out rather than a merger, and Mugabe reigned supreme. It would not have been unreasonable to suppose that this period of political hegemony and stability would serve as a springboard to economic success. Instead it proved to be exactly the opposite, and the nineties saw Zimbabwe nose-dive into economic penury and political intolerance.

It's difficult to explain this extraordinary transformation not just in the country, but also in the man, though the two are inextricably linked. Just how did this hero turn into a villain? It is too easy to write off Robert Mugabe as just another incompetent, ruthless, corrupt African leader in a long line that includes the self-proclaimed Emperor Bokassa of the Central African Republic, Samuel Doe of Liberia, Mobutu Sese Seko of Zaire and Idi Amin of Uganda. That is to fall into the trap of assuming that the road to damnation or prosperity must be identical regardless of geography, culture or history. For Africa, with its myriad ethnic groups and 2,000 languages, is more diverse than any other continent.

Mugabe's fall from grace is disquieting precisely because he is *not* a Bokassa, a Doe, a Mobutu or an Amin. Their failings were obvious from the beginning, even if, in the world of realpolitik, many chose to ignore them. In Robert Mugabe's case, even a cursory examination of his past reveals a retiring but diligent child who matured into a disciplined, principled and dedicated freedom fighter. Though he was labelled an unreconstructed Marxist-Leninist (and he did have more than a passing interest in the ideology), his first years in government were a lesson in economic pragmatism. It is his journey from prospective peacemaker to trader in racial division that is so perplexing.

When, in March 1980, the victorious Robert Mugabe talked of the 'love' that bound him to his white citizens, one must assume that he was not being literal. All the same, his speech would have been painstakingly crafted and delivered with care. He was making a statement not just about his politics, but about himself.

For a politician, to talk of love and hate, of forgiveness and reconciliation as he did, and in such personal terms, is to expose
yourself. To do so at the end of a dirty war for independence takes
a certain kind of courage.

There were two Robert Mugabes making a speech that night.
One was a statesman with a job to do. The other was a man susceptible to the thirst for revenge and recompense that preys on all
those who have fought oppression. Each pulls in opposite direc-
tions, working against the other. One of them has to give way. I
have spoken to several freedom fighters who acknowledge the
psychological tug-of-war involved in deciding whether they are
willing to bury the past and give everyone a new start, a fresh
chance to redeem themselves. The alternative is to live with the
corrosive effects of hate. In his victory speech Robert Mugabe
signalled his choice: he had opted to wipe the slate clean.

There were plenty of pragmatic reasons for such a decision. He
had a country to govern, an economy to nurture. He was keen to
ensure that white people did not head straight for the border: he
knew he needed their skills and experience if he was to have half
a chance of turning a faltering Rhodesia into a successful
Zimbabwe. That was the reasoning of the Mugabe who was on
display, the man who addressed the country's white people packed
into country clubs and each other's sitting rooms to hear what he
had to say. This Robert Mugabe talked about continuity and security. He told them their pensions would be safe. He invited the
commander of the white army, the man who had dedicated his
military career to destroying Mugabe, to stay on and help fashion
a new national army. It was a bit like calling on Jean-Marie Le
Pen in France, or the British National Party, to join the fight
against racism. He asked the head of the Commercial Farmers'
Union, the repository of white power over the land, to be the new
minister of agriculture. He was offering the white community a
chance they had never bothered to give their black countrymen.

Political expediency might have dictated much of that, but we must nonetheless allow a measure of personal conviction. Mugabe, like so many who have fought for freedom, must have had his own demons to bury. There was much to despise in what the white man had done to Robert Mugabe personally, let alone to the people he led. As he prepared his speech, he may have recalled the eleven years he spent in jail. He must have remembered the authorities' refusal to allow him out of prison to bury the son who died while he was incarcerated. Perhaps he thought of the way Ian Smith's propaganda machine had made him out to be a psychopath and child-killer. He had to set all this aside, to convince himself that the country's white people were worth this self-imposed amnesia. He also had to persuade himself that the settlers would, in turn, reach out to grasp the hand of partnership he was extending.

But the white man did not respond. Many white Zimbabweans simply withdrew into the isolated comfort zone of fenced-off farm compounds or suburban walled gardens. Their prosaic response to this historic opportunity to help build a better nation was to keep their heads down. Their biggest flaw was a lack of imagination. Perhaps that wasn't surprising in a people who, according to Anthony Verrier, had been led by men with the 'mentality and outlook of county councillors'.

On the land question in particular, they failed to take the initiative. Instead they waited till they were pushed. What they didn't understand is that one acre of land freely given is worth a lot more in goodwill than ten acres grudgingly dispensed under pressure by the courts. White Zimbabweans often point, in mitigation, to the corruption and other problems that blighted what little legal land redistribution there was, but the truth is that many of them enjoyed the spectacle of black people mucking it all up. It rekindled old theories justifying white control on grounds of black incompetence.

Even at the height of the land invasions in 2000, when you might have expected white farmers to seek allies among their black countrymen, too many of them were happy to deride the humble achievements of their black neighbours. They would not have been so cavalier in their judgements had it been a white farmer who was struggling to make a go of it. In their mind's eye, they did not see fellow farmers, they saw white farmers and black farmers.

As far as land is concerned, the issue is not whether white people have legal title to it (that is beyond question), but whether they have moral title to it, which is a far more complex proposition. When deciding between doing only what the law requires them to do and doing as much as morality dictates, most white people have tended to choose the former. That has left them on the right side of the law, but on the wrong side of the social and emotional construct we call community. It's the difference between saying sorry because you have to and saying sorry because you mean it.

This myopia, exhibited most dramatically over the land issue, confirmed the visceral distrust in which they were held by so many former freedom fighters and black activists. The black Zimbabweans had tried to keep it in check, but it returned like a bout of recurrent malaria. Old hatreds were exhumed, historic enmity was, once again, laid bare. Robert Mugabe, too, gave vent to these splenetic emotions, demonising white people as everything from racial supremacists to purveyors of sodomy. As farm after farm was attacked by the lumpen gangs, his manic verbal tirade was the antithesis of the solicitous words with which he had wooed them just two decades earlier.

Robert Mugabe had come full circle. In his late seventies – many would say his dotage – he returned to the only thing he had ever really been any good at. He fought the white man. He employed the language of militant struggle and unleashed the hordes of neo-revolutionary violence.

Curiously, Mr Mugabe's hate speech has wrought a profound, if still embryonic change in Zimbabwe's racial dynamics. In the face of their president's blatant misappropriation of the race card, both black and white Zimbabweans have begun a more honest and open discourse about race and identity than they have ever entered into before. Progressive white people have felt able to speak up against Mr Mugabe's malign tactics without being accused of being diehard racists. And black people have felt able to point to the failure of white Zimbabweans to pull their weight without being accused of being anti-white.

More and more people now reject the notion that white Zimbabweans are solely responsible for what has gone wrong in the country. Far from it. Zimbabwe's economy has the dubious honour of being the fastest-shrinking in the world, and the reason for this is that black government has failed, and failed spectacularly. Robert Mugabe knows this, but he cannot accept it because to do so would be to accept that he has mishandled the great prize of freedom. Like a lawyer in search of a legal loophole, he has found a bewildering array of scapegoats for his incompetence. In the months before the 2002 presidential election, land remained the constant motif but added to it were several others, usually revolving around an alleged conspiracy between white Zimbabweans and the old colonial power, Britain. Zimbabwe's white people were accused of being everything from racial supremacists to purveyors of sodomy. He even accused Tony Blair of leading a government of 'gay gangsters'.

But by then even Mr Mugabe must have suspected that nobody, except for those on the rabid fringes of ZANU such as the party militia, believed him. Twice before – in a constitutional referendum in February 2000 and the parliamentary election in June of the same year – he'd been handed a stiff rebuke by his people. He had lost the referendum outright and in the election the newly formed Movement for Democratic Change had won fifty-seven seats, just five fewer than ZANU. And that despite a campaign of harassment, torture and murder in which, according to the Zimbabwe Human Rights Forum, thirty-seven people were killed and over 2,500 assaulted. Mr Mugabe's Machiavellian instincts for power told him he would have to resort to even more despotic measures if he was going to cling on to the presidency in 2002.

The violence continued unabated; the farm seizures multiplied, despite a high court injunction delivered by the last of Zimbabwe's independent judges. But there was more. In the final weeks before the March vote, Zimbabwe's Parliament passed a series of laws that made it virtually impossible for the MDC to campaign freely. An Information Bill outlawed all but the most anodyne comments about the president and severe restrictions were placed on foreign correspondents. The number of polling booths in Harare (an MDC stronghold) was cut and the opposition's election agents were not registered. Mr Mugabe must have studied every rigged election in the world because he did not miss a trick.

As the election dates – 9 and 10 March – drew closer, the international community was divided over just how to react. Some countries thought Mugabe was already beyond the pale and should be penalised, while others felt there was still a chance to exert some influence, to ensure that Zimbabwe's hapless people got their chance to cast a vote. The split was most obvious within the Commonwealth, not least because it separated the white countries – Britain, Australia, Canada – from the majority of African ones. Thabo Mbeki, South Africa's president, who had dedicated his adult life to gaining the right to a free and fair vote for his own people, balked at the idea of taking any action. He stuck to the hear-no-evil, see-no-evil formula, even when his own election observer team in Zimbabwe was attacked. It was a depressing return to the days when the likes of Idi Amin had been tolerated by their African counterparts.

The result, for what it's worth, was a victory for Mr Mugabe, who received 56 per cent of the votes cast. Fortunately, the Commonwealth observer mission was more scrupulous than the South Africans and exhibited a degree of independence many had not expected. It declared that the vote had been held in a climate of fear and did not reflect the will of Zimbabwe's people.

Zimbabwe was suspended from the Commonwealth for one year. So the man who in his heyday had hosted a summit of the Commonwealth and given his capital's name to a declaration on good governance was finally and officially deemed to be a pariah.

Mr Mugabe, like so many African nationalists, is a product of the old era, whose political imagination was fired by the need to free his country of white colonialism. The power of the settler was the single most important fact in his life. Liberation is the key word in his lexicon, not growth or efficiency or competence. The most effective rebuttal of white recalcitrance is not revenge, but black competence. Deeds are more important than words. This is what men such as Yoweri Museveni in Uganda have begun to understand. Yet, like many of his generation, Mugabe has allowed himself to be defined not by what black people can achieve, but by what white people have failed to achieve. He has, in a sense, allowed himself to be psychologically held hostage by the white minority.

There is a personal cost to be paid even when you come out on the victorious side. It is exacted from different people in different ways. Southern Africa, in particular, is awash with both black and white freedom fighters struggling to come to terms with their actions and what to do with their lives now that the big battle is over. There are men who can't settle down and women who don't even want to settle down. There are some who still hanker after the hero's welcome and others who want to put it all behind them.

Mr Mugabe has been warped and scarred by the very struggle that freed his country, and indeed, there are very few who have emerged from the cauldron of racist conflict free of rancour and beyond reproof. It is manifestly difficult to fight a system without hating the people who propped it up. Yet one man appears to have done just that. His name is Nelson Rolihlahla Mandela or, as his own people prefer to call him, Madiba.

11

Mandela's Miracle

'He is only one pebble on the beach, one of thousands.' The epithet was delivered with all the impishness for which Archbishop Desmond Tutu has become famous. 'Not an insignificant pebble, I'll grant you that, but a pebble all the same.' Only Desmond Tutu could get away with comparing Nelson Mandela, probably the most widely recognised and respected leader on the planet, with a round, lifeless stone on the seashore.

The Archbishop was speaking at the foreign correspondents' association annual dinner in Johannesburg, where he was the guest of honour. It was 1996, and although Mr Mandela's presidency had a few more years to run, some foreign correspondents were already beginning to fret about what the future would hold for the country without the man who personified its freedom. Tutu was trying to point out that even Mr Mandela was not indispensable. The sentiment was not new: it was a point Mandela himself, in his self-deprecating way, had made more than once. But the metaphor was vintage Tutu.

The two old friends had a history of scoring points off each other. Together, they were something of a double act, an African odd couple. They had reached the same conclusions about South Africa's destiny from very different perspectives. For Tutu, the equality of one person with another was underpinned by a deeply spiritual element; for Mandela, it was a matter of human rights and political legitimacy. At times their differences could be significant; mostly they were not. Early on in Mandela's presidency they are said to have verbally crossed swords over the lavish pay and benefits the newly enfranchised members of parliament had awarded themselves. Mandela gave as good as he got. On another occasion the Archbishop is reported to have taunted the president about his sartorial taste, criticising the bold, silky shirts Mandela preferred to grey suits as inappropriate for a head of state. Mandela quipped back: 'That's a bit rich coming from a man who has spent most of his adult life wearing a dress.'

Since Nelson Mandela stepped down as the president of South Africa in May 1999, much to the chagrin of those who predicted the worst for a South Africa ruled by the indigenous population, the economy has not collapsed and the nation's politics are as lively as they were when the African National Congress (ANC) won the first free elections in 1994. If it has failings – and there are certainly some – they are no greater or more numerous than those occurring in other countries in transition. Ask West Germans how difficult reuniting with their partners in the east has proved, take a look at the graft and corruption in post-Soviet Moscow, and you can only conclude that South Africa has done quite well after all. The country is not only alive and kicking, it has passed that most difficult test of political maturity: the democratic rite of passage of replacing one leader with another.

Part of the reason for all this is the manner of Nelson Mandela's departure, the way he managed it, the way he began planning for it almost as soon as he took office. He said from the outset that he would serve no more than one five-year term. It was a brief stewardship for a man who had waited a lifetime to lead his people, but he kept his promise, a rare thing for a politician in post-colonial Africa. Like that other old man of African politics, the late Julius Nyerere of Tanzania, he gave up the presidency voluntarily, but unlike Nyerere, Mandela did it straight away. It wasn't even a case of jumping before he was pushed: there were many in South Africa, and even more overseas, who would have been happy to give him another five years in the presidential suite of the Union Buildings in Pretoria.

Indeed, history may judge his withdrawal from the country's post-Apartheid political scene to be just as important a contribution to South Africa's long-term stability as his dramatic entry into it just under a decade before. It is a tribute to his presidency that the institutions of state – the legislature, the judiciary, the civil service – were as vibrant on the day he left office as they were when he was sworn in as South Africa's first freely elected president.

It was his government that had handed these institutions their independence in the first place, an independence that was demonstrated in 1997, when a judge subpoenaed Mandela himself to give evidence in a wrangle between the government-backed National Sports Council and the Rugby Union. The council was unhappy with the failure of rugby's governing body to open up the game to all races and was trying to push it into doing so. The president's lawyers and political advisers were adamant that Mr Mandela should refuse to attend. They feared that his appearance before a judge would set a precedent, leaving every aspect of government decision-making open to perusal by the courts. Mandela argued the reverse: he said that the people had to know that no one, not even the president, was above the law. He appeared in court, where the judge's verdict went against him and the sports council. It was a perverse decision, but that's another story.

The contrast between the new South Africa and the country

inherited by the African National Congress could not have been more marked. The whole machinery of state had been politicised and subservient to a single party. Mandela's government introduced genuine multi-party politics to what had, in effect, been a one-party state since the 1950s. This was a reversal of what had happened elsewhere on the continent. Africa's post-independence leaders were generally known for shutting down their political systems, not nurturing them.

This refreshing break with the appalling record set elsewhere in Africa led many to see in Mandela something wonderfully ground-breaking. The president himself, as we've seen, spoke of a new era for Africa, a continental renaissance. Though he did not place himself at the cutting edge of this revival, others did. Almost immediately, he became the thing he feared most: the object of a personality cult.

Hero-worship of presidents – on the surface, at least – was commonplace in Africa, from tiny countries such as Togo to mammoth nations like Zaire, where leaders had worked hard to ensure that they were the arbiters of all things. Their touched-up portraits were hung everywhere from hairdressing salons to airline offices, even those belonging to foreign carriers. In South Africa it was different: here the mantle had not been appropriated by personal command, or bestowed by party apparatchiks, but was foisted on Mandela by public acclaim. The adulation was as great abroad as it was at home, and it started the minute Nelson Mandela walked out of Victor Verster Prison after serving twenty-six years.

Even his most conservative detractors had to admit to a grudging respect for this man who seemed a million miles from the fly-swatting caricature of African leadership the world had come to expect. He was, many argued, a new man for a new age. People began to talk of the new South Africa as a miracle, and of Mandela as the magician who had made it possible.

In truth Nelson Mandela was not so new and the defeat of Apartheid was merely the last battle in a very old war: the war against colonialism and settler domination. Technically, South Africa may not have been a colony but, in every other respect, its freedom represented the last piece of black Africa's post-colonial jigsaw.

Nelson Mandela was not Africa's first political prisoner turned president. The colonial authorities, whether the Belgians in Zaire or the British in Zambia, had a knack of creating heroes out of the men they tried to suppress. Looking back at Africa's history, it is tempting to view a spell in jail courtesy of a colonial power as a prerequisite for ultimate victory at the polls. But while Mandela's release from prison was an event as old as the process of decolonisation itself, in 1990 it seemed new and fresh to far-off audiences who tuned into it, courtesy of the live television age, to see history unfolding in real time. Indeed, the occasion was a prime candidate for the full-on TV treatment. If Kwame Nkrumah's swearing-in as Africa's first black leader had occurred in the 1990s instead of the late 1950s, he too would be remembered today and be given his rightful place among the continent's liberators. What Nkrumah had begun, Mandela finished.

Nor was Nelson Mandela the first black man to walk out of jail apparently free of bitterness. Jomo Kenyatta preached reconciliation after the bloody Mau Mau campaign against the whites during Kenya's struggle for independence. In a speech at Nakuru in 1961 he, too, charmed the white settlers and assured them of a place under Africa's sun. 'We are going to forget the past and look to the future,' he told an audience of white people. 'I have suffered imprisonment and detention, but that is gone and I am not going to remember it. Let us join hands and work for the benefit of Kenya.' Robert Mugabe did it again in Zimbabwe in 1980. In fact, the independence leaders who excoriated their colonial enemies, such as Patrice Lumumba in the Congo, were the exception rather than the rule.

This willingness to forgive, this yearning for consensus, this desire for inclusion is much more than mere political expediency.

It is a part of the African psyche, as old as the people themselves. For centuries chiefs have been gathering together their subjects and trying to reconcile the seemingly irreconcilable. The search for togetherness finds expression in the uniquely African spirit of *ubuntu*. It is not an easy concept to define. Broadly, it is the notion that one person's humanity is inextricably linked to the perception of humanity in others. The humiliation of a former enemy, therefore, has no place in *ubuntu*.

On the face of it, Africa is littered with conflicts that show little sign of the spirit of *ubuntu*. Liberia, Somalia and, above all, Rwanda appear to prove a more savage reality in the communal relations of the continent. But these conflicts are almost always the result of leaders manipulating tribal and ethnic loyalties for political ends. They prove only that, like the imported hyacinth that is suffocating all the indigenous flora in Lake Victoria, adversarial party politics can undermine even the most ancient of Africa's traditions. The tribe, once the guarantor of social stability, has been misappropriated to achieve quite the opposite effect.

In the established democracies of Europe and North America, old allegiances to regions or clans long ago gave way to new loyalties. After the Industrial Revolution, people began to worry more about which politicians would protect their factories from foreign competition, or who would safeguard the interests of the countryside as urban demands came to the fore. Class became more important than bloodline as working people in one area started to realise that they had more in common with labourers from other parts of the country than they did with people of a different social standing in their own. Politicians saw this and tailored their policies accordingly. More recently still, political parties have had to prove above all that they are competent managers of a nation's wealth.

In much of Africa, however, it is not a nation's economic growth that requires careful husbandry but its ever-dwindling resources. There is less to share out in Africa today than there was forty years ago. A system of patronage and loyalty has become the key to a slice of this shrinking cake. When there is not enough to give everybody, you give first to your tribe. But to do so you have to be in charge. So tribe and family have become the passport to political power. Curiously, then, it's possible that the imposition of multi-party politics on societies that were simply not ready for the attendant winner-take-all electoral systems has strengthened, rather than weakened, tribal affiliation.

Nelson Mandela resisted the allure of tribal politics, but even in this he was not unique. Other African leaders followed the same path, though they fell by the wayside when their political future was put to the test.

So Mr Mandela was not the first of a new order but the last, and best, of the old. He just took things a stage further than other leaders, with more success and in a shorter time. He was what Kwame Nkrumah promised to be; what Kenneth Kaunda should have been; what Hastings Banda might have been; what Robert Mugabe ought to have been; what Samora Machel tried to be; what Milton Obote could have been; what Julius Nyerere very nearly became. He is special because he got it right, not because his was a new or different approach. His presidency marks not a departure from Africa's post-colonial values, but a reaffirmation of them. His five years in office closed one chapter in Africa's history – the era of national liberation – rather than opening a new one.

In a sense, Mandela was out of step with the rest of the continent's leaders. When he was sentenced to his first term of imprisonment in 1962 as an angry, young(ish) man, the rest of Africa was gaining its independence. He returned an older and wiser man with all the lessons of thirty-odd years of self-rule in Africa to work from. At first his instincts had been to repeat some of the old mistakes. It took a while, for example, for him to be persuaded to drop nationalisation as an ANC policy. If he managed the transition from freedom fighter to government leader more successfully than others, it was partly due to the fact that the world had changed so much. Africa had changed; it had learned some very hard lessons.

What Nelson Mandela didn't do, and may not even have tried to do, was to find a new way to meet Africa's biggest challenge: to lift the planet's most wretched people from the grinding poverty that keeps them at the bottom of the global pile. That he has left to others. He bowed out of politics at precisely the point so many other leaders in Africa were starting off. History has shown that this next phase, the economic consolidation of independence, is every bit as hard, perhaps even harder, than the struggle for national liberation.

This is not to denigrate Mandela's achievements; merely to put them into context. I wouldn't go so far as to call Nelson Mandela just another pebble on the beach, but I know what Desmond Tutu was driving at.

The image of the tall, silver-haired old man walking out of the prison gates on a sunny February morning in 1990 with his hand held high in the air in a clenched-fist salute is one of the most enduring of the twentieth century. It is etched into the collective global memory along with Neil Armstrong's moon landing in 1969 and Muhammad Ali's reclamation of the world heavyweight boxing crown in 1971. In a world that had become cynical and tired of politicians, to people bored with the tawdry promise of an ever-better tomorrow, Nelson Mandela represented moral certainty and personal dignity.

He was a man for all people and all seasons. In the years to come, as he travelled across the globe he met people – rich and poor, high or low caste, progressive or conservative – who sought in him a solution to their own needs and fears. Totalitarian governments in Europe had collapsed one after another, the Cold War was over but, tumultuous as those events were, they had not thrown up a defining vision or icon. Too often in these newly liberated countries, accumulating wealth, whatever the cost to the community, appeared to be the guiding principle. George Bush senior, the American president when the Berlin Wall came crumbling down, was an unlikely hero; still less Margaret Thatcher, Britain's leader at the time. Vaclav Havel, president of the newly freed Czech Republic, had all the right credentials, but his fame remained firmly confined to Europe's liberal cognoscenti.

Mandela was sucked into this vacuum in international affairs, and he did not disappoint. His effortless star quality shone through for the world to see. Whereas most African leaders were merely tolerated in great gatherings of the rich and powerful, Mr Mandela had to do no more than sit back and wait for them to arrive on his doorstep. Monarchs and maestros, princesses and presidents, entertainers and entrepreneurs all beat a path to 'Mahlanbandhlovu', the renamed presidential residence in Pretoria. It was as if they hoped some of his moral authority and pulling power might rub off on them. Not a bad word was said against him anywhere, except in the most rabid corners of Afrikanerdom and the dark recesses of international right-wing politics. And churlish criticism from these quarters served only to show how out of tune such people were with the global zeitgeist.

At home he had to combine two roles, loyally serving his disenfranchised black countrymen while at the same time reassuring white people that a South Africa under him would be a place where all could prosper. This balancing act between black need and white fear would become the overarching theme of the four-year negotiations with the incumbent president, F. W. de Klerk, that led to elections, and of Mandela's subsequent five-year presidency. These two vital concerns were not mutually exclusive, whatever the beliefs of some of those on the more radical wing of his party. Mandela understood that satisfying the pent-up expectations of a people oppressed for three and a half centuries depended in no small measure on ensuring that skilled white people continued to pull the levers of economic growth.

He needed a unifying vision, something that would bind together these two potentially conflicting goals. He found it in reconciliation. To black people this was a call to forgive (but not forget), to resist the temptation to seek revenge, in the interests of greater prosperity, while white people were offered a chance to atone for their past sins, to make up for what Rian Malan called 'genetic complicity' in his book *My Traitor's Heart*. That was the deal implicit in Mandela's policy of reconciliation and nation-building. To those who carped from the sidelines, who said there were more urgent tasks than to go around making friends with white people, Mr Mandela had a tart reply: 'Forgiving your enemy does not cost a penny from the national coffers.'

One of the biggest challenges facing the country was precisely how to deal with its past. There was no question of a victors' tribunal such as the one held at Nuremberg after the Second World War. Black South Africa had not conquered white South Africa; this had been a negotiated settlement in which both sides had had to compromise. Many in the white community had wanted a general amnesty; many in the black community argued that that would be tantamount to rewarding racism and torture. Mr Mandela understood that to drag each and every servant of Apartheid through the courts would have been a lengthy, expensive and, above all, divisive process. The negotiators found a middle way, a halfway house between justice and impunity. It was called the Truth and Reconciliation Commission.

The commission's guiding principle was to be that very African recognition of a common humanity. Its task was written into South Africa's new constitution: 'There is a need for understanding but not for vengeance, a need for reparation but not for retaliation, a need for *ubuntu*, but not for victimisation.'

From an original list of about 200 names representing all shades of colour and political opinion, an interviewing panel produced a shortlist of forty-five candidates for the commission. This was later honed down to the twenty-five names that were sent to

President Nelson Mandela. From that list Mr Mandela chose the seventeen men and women who would have the unenviable task of shining the torch of truth into the murky depths of South Africa's recent past. Together they would have to find the strength to listen to Apartheid's many victims and the forgiveness to grant amnesty to those who were willing to admit their misdemeanours.

In a typical example of the ironies that peppered this new South Africa, the minister of justice, Dullah Omar, who steered the commission's founding legislation through Parliament, found himself championing a bill that would allow the people who had tried to assassinate him years before to seek amnesty.

For Archbishop Desmond Tutu, the commission's chairman, this job was the culmination of a ministry in which he had always placed his Christian beliefs at the service of the struggle against Apartheid. In his account of the commission's work, *No Future Without Forgiveness*, he described his role in pastoral terms. He had, he said, 'to distinguish between the sinner and the sin; to hate and condemn the sin whilst being filled with compassion for the sinner'.

For two years the commission held meetings around the country. Its hearings on human-rights violations became platforms where the victims of Apartheid could reclaim their dignity, speaking publicly, often for the first time, about the horrors they had kept locked up in what one South African judge called 'wounded memories'. It wasn't a courtroom; there was no judge to pronounce a guilty verdict. Its purpose was to establish the truth so that no white South African could ever again utter those Judas words of disguised culpability: 'We didn't know.'

The first-ever witness to come before the Truth and Reconciliation Commission, on 15 April 1996, was Nohle Mohapi. As it happened, I had got to know Nohle some eighteen months earlier when I was making a film for the BBC's *Correspondent* series. She had worked with Steve Biko, the young and brilliant leader of the Black Consciousness movement of the

1970s. Biko had been arrested, tortured and left to die in a police cell in Pretoria, a thousand kilometres from his home in the Eastern Cape. Like others associated with him, Nohle had also been held in solitary confinement and humiliated by the white police officers who arrested her. Worse, her husband, Mapetla, had died in detention.

That Nohle consented to appear before the commission at all was a testament to the willingness of thousands of black South Africans to set aside their deep yearning to see their abusers put behind bars. I remember standing with her in one of the cells where Biko had lain damaged and inert. I asked her then, a year and a half before the commission set to work, whether she could ever be reconciled with the people who had so mutilated her life. She turned on me, her eyes cold and piercing, her body taut with controlled anger, and said: 'There is hatred in me, and it is for them to try to rub out that hatred. You must have the truth first and then you can think about reconciliation. I don't agree when they say, "Let bygones be bygones, let's try to forget about the past and try to reconcile." Reconcile what?'

In that instant I understood that although all I could see were whitewashed walls and an empty steel bed in Cell 4 of Walmer Police Station, Nohle could see a once strong, proud black man lying prone and injured on a cold cement floor. The Truth Commission asked its witnesses to make huge personal sacrifices; without fail, all of them lived up to the challenge.

While the commission gathered its evidence, Nelson Mandela was making his own pilgrimage of peace and nation-building. Even as the commission was unearthing all the gruesome details of South Africa's divided past, Mr Mandela was showing his people the way to a united future. He found allies in the most unlikely places. I remember talking to a Boer farmer deep in the *platteland* that lies north and west of Johannesburg. This is the land of the diehard Afrikaners, the descendants of those who fled what they saw as the licentious Cape in the Great Trek of the 1830s. It was from among these communities that right-wing groups such as the Conservative Party and the Freedom Front recruited their supporters. Even the militaristic but largely ineffectual Afrikaner Weerstands Beweging (AWB) had its adherents in these parts. I'm not sure which, if any, of these organisations my farmer friend belonged to. 'Ah, man. Munndela I can live with,' he said. 'He is an honest man and he has done well by his people. He is a chief and he's looking after his tribe. It's that snake De Klerk that I can't stand. He's a traitor to his people. Munndela can come here any time he likes, but not that bastard De Klerk.'

Nelson Mandela's courting of white opinion was as relentless as it was breathtaking; as shrewd as it was surprising. He sought out his old adversaries one by one and made his peace with them. But this was not some private mission, it was a form of public therapy. Almost always the cameras were allowed to record these meetings.

There was Percy Yutar, the chief prosecutor at the Rivonia Trials. The man who had helped to put Nelson Mandela behind bars in the early sixties was invited to lunch over thirty years later.

There was the widow of the man often described as the architect of Apartheid, Dr Hendrik Verwoerd. To meet her, Mr Mandela had to travel to Orania , the Afrikaner-only town in the Northern Cape province. Its residents viewed it as the embryonic Afrikaner *volkstaat* of their far-fetched political fantasies; in fact, it was no more than an inoffensive little enclave cut off from the outside world. Even so, by visiting Orania Mandela would be seen to be conferring on it a kind of blessing. He went ahead anyway, even helping the poorly sighted widow to read from a text which called for an independent Afrikaner state. The following day, a cartoon by Zapiro, who offered some of the most mordant analysis of South Africa's transition, showed the president bending over backwards and shaking hands through his legs with Verwoerd's wife.

Then there was the Rugby World Cup in June 1995, hosted by South Africa. Their isolation from international sporting contacts during the years of sanctions against the country was perhaps one of the hardest things for white South Africans to swallow. Sport was a central part of their lives. Playing hard and playing to win suited the backs-to-the-wall mentality in which so many wallowed. Rugby, so beloved of the Afrikaners, more than any other game encapsulated this spirit, this fight to the death. And for precisely this reason, most black people hated the sport, seeing it as the racists' favourite pastime. The Springboks, as the national team were called, won through to the final. If they were the gladiators, then Ellis Park in Johannesburg, the venue for the final, was their amphitheatre.

Into this cradle of white myth-making strode President Nelson Mandela, resplendent in the green and gold Springbok jersey. To many black South Africans it must have been a bit like seeing Martin Luther King dressed in the white robes of the Ku Klux Klan. The applause was rapturous. For minutes all you could hear was 60,000 people, a capacity crowd, almost all of them white, shouting 'Nelson! Nelson!' New Zealand were the favourites to win the competition but it was the Springboks who took the trophy after the final whistle was blown. Mandela had worked another little miracle. Afterwards, as captain François Pienaar hoisted the World Cup, Mandela pumped the air with his fists as if he had kicked the winning drop-goal himself.

We, a family that couldn't tell a knock-on from an offside, watched the whole spectacle with friends on TV at home with goose-pimply fascination. We wore beatific smiles as the captain, in a post-match interview, captured the mood set by his president. 'How did it feel to have sixty thousand people behind you?' the commentator asked. 'It wasn't sixty thousand people behind us,' said François Pienaar. 'It was forty-three million.' And indeed the victory captured the hearts of the whole population. Our friend

Janie, a white woman, was in tears. 'It's just so good to be able to be a part of all this without feeling guilty,' she said.

That was Nelson Mandela's secret. After years of being regarded as the 'skunks' of the world – which is how he described the old South Africa in his inauguration speech – he had made it possible for white people to feel good about themselves. It was part of the plan. He knew that a demoralised, isolated, victimised white minority was never going to make the kind of contribution that was needed to lift the whole country out of the morass into which Apartheid had plunged it.

And Mandela played his part to perfection, often in the face of ridicule and worse from his own supporters. But pretty soon it became obvious that too many among the white community were unwilling to reciprocate his generosity. They liked the reconciliation part, but were reluctant to accept the transformation that went with it. For many, Mr Mandela's policy of forgiveness was a licence to carry on as if nothing had changed. White South Africans were afflicted by a collective amnesia. It became almost impossible to find anyone who had actually supported Apartheid, or acknowledged that they had benefited from it.

People who'd been cosseted by an educational system that budgeted eight times as much money for teaching white children as black children now balked at the idea that schools should be opened to all pupils. In February 1996 a group of white, largely Afrikaner parents at a primary school in the rural town of Potgietersrus kept their children out of class. The reason? A court had ruled that the school had an obligation to accept black children from the local township. Eighteen neatly dressed, eager black children showed up, ready to receive the kind of education that had been denied their parents. Eighteen black children out of a school roll of around 700. But it was eighteen too many for the Afrikaner parents. In keeping with the times, they found a new language to press home their claims for the old privileges. Where once they simply cited racial preference they now talked of diversity, arguing that Afrikaner culture was being threatened.

While that boycott was exceptional, the sentiments that underpinned it were far more widespread than white parents in other areas of the country were willing to acknowledge publicly. We saw them at work in Johannesburg, at the local state primary school to which we sent our two sons. When they enrolled in 1994, the year Nelson Mandela was sworn in as president, the school was evenly mixed between black and white children. By the time we left, just under four years later, nine out of ten were black. Nothing had happened to our suburb. It was still largely what it had been in the Apartheid era: a comfortable, wealthy part of the city with neatly trimmed lawns and sparklingly clean swimming pools. There were still plenty of white children around, but they were being sent to school elsewhere, somewhere a little bit whiter.

The defence, as ever, was standards. It is true that teachers did find life more difficult. Classes were bigger and the endemic disadvantages endured by black households certainly manifested themselves in the children who came from them. But the drop in standards was always perceived as greater than it was in reality. A steady nerve on the part of white parents, and a little bit of extra tuition (which most white families in the kind of area we were living in could afford) would have seen their children through to secondary school, but only a few chose this path. Many opted to spend even more money on private schools and the phoney security of the enclave, the *laager*.

This is not an argument against South Africa's private schools as such, more an observation about the largely Eurocentric culture most of them continued to represent. We looked at some of these schools ourselves when we first arrived in South Africa. What we found were institutions that were far less racially mixed than most city schools, even selective ones, back home. It seemed perverse to travel all the way to Africa only to educate our children in a narrower environment than anything they might have enjoyed in Britain.

The tensions in education were mirrored in other spheres. White people complained about crime, despite the fact that their suburbs received the lion's share of the police budget and certainly a lot more than the townships where most of the crime occurred. They complained about affirmative action, despite the fact that the vast majority of office jobs in the private sector, especially those carrying any real clout, remained in white hands. They complained about corruption without ever really acknowledging that under the African National Congress, it was at least possible to expose it. They complained about government interference in the press when there was far greater freedom of expression than there had ever been under Apartheid governments.

Some time towards the end of our stay in South Africa – it was wintertime, about June 1998 – my elder son, Adam, had a friend to sleep over. He was a white boy from a typically wealthy family. He was eleven years old or thereabouts. The next morning, we sat down to breakfast. Outside, the round camellia bush with its deep green leaves was in flower. The ground beneath it was like a carpet of blood-red petals. The palm tree down near the swimming pool swayed in the gentlest of breezes, swinging the bauble-like weaver birds' nests from one side to another. Beyond that was the treehouse, a favourite hidey-hole for my younger son, Matthew. Over to the side of the compound, the cricket stumps were still standing, a reminder of our game the day before. Jericho, our black Labrador, was chewing one of the bails.

Looking out at this picture of domestic bliss I repeated what had become virtually a daily mantra. 'Remember boys, you have grown up in Madiba's country.' As the day of our departure drew nearer, both Frances and I feared that we might not have done enough to make our sons aware of how privileged they were to have lived in South Africa in these momentous times. I suppose, subconsciously, I was harking back to my own childhood in Ghana. There was a neat symmetry to it: I had grown up in the first country in Africa to win the right to run its own affairs; they had spent their early lives in the last to gain the same right. I wanted them to enjoy these years as I had savoured my time in Ghana. I wanted them to feel, deep down, that Africa was still a place of hope.

'It's not that great.' The words crashed into my quiet reverie like a rogue note in a perfect tune. It was our young guest. 'Things are getting worse in South Africa,' he said. 'Black people are getting jobs when they're not good enough to do them. The government can't even make sure the lights on our street are repaired.' Our children sat in shocked silence, for they had been told that Madiba had embarked on a noble project.

My son's friend had always been a precocious child, but I sensed that these sentiments had been planted in his mind by others. Where did they come from? We knew his parents, an enlightened couple, apparently committed citizens with a social conscience. It couldn't have been them, we said to ourselves afterwards. The truth was that these thoughts were just out there, ubiquitous. Leaching from conversations overheard between racks of designer label clothing in a glistening new shopping mall; from a bit of gossip around a weekend *braai* and beer; from a chat between two parents picking up their children from school. The ideas spread, floating around like those fluffy seed-heads that are blown hither and thither on a puff of wind.

It didn't sound as if anyone had told this child that Apartheid had been the most comprehensive affirmative action programme in the world, or that people like his parents had benefited from it. It was doubtful that anyone had reminded him that for every streetlight that flickered uselessly in Johannesburg's fragrant suburbs, a thousand South African children in a township he was unlikely ever to venture into were reading books under an electric bulb for the first time.

Some time after the election, I'm not sure exactly when, a lot of white South Africans became better at whingeing than at hoping. To be sure, there was and still is a lot that is wrong with the new South Africa. But their incessant carping began to have a corrosive effect. It was like being in a team with one player who is always a bit sullen. Writing in a newspaper at the time, a (white) academic compared elements of the white population with an army that had lost its morale. 'They are,' he said, 'listless, cynical, pessimistic, voracious consumers of rumour, twisting everything to confirm some undefined but nightmarish vision.' It became a self-perpetuating exercise. The less they admired their country, the less they contributed to it; the less they contributed to it, the less there was to admire in it.

Thabo Mbeki, the man destined to take over from Nelson Mandela, gave vent to black exasperation in a way no senior politician had done before. He said that South Africa was one country but two nations: one white and largely comfortable, the other black and predominantly impoverished. With that summary he stripped away the feelgood veneer that had masked the truth for the four years since the election. He was merely saying out loud what many black people had thought privately for some time: that their white compatriots had not kept their side of the bargain. They had done the forgiving, what had white people done in return?

Many white South Africans took comfort from the fact that it was Thabo Mbeki who had launched this broadside and not their beloved Madiba. They could put it down to Mr Mbeki's communist past, or dismiss it as an attempt to win over radicals in some internecine power play. The last thing they were willing to do was to concede that he might have a point.

A measure of just how out of touch the white community had become was their response when Nelson Mandela, the reconciler-in-chief, said much the same thing in his valedictory speech at the ANC's fiftieth congress in Mafikeng. Mafikeng, in the hot, dusty north-west of the country, was precisely the kind of place that the struggle against Apartheid had been about. Here, in the settlements around the city, you could still see barefoot children, homes without piped water or sewerage, teachers trying to educate their pupils in classrooms that consisted of nothing more than four poles holding up sheets of corrugated metal. Mr Mandela lashed out at white business and, by implication, the whole community, accusing its denizens of not doing enough to relieve the poverty in places like Mafikeng.

The white community reacted as if Mandela had betrayed them. In the years since the election, they had adopted him as their own champion – it was not unusual to hear white people say things like, 'I don't know what's going to happen to us once Madiba goes.' It was as if his sole purpose in life was to protect them from the masses. In this twisted version of post-Apartheid history they saw themselves as the victims who needed protection. Seduced by Mandela's dramatic gestures of reconciliation, they had convinced themselves that he was just a sort of kindly great-uncle. 'They shouldn't work the old man so hard,' they would say in proprietorial tones. 'Ah, he's so sweet, man,' they would gush over coffee and cakes.

They had hijacked the man who spent twenty-six years in jail in order to free black people, and morphed him into a political eunuch, someone who merely decorated the political landscape. They were denying all that his life had actually stood for, seeing only those parts of his nature and language that made them feel cosy and comfortable. It was the ultimate insult, though few were sensitive enough to see that for themselves. So it was a shock to the system when Mandela returned to his political roots. They'd forgotten why he had been described as a revolutionary; they didn't remember that this was the man who had been willing to take up arms to free his people.

It wasn't a shock to black South Africans, of course. It was a relief. Many had slipped into quiet dismay as Mandela pursued his

policy of reconciliation, apparently above all else. I remember
Milton Nkosi, my producer at the BBC's Johannesburg bureau,
declaring: 'Now, this is why we voted for him.' Milton wasn't a
hothead; he wasn't a radical who wanted to tear down the walls of
white privilege brick by brick (though he confessed to such
dreams in his febrile youth). He was just a black man who wanted
a better deal. And that was all Mandela was asking for.

The largely white-owned press reacted with fury. Perhaps the
most telling comment came from *Business Day*, which opined
that Mandela was naïve if he ever believed that whites would
'voluntarily take a drop in living standards to help the poor'.
That was it in a nutshell. They had taken so much from him
and now, on the eve of his departure from politics, when he
asked for something in return, they charged him with being
dimwitted. The accusation of naïveté raised a question: would
white people have preferred a touch of the coercion so common
elsewhere in Africa? What they wanted was to have their cake
and eat it.

The British press chimed in, too. Newspapers that had once
been ridiculously generous in their praise now unburdened themselves of their collective bile as they tore into Mandela's speech.
The *Independent* described it as 'antiquated gibberish'. *The Times*
said that for a 'man who embodies reconciliation, the attack on
opponents and whites did not promote confidence for pluralistic
politics'. Really? A speech asking white people to play their part
was a step towards dictatorship? And, not to be outdone, the
Daily Telegraph called the speech a 'depressingly paranoiac tirade
that marks the end of rainbow politics'. To which most black
people would have replied: 'If that is what rainbow politics was all
about, then good riddance.'

Curiously, the charge of naïveté was also levelled at Mandela by
black radicals, who had told him from day one that the leopard
could not change its spots. Nobody, least of all white South
Africans, should be surprised if Nelson Mandela's successor feels

he has to resort to something a little more robust than avuncular persuasion.

The last word on this whole sorry episode must go to the white man who called into Tim Modise's drivetime radio news programme on SA*fm*, the public-service broadcaster, as I was driving back to Johannesburg. His comments encapsulated the way white South Africans had simply failed to understand the meaning of Nelson Mandela's long walk to freedom.

'Yah. Hello, Tim. Are you there?'

'Yeah. How's it. Go ahead.'

'Look, I just want to say something about Madiba's speech yesterday.'

'Sure, sure. Everybody's been talking about it.'

'Look, man, I think Nelson Mandela is a great man. He's a statesman. But, you know, I really think he should stay out of politics . . . Hello, Tim? Are you there?'

As I stopped the car and jotted down the conversation, I was convulsed by a rib-aching bout of laughter. The only other reaction that would have made any sense at all would have been to go off and tear down some of those walls of privilege, brick by brick. But that simply wouldn't do. Not in the new South Africa.

Freedom is a textbook on accounting. Freedom is studying late into the night in dim light till the words and numbers blur. Freedom is getting up early and doing it all over again. Freedom is tough. Freedom is the opportunity to try hard and be rewarded for your pains. Freedom is Khethiwe Badela's slow but determined journey towards a better life.

Khethiwe wouldn't stand out in a crowd. She dresses sensibly: a skirt for work and jeans when she's at home. She doesn't do much with her hair, except to keep it clean and tidy. She doesn't really bother with make-up. She doesn't go in for rings and bangles, either. She's happy with her looks just the way they are: wide-set eyes, high cheekbones and a smile for Africa. She doesn't go to the gym and she doesn't hang around in cafés. That's because she hasn't got the time. Like thousands of other single mothers, she's sorting out her life, making the best of the opportunities that became available to her on 27 April 1994.

Khethiwe's sons, Thando and Sephiwe, and her niece Cassandra attended the same school as our boys. They were freedom's children, the first to benefit from the opening up of the well-endowed suburban schools to all. What my generation was to Ghana, they were to South Africa. Nearly forty years on, here was another group of children who dared to dream, whose parents willed them on to something bigger and better.

Like so many others, Khethiwe's kids were dropped off at the school gates early in the morning. They came from rundown apartments in Hillbrow, a once-hip city-centre residential block that had fallen on bad times. They came from Soweto, the sprawling township that provides Johannesburg with most of its labour. They came from house workers' quarters at the bottom of big gardens in nearby houses. And, like Khethiwe's brood, they came from Vosloorus, another township, on Johannesburg's eastern fringes.

By the time lessons started at 7.30am, most of these children had already been up for several hours. While our sons were rolling out of bed, their classmates from the townships were nodding off in a swaying taxi – as they call the minibuses that run from the townships – heading into the city.

Thando's day started at 5am, when his mother woke him. She would have been up half an hour earlier to wash before the children needed the bathroom. Thando was eleven, the eldest. He would prepare breakfast for the others. By 6am, Khethiwe, Thando, Sephiwe and Cassandra would be queuing at the taxi rank. Once in the city, they would catch a bus down the Oxford Road, from where it was a short walk to our school, Saxonwold Primary. Khethiwe would then catch another bus, if she was lucky, or walk to the First National Bank in the suburb of Rosebank, where she worked as a clerk. At 1.30pm she would come back, pick up the children, take them to the public library on Jan Smuts Avenue, leave them there and return to the bank. At 4.30pm, by which time she had already been up for twelve hours, she would collect the children again and make the journey back to Vosloorus. Then Khethiwe would prepare supper. They ate at 7.30pm, and then the children bathed and went to bed. At about 9.30pm Khethiwe would start working for her credit management exams. She stopped when she was too tired to go on. Usually she got about five hours' sleep.

We knew Khethiwe long before we were able to call her a friend. I say 'we', but it was really Frances who got to know her. I was always somewhere else, covering yet another African disaster. But even if I'd been around, I doubt if I'd have formed the same kind of relationship with Khethiwe as Frances did. As they say, men talk, women communicate.

It started in stereotypical fashion: rich white woman – which is what Frances was by South African standards – helps out poor black woman. Very soon after the school opened up to township children, it became obvious to the staff that these kids were at a disadvantage simply because their parents were in no position to supervise homework or any other extracurricular activity. Sometimes it was because the mothers and fathers were themselves hampered by the woefully inadequate education they had received under Apartheid; more often it was because, like Khethiwe, they were at full stretch just getting their children to and from school each day, and had no time or energy left for anything else at the end of a hard day in the city. So a group of women, Frances included, started a homework club. Children would come to their homes, work a bit, play a bit, and their parents would pick them up in the evening.

Thando, Sephiwe and Cassandra were regulars at our house. For a long time, as long as a year, little more than a greeting, a perfunctory conversation and a hurried farewell passed between Frances and Khethiwe when she came to collect the children.

Khethiwe was very reserved and Frances was not confident enough to push things. We asked Khethiwe about it years later. 'At first it was strange coming to your big house,' she explained. 'Though, of course, I was proud that Thando had made a friend from the suburbs. I knew George was an Indian, but I wasn't sure about Frances. You know, many whites can pretend to like you but it is not genuine. So I was careful.'

It all changed when my father visited us in South Africa. Over the twenty-odd years she has known my family, Frances has come to understand the little courtesies and habits that oil social contact among Sri Lankans and people in the developing world generally. One of the most important of these is deference to age. In the rich world the elderly are often regarded as a burden; in the poor world they are respected for their years and cherished for their wisdom. When Khethiwe came over to fetch the children, she saw Frances and my father together. 'That was the day I knew I could be friends with Frances. She showed respect to your father, like a proper *makoti*, a daughter-in-law. I knew she was not like the white women I saw at work. She could be like us, even if she came from London.'

And so it was that a lawyer's daughter from the gentle, undulating acres of southern England struck up a friendship with a woman brought up in harsh, overcrowded Emdeni, one of Soweto's poorer quarters. Through knowing Khethiwe, we gained much more than a friend: we also gained an insight into the real South African miracle. We saw the gradual fulfilment of some of the lives Apartheid had sought to suppress for so long. We saw the dedication and discipline it took. We saw that a vote stuck through a slot in a ballot box was only a beginning. But most of all, we saw what happens on the other side of the wall of suspicion, fear, prejudice, culture and habit that still separates so many white South Africans from their black brothers and sisters.

When Khethiwe got a new job, having passed her exams, she invited us to a celebratory party at her home in Vosloorus. In the

1980s and early 1990s, the township had seen some of the worst violence in the country. It was, as Khethiwe put it, 'a bad location'. Apartheid governments certainly fomented 'black-on-black' aggression, but it soon developed a momentum of its own. Like 'necklacing', killing people by setting light to a tyre placed over the head, the violence was evidence of the brutalisation of politics in a system that provided no legal channels through which people could express themselves.

By our time, though, Vosloorus was simply another of those shapeless, drab estates you found all over South Africa. You could see it from the highway out of Johannesburg, a vista of unremitting tedium, row upon row of matchbox houses. The huge pylons with their floodlights added to the impression that you were entering a concentration camp – which, in a sense, is precisely how such townships had been perceived by the town planners of Apartheid South Africa.

As we prepared to set off for Vosloorus on the Sunday morning of Khethiwe's party, all the visceral anxieties that can divide black from white, township from suburb, surfaced. I had been to many townships on reporting assignments, but always with Milton, my producer, and Glenn, my cameraman. I felt safe unless Milton told me not to feel safe. They always drove and we never got lost.

As Frances pulled out the map and I read out Khethiwe's instructions, I found myself recalling the opening scene of Tom Wolfe's *Bonfire of the Vanities*, the one in which the rich commodity trader panics after mistakenly driving his Mercedes into the Bronx at night. My car was that other example of German automotive excellence, a BMW. I decided to leave it in the garage. We opted for Frances' trusty old Volkswagen instead. When we had bought it a couple of years earlier, and the dealer had delivered it to me at the BBC office, the picture editor, Mike Purdy, had teased me about it. 'Shame, man, they're going to laugh at her if she turns up in a thing like that.' To which Glenn replied: 'Yeah, but that's fuck of a sight better than getting hijacked and raped, eh?' Never one to mince words, was our Glenn.

What to take with us? If we'd been going to visit the Lenahans, the Kennedys, the Naickers, the Lewins or the Randeras, it would have been obvious: a nice bottle of Cape Red, and perhaps some chocolate truffles to have with coffee. But for Khethiwe's party, every option seemed to have its downside. We could take something quite substantial – we were certainly well off enough to contribute more than most – but that might have seemed patronising. The usual bottle of wine didn't seem appropriate, either. It looked mean. Besides, we didn't know who would be there, and whether they would be wine people. It sounds ridiculous, and I'm embarrassed even to write about it, but that's the way it was. I think in the end we settled on a crate of beer and a pudding.

We needn't have worried. Khethiwe scolded us for bringing anything at all. It was a gathering of Khethiwe's clan, her extended family. Parents, brothers and sisters, nieces and nephews, friends and relatives. A sheep had been slaughtered and the drinks were on ice. There was an awning to keep the hot sun off the old folk. Khethiwe's father, his face exuding the serenity of a man who has done well by his family, said a prayer, partly in English, partly in Xhosa. A fusion of Christian and ancestral, reflecting the way so many Africans continue to straddle the old and new worlds.

Later in the afternoon, Adam came over and said that he, Thando and the other children were going to walk into the township to get some ice-creams. I tried not to show any outward sign of the alarm bells that rang loudly in my head. It was a measure of the extent to which we, as expatriates living in the suburbs, had been affected by our perceptions of life in the townships. I asked Khethiwe's brother, Gandhi, if he thought it would be OK. 'They will be safer here than anywhere in Rosebank or Sandton,' he said. 'They are children going to get some ice-creams, that's all. No one is going to touch them. They are guests here.'

It was the first time our children had walked anywhere on their own in South Africa. That was the paradox: they were freer in the township, with all its supposed dangers, than they had ever been in the seemingly secure suburbs. As we drove home that evening we became painfully aware of just how cut off we were from most of South Africa. There was also the depressing realisation that it wasn't going to get much better, not in our time.

In his book *The Mind of South Africa*, Allister Sparks wrote about the wild almond hedge planted in 1660 by Jan van Riebeeck, leader of the first white people to settle on the Cape. The hedge, Sparks said, 'cut off Van Riebeeck's little white community from the great African continent stretching away to the north, creating their own little enclave of Europe six thousand miles from home'.

Today, in modern Johannesburg and other major cities, the suburbs remain largely white enclaves. The hedges have given way to solid walls six feet high, sometimes higher. We had one round our rented house in Saxonwold. Some of our neighbours installed electric fences on top of their walls. We visited houses where there would be an outer gate and an inner one. The space in between, where you parked your car, was like a decompression chamber in which you prepared yourself for the mean streets outside.

In our four years in Johannesburg the only real contact we had with our immediate neighbours was when there was a move to arrange a security patrol for the area. One of the suggestions offered at the community meeting was that we should have a 'wog and dog patrol'!

There's no denying the crime that blights far too much of South African life. Virtually every significant political leader, including Nelson Mandela and Thabo Mbeki, has acknowledged as much. But it's impossible to avoid the conclusion that the debilitating effects it has had on the white psyche have as much to do with history as with crime. If over 350 years of occupation you have been drip-fed the notion that the black man is a sly and rapacious enemy, it is not surprising if you spend half your time looking over your shoulder. Where once the white people turned the ox wagons into a *laager* for protection, they have now become world experts in urban security.

South Africa's contribution to the art of town planning is suburban siege architecture, and some of the best examples are to be found in Johannesburg. Its premise is that no one ought to walk anywhere; that it is too dangerous to live life out in the open. There are very few high streets in the way we have them in Britain; not many children get to nip down to a corner shop for a bag of sweets or the morning papers. There are very few open-air markets of the kind that give the districts of other cities round the world their distinctive character.

What you do is get in the car and head for the malls, the emporiums of fear and insecurity. Once inside, you're supposed to feel safe. Each shop and café will have its own security guards. These are large, brash capsules of imported culture. You could be in Dallas. And that's the whole purpose of these buildings: they are there to keep the chaos of Africa at bay.

For those who really want to get away from it all in South Africa, Cape Town is the place to go. There the atmosphere is more relaxed and it is a bit easier to pretend you are in Europe. The vineyards help, of course, and Table Mountain is quite useful for obscuring the more disagreeable aspects of the city's life – like Khayelitsha, probably one of the largest slums in the southern hemisphere.

Recent years have seen a sort of reverse trek as white families head back to where it all started. A manager of one removal company told me they were moving about three families a week from Johannesburg to Cape Town. It's probably more now. But where next? What happens when Africa catches up with Cape Town? There's only the Atlantic Ocean after that.

White people are going to have to decide whether or not they like being Africans. Africa is on the march and it's time to make a choice. If you drive south from the frightened suburbs of Johannesburg and across the railway line, you will find a new city taking shape. Go to the Rand Supreme Court, where the hawkers will sell you everything from a fake Rolex watch to a kilo of oranges. From there, travel eastwards to the shops around the Ponte Building. Listen and look carefully, for you will find Africa in all its vitality, mischief and flamboyance. You will hear the way Zairean Lingala competes with the local Xhosa or Sotho; or how Nigerian Yoruba contrasts with Zulu. Over there is a man from Mali. He does a weekly round trip bringing cheap clothes from West Africa and taking back radios and microwave ovens. Further on, sitting in the shade, is a chap from Zaire. He'll tell you the carvings he is selling are all genuine antiques. And if you hang around long enough, you'll catch him rubbing a bit of antique dust into them.

There is a seamier side to this African invasion. South Africa has become a favoured destination for a vast array of crooks and gangsters from all over the continent. Some come to peddle their illicit wares; many others choose it as a place to enjoy their ill-gotten gains. A police force trained chiefly to act as Apartheid's henchmen has in the past proved easy meat for gangs who learned their skills of evasion and deceit in places like Paris, London and New York. In comparison, South Africa has been a breeze. What's more, its reliable and well-connected financial system has made it an ideal venue for money-laundering.

But the crooks are in a minority. Most of the foreigners who come into South Africa are simply looking to make an honest buck. Once they might have tried their chances in Europe; now there is somewhere much more convenient. It isn't a conspiracy, just a matter of geography. They have found a new land of opportunity.

The reaction of many black South Africans to this steady, but not overwhelming, flow of economic migrants has exposed the extent to which they, too, have been infected by the *laager* mentality. It has shown that they are willing to put up their own walls. The African migrants are seen as a threat even though few of them have taken up jobs in the formal sector. The one-Africa sentiment that underpinned so much of the struggle against Apartheid has simply evaporated. The solidarity engendered by shared colour and experience of oppression turned out to be a weak link in the chain: it snapped as soon as it was put under pressure. In its place there has been an upsurge of the kind of xenophobia one would normally associate with the fascist right in Europe.

In Mpumalanga province, which adjoins Mozambique, we heard reports of white farmers and their workers getting together for some rudimentary training in how to tackle anyone who slipped through the electrified fence (the voltage had been reduced after 1994) that stretched across the more vulnerable parts of the border between the two countries. In Johannesburg I listened to an activist at a rally of small traders. 'Our exiles, our freedom fighters have come back to find all the flats and jobs taken by these foreigners!' he ranted. A murmur of agreement ran through the crowd. The man warmed to his theme. 'When our exiles were abroad, they didn't live in cities – they were put in camps.' This time a cheer. From the back of the group somebody else shouted out, 'It's no good meeting in a park like this. We need to act.' The truth is that black South Africans are nearly as ignorant as white people about the continent they glibly call their home.

My stint as the BBC's correspondent in Johannesburg coincided with the decision to turn our bureau there into one that would cover the whole continent. Up to then its main task had been to follow the vicissitudes of South Africa's liberation struggle. The story inside South Africa after Nelson Mandela's victory was less compelling, at least in terms of television news pictures. So over the four years I was there, my colleagues and I saw more of the rest of Africa than we had expected.

Much of it was already familiar to me, so much so that sometimes I felt that I, an outsider, was helping the local members of the BBC team to discover their own continent. I tried to teach Byron Blunt, a man with a temperament like taut elastic, the value of patience as lethargic immigration officials took their own sweet time to check our papers. In Sierra Leone I persuaded the fastidious and frugal Jerry Chabane to resist yet another order of chicken and chips in favour of a helping of boiled cassava and smoked-fish relish. I enjoyed the way Glenn Middleton amused hordes of children all over the continent with the football flip-kick he'd perfected in the days when he'd played truant from school. I listened as Mike Purdy, wiry, nervy Mike, confessed that he couldn't take much more of the killing and maiming. I laughed as Hamilton Wende got better and better at mimicking the petty officialdom that passes for a civil service across Africa. And I admired the pains taken by Debbie Morgan to understand what lay behind the pictures she edited so deftly. But most of all, I watched with pleasure and pride as Milton Nkosi hit his stride in places like Zaire. Africa suited him and he wore it well. They liked his manly belly and his appetite for life.

All of them, black and white, had one thing in common. When they saw what other countries were going through, they began to understand the challenge that faced theirs. I would not blame them if they privately thought, 'Let's keep Africa out. Let's just enjoy the fruits of our own freedom.'

And I cannot find it in me, either, to dismiss outright the insecurity felt by white South Africans. Many are trying hard to make a go of it. They are not all racists. Most of them are like you and me, parents worried about whether the degrees their children will get in fifteen years' time will be recognised outside the country; wives concerned about whether their husbands will manage to keep their jobs until their retirement. Who can censure them for worrying that an opportunist at their workplace might play the race card? It's happening already. They are right to be indignant when they hear that politicians in a rural province have elected to drive around in BMWs more suited to the motorways of Europe than the farm tracks of Mpumalanga. This new culture of entitlement is as dishonourable as the old ideology of beggar thy neighbour.

The South Africa I left in 1998 was not so much a miracle as a microcosm of the globe. Its borders contained the great unresolved war between the rich world and the poor world. To be sure, racial bigotry has bestowed on this land a veil of bitterness and mistrust you will not find anywhere else. But now, in this new struggle for equality of opportunity, both black and white South Africans have a vested interest in finding a solution. The alternative is too depressing to contemplate.

You can see what might happen. Perhaps this great white tribe of Africa will fall apart. Some will pull down the shutters and withdraw into the isolation of their dim sitting rooms. Others will disperse to all corners of the earth. From their new, rootless homes, as they look towards the horizon and beyond that towards the continent of their forefathers, one question will keep returning to their lips. 'How did we let it all slip away?'

And perhaps black South Africans will find themselves sole masters of the land on which they fought that most noble of battles, the battle for freedom. They will look north to the troubled continent over the Limpopo and they will see that their beloved country is beginning to look exactly the same. Then they will turn to each other and ask: 'How did we come to make the same mistakes as our brothers and sisters?'

So Africa has come full circle. There is now a generation in charge that looks back not so much in anger as in regret. The people at the top, the men and women who run everything from governments to game parks, radio stations to restaurants, are my people, freedom's generation. They were born under the rule of black men. They know that what is happening to their continent is not what was promised in those heady days when my schoolfriends and I talked about putting an African into space. But they know, too, that the power and responsibility to change things rests with them in a way that it rested with no previous generation. They are holding the reins at a time when the world is moving so fast it is no longer patient enough to wait for Africa.

Thabo Mbeki, who took over as South Africa's president in May 1999, has a unique position in Africa's story. It is one that has been foisted on him regardless of whether he wants it or is capable of living up to its demands. If you accept, as I do, that Nelson Mandela's presidency marked the last phase of Africa's decolonisation, Mr Mbeki's rise to power heralds the beginning of the continent's journey onwards, utterly free, for the first time, of foreign or settler occupation. Other leaders, such as Uganda's Yoweri Museveni, have already started to clear a path through the litter of false promises and betrayed hopes, but it is Thabo Mbeki who runs Africa's strongest nation. With that responsibility comes the historic obligation to get it right.

I left South Africa before Mr Mbeki took over, but like the migrant I am, I look back from time to time at the land that was my home for nearly four years. And I see things now that I didn't notice then. I appreciate, with the clarity afforded by distance, what a favoured birth and charmed infancy South Africa enjoyed. Right up to the day before the elections in April 1994, it was possible that the whole process could have been derailed by the extremists who couldn't bear the thought of a black man in charge. But, come the bright new dawn, all that seemed to evaporate. The colossal presence of Nelson Mandela, as near as the modern world has got to the ancient ideal of a philosopher-king, overshadowed the faultlines in this most divided of nations. But Madiba did not solve the country's problems so much as bury them under the sheer weight of his personality and conviction.

Thabo Mbeki understood all this long before he moved into the presidential wing at Union Buildings. That's why it used to infuriate him when journalists habitually asked him how he would fill Mr Mandela's shoes. The point is that this was the last thing he wanted to do, and the last thing South Africa needed.

Mr Mbeki knew that, for all the open doors Madiba found to the staterooms of the powerful, his country's access to the trade markets of the rich world was still constrained by old-fashioned protectionism. He knew that for all the promises of fraternal support and financial help, it was up to him to take on the corporations which happily overcharged his people for the drugs that would save their lives. And for all the talk of a new era he must know that the challenge confronting South Africa today is not so different from the one Ghana faced back in 1957: to make and grow the goods that the world will want to buy and to sell them at a price that leaves enough to spare to build a better South Africa than the one he inherited. In the end that is what freedom is about. It isn't rocket science, but it does take honesty and commitment.

As for me, I have watched it from first to last. When I was an impressionable child, Kwame Nkrumah's position in my universe was all-consuming. As an adult, I understand that Thabo Mbeki can be no more than the man he is. I look to him now not for grand gestures or heady rhetoric, but for the little things. The decisions made on time, the appointments made without fear or favour. I hope he will develop the humility to listen to the voices of his critics and the perception to see through the blandishments of his supporters. So far neither quality has been evident in abundance. Political opponents have been harshly disparaged and the misdemeanors of his cohorts too readily indulged. But I am not beyond hoping that Mbeki will live up to the promise he showed as the freedom fighter I trailed in the old days of exile. Most of all, I look for a man who will be true to his word. That is all his people need. It is all Africa wants of its leaders. They will do the rest.

Epilogue

If Only the Baobabs Could Speak

When I started out on this passage through Africa I had two aims: to tell the truth about the continent, but at the same time to ensure that, whatever else this book is, it should not be yet another addition to the library of despondency. I wanted to show that understanding Africa's failings is not the same thing as condemning it for them.

If it has taken an all-too-familiar path through famine and fear, conflict and corruption, it is because these are the raw materials of a foreign correspondent. Like a sculptor who has to work with a flawed stone rather than the solid piece of granite he would prefer, I have had to work with Africa's many imperfections. But as I have chipped away at the friable outer layer of the continent's most recent history, I have sensed a solid core underneath. I have rediscovered simple truths I knew about Africa when I was a child growing up there, above all, the capacity of its people to survive against all the odds. Contrary to the prevailing perception, the vast majority of Africans are both industrious and strong-willed. If they were anything less they would long ago have succumbed to what has to be one of the harshest environments on the planet. There nature can be unkind and, as we've seen, the rulers even worse.

Africa is of course much bigger and much more varied than my personal journey can express. If you look at a map of the continent, the first thing you see is just how vast it is. The distance from the Equator, which runs through the heart of Africa, to its most northerly point, Ras Ben Sekka in Tunisia, is about 4,000 kilometres. You'd travel more or less the same distance from the Equator to get to the most southerly point, Cape Agulhas in South Africa. Eight thousand kilometres – 5,000 miles – from top to bottom. And over 7,000 kilometres separate its western and eastern extremities, Cape Verde in Senegal and the Ras Hafun peninsula in Somalia.

Look at all those blue lines – the rivers. The Congo, the Niger, the Zambezi, the Limpopo, the Nile, the Okavango, and many others. Their very names suggest a torrent of untrammelled power. According to the Africa Institute in Pretoria, the combined hydropower potential of the continent's rivers is the greatest in the world.

Then there are the other lines, the political ones which mark out the borders between fifty-three countries. Many are meaningless, artificial divisions that reflect the power politics of nineteenth-century Europe, on each side of which live people of the same culture and language. In his authoritative work *Africa: A Biography of a Continent*, John Reader points out that the continent was carved up into three times as many countries as Asia, which boasts a land mass 50 per cent bigger. The borders between these countries cut through 177 ethnic 'culture areas', to use Reader's term. Apparently, every single border in Africa divides at least one such area. A political map that reflected the uninterrupted evolution of Africa's indigenous kingdoms and nations – the Nubian civilisation under the kings of Meroe, the Kongo,

Great Zimbabwe, ancient Ghana and so on – would have looked completely different. It also might well have led to greater stability.

From the very earliest meetings of the Organisation of African Unity way back in May 1963, the continent's politicians decided to respect the borders bequeathed by the colonial powers. To try to rearrange them would have led to virtually every country making some sort of claim on its neighbour, and thence, the leaders felt, to conflict. But conflict is what has happened anyway. Except that it has flared up within nations rather than between them. More often than not, the belligerents have sought to explain their grievances along ethnic or tribal lines.

Perhaps Africa's leaders should no longer be so conservative. It's possible that the only genuine African Renaissance is one in which its people rearrange themselves into the units with which they feel most comfortable.

In a sense this is already happening, whatever Africa's politicians and diplomats say. Every day, in every corner of Africa, borders are crossed and goods traded by people who ignore the line drawn in the sand. And the more inefficient and decrepit central governments have become, the more their people have begun to rely on old allegiances. When the experts at the Economic Commission for Africa or the Southern African Development Community bemoan how little of Africa's total trade is conducted within its shores – a mere 4 per cent of its trade with the rest of the world – they're really only sure about what's going on at the official border posts. As for the rest, we can only guess. It's almost certainly much more than anyone dares admit.

There is also a third, invisible, line. You will not find it on any map but it's one I have discerned as I've criss-crossed the continent. It divides Africa into two sectors: the part in which the colonisers decided to settle and the part they found less congenial. It separates the Africa of borrowed ideas and imported customs from an older, more genuine Africa.

This line would be drawn from the tip of the Horn of Africa in the east, up there in the arid, dust-devilled vastness, through the north of Kenya, over the top of Uganda, under most of Congo, and would finish up in Pointe-Noire on the Atlantic coast. Below this imaginary border, with its mosquito-free highlands, lies the Africa where the colonialist decided to stay. He supplanted local traditions with his own, sometimes to ludicrous effect. Many of the regulations dreamed up in some Victorian club off Piccadilly still hold sway. I was once, for example refused entry into the national assembly's press gallery in Robert Mugabe's independent Zimbabwe on a hot, summer afternoon because I had a tie but no jacket.

Other legacies are more subtle. Black people in places like Malawi or Kenya still show a vestigial diffidence in the company of whites, the result of the drip-drip draining of confidence over more than a century of playing second fiddle. They feel ill at ease; they feel their clothes are not stylish enough, or their homes not big enough. I remember the way my own parents would fuss if they expected a visit from one of their few white friends. The unannounced arrival of our Asian or African friends, on the other hand, they always took in their stride.

Above my make-believe line there is a different kind of Africa. The colonialist plundered this land, too, and exploited its people, but the climate and terrain dissuaded them from ever really settling here. There would be no louche and decadent band of English aristocrats, like the Happy Valley set who turned the Kenyan highlands into their playground, in the steamy backwaters of Nigeria or Sierra Leone. Here were Graham Greene's Scobie and Wilson, the kind of chaps who'd been passed over in the game of colonial Snakes and Ladders. They didn't hang around long enough for their insistence on kippers for breakfast and black tie for dinner to become *de rigueur*. When they left, bent and disillusioned, Africa reasserted itself with vigour and vitality to engulf all traces of their presence.

Consequently, in places like Lagos and Accra you will find a robustness of culture and flamboyance of character that has been largely erased in that other land. This is where it is easiest to glimpse the old Africa. When a man from the Ashanti region of Ghana wraps himself in a *kente* cloth he is not simply putting on some clothes, he is asserting an age-old tradition. Not for him the tie and jacket borrowed from a foreign culture. And when a Nigerian dresses in the flowing, brocaded robes of the three-piece *agbada* he is following a sartorial code that has been centuries in the making.

When our Nigerian friend Funke Abu invited us to lunch, her table was laden with a cuisine that you would find nowhere else. There would be some *joloff* rice, perhaps some *egusi* and *eba*. If she was feeling extravagant she might garnish the spinach-like *ewudu* with dried, smoked fish. If she was going to borrow from another culture, she was more likely to serve a groundnut stew from Ghana than roast chicken and potato chips from a recipe left behind by erstwhile colonial masters.

When Barbara Azu Ackah-Yensu, an old classmate of mine from Christ the King school, meets other members of staff at the Ashanti Gold Field's headquarters in Accra, she is continuing a business that first flourished a thousand years ago. In those days, West African gold fed a web of trade links that stretched across the Sahara and as far afield as the Mediterranean, India and China. For the next 500 years or so the great African kingdoms of Ghana, Mali and Songhay rivalled those of Europe and Asia for splendour and power.

This is not the victim-Africa that you see on the television news. It is not the beggar-Africa you are asked to help in end-less emergency appeals or the corrupt-Africa you run into when you try to do business there. Too often we see only Africa's demons and disasters. But for every victim, someone, some-where pulls through against the odds – little victories in remote places.

Take Yanai Dolo, for example. She lives in Gogoly, a hilltop Dogon village in central Mali. The Dogon people have occupied the Bandiagara hills for centuries now. This is arid country, not an easy place to live, yet they have flourished here. Their houses, tightly packed together on either side of narrow alleys, look as if they have grown out of the ground. The ochre-brown walls form a part of the landscape. The Dogon are linked to their land and history. It is not so much that they own the land as that the land owns them, and they belong to it. They are growing out of their past naturally, not being yanked away at a speed dictated by others.

The square door to Yanai's granary is exquisitely carved. The little figures, the fertility symbols, tell the Dogon story of creation. Whenever she opens the door, she is reminded that she is part of a grand plan, and that she and her community play an important part in it. It is an affirmation of her place in the world.

Every morning Yanai and the other village women walk down to the fields hundreds of feet below. The rock steps they tread have been worn smooth by the generations who have made the journey before them.

When I visited Yanai she was tending her plot, pulling out the weeds, making sure her crop of millet would survive till the harvest. As she worked she bent so far forwards that her shoulders were below her hips, her legs very slightly bent at the knees. Her face glistened with sweat. As I watched her, my mind registered this as oppressive labour. But my experience told me it was the great, fecund strength of African womanhood. Here was the embodiment of the marvellous creative force that will never let Africa die. For me, Yanai is a symbol of the vast, untapped potential of this troubled continent.

On the way back up to the village, Yanai carried a heavy basket of compost for her vegetable garden on the hilltop, her insurance policy, something she can fall back on if all else fails. That year she was growing onions. The money she earns from selling her vegetables at a nearby market goes towards her children's school fees. If she can, she keeps a little money aside for the bad times when the granary is empty.

Of course Yanai wants more, deserves better. It is as easy to romanticise life in the African countryside as it is to ignore the communal spirit that underpins it. For it is not Yanai's standard of living that is appealing, but the quality of her life. Across the continent, hundreds of millions of people are in touch with who they are and where they have come from. They know they are much stronger working together than they would be if they set off on the lonely path of individualism.

To see this Africa you have to find a new vantage point. It will have to be a place in your mind, for I don't know anywhere else that will work quite as well. Picture yourself high up on a hill, so high up that you can see the whole continent. All of Africa is spread out like a living carpet below you. Yes, there are places where the carpet has been worn away, but the fibres underneath are still visibly strong and intertwined. For every child who is brandishing a gun, you can see ten more helping their parents in the field, and another ten hard at work on their exercise books under the shade of a tree. Over there, by the river, where all those colourful cloths are laid out on the smooth boulders to dry, you can hear women joking about how much easier their life would be if they could get rid of their men. Further away, in the shack at the edge of that smoky city, you see a man knotting his tie in front of a cracked mirror that hangs from a rusty nail. It is five in the morning, and he is about to set out for work, determined to earn the money that will ensure that his children grow up with more opportunities than he has had.

I hope what this book has shown is that life in Africa is much more complex than its detractors often suggest. If you carry away one thought, let it be this: that although Africa's failings are many, so, too, are the reasons for them. Africa's conundrum is not its own. It got where it is today because the vast majority of its people were let down, primarily by their own leaders but also by those in the rich world who made common cause with dictators and despots.

When it was time for me to leave the Africa Bureau in Johannesburg and return to London, Frances and I decided to spend a little while in Zimbabwe, where we had started our married life, and where our first child had been born.

We were speeding up the Great North Road towards South Africa's northern border with Zimbabwe, Kipling's 'great, green, greasy Limpopo'. The road is straight and true. The Apartheid government's attempt at social engineering may have been an affront to civilisation, but their efforts at more conventional forms of engineering were commendable. They knew how to build roads and – a rarity in Africa – how to maintain them. I was at the wheel, Frances was comfortably settled in the passenger seat and there hadn't been time for the boys to get bored. Manu Dibango's *Waka Afrika* was in the CD shuttle. As places with names like Hammerskraal and Petersburg flashed by, testament to the country's history of occupation, my mind began to wander. Just two days earlier I had been on a very different road in a very different Africa.

I had been travelling south, leaving the northern Ugandan town of Gulu. The road was rutted and the car well past its sell-by date. I had spent two days in the company of a Brigadier Kasini, reporting on his attempts to see off the Lord's Resistance Army. The ten-year-old conflict was making a mockery of Uganda's new-found status as Africa's success story. As is the way with these nasty, brutish little wars, civilians were the main casualties. My notebook was brimful of stories of near-ritual cruelty and senseless killing.

Now, as we devoured the kilometres to Zimbabwe, it was difficult to believe that both roads belonged in the same continent. It wasn't simply a matter of distance but of time. Northern Uganda, like so much of Africa, seemed to be in another era. What, if anything, linked these two Africas? Did the town of Louis Trichardt, with its supermarkets and hole-in-the-wall cash machines, have anything in common with the tatty little village by the Lira junction in Uganda where I'd stopped to cool off an overheating car radiator?

I asked the question out loud, interrupting Frances, who was now reading an extract from our travel book to our sons. It was a passage about the 'upside-down' trees, the baobabs, that we could see on both sides of the road, standing there like massive, weathered monuments to a bygone time. 'It says here that some of these trees are four thousand years old,' she told the boys. 'If only the baobabs could speak, Dad,' one of them said. 'I bet they'd know the answer to your question.'

And indeed, these silent witnesses have seen it all. They were there, young and vibrant, 2,000 years ago when the first Bantu migrated south from the Congo basin. They can remember a time when Africa's polyglot tribes were at peace with each other and when the fruit of the land was abundant. They looked on as the great king Munhu Mutapha built his empire in this region in the fifteenth century, keeping a watchful eye on his pampered emissaries as they travelled to the coast, where they traded gold for Indian cotton and Chinese silks.

And the baobabs were still there when the great kingdom began to crumble, leaving only the towering walls of Great Zimbabwe as a record of its former glory. A few hundred years later, they may have winced at the wanton destruction that was the hallmark of the great Zulu *mfecane*, the punitive raids that gave the tribe power over a vast tract of territory that stretched to modern-day Bulawayo. They would not have had to wait much longer to hear the Pioneer Column pushing its way north, the foot soldiers of another empire, one that would have a more profound effect on this land than any other.

But after what, to the baobabs, must have been no more than a brief pause in time, their far-reaching roots felt the earth shake as the march of liberation gathered pace and, under their serene and solid presence, the peoples of Africa began their joyous journey out of oppression.

Less than fifty years later, the baobabs' small, oval leaves may have caught a chill in the wind as it floated down from the killing fields of Rwanda.

They have seen it all: the best and the worst. They have known incredible beauty and terrifying ugliness.

So today, in their gnarled and knobbly old age, perhaps they are not confused or worried about what is happening in this most blighted of continents. They have experienced the ebbs and flows of history. They understand that no condition is permanent. They know that Africa is not as fragile as she sometimes looks.

Africa will change.

Its people will be strong.

Nkosi sikele Afrika. God bless Africa.

Ye mre bé bà bio. Our time will come again.

Bibliography

Archer-Straw, Petrine: *Negrophilia*, Thames & Hudson, London, 2000.

Bennet, Ronan: *The Catastrophist*, Review, London, 1998.

Benson, Mary: *Nelson Mandela: The Man of the Moment*, Penguin, London, 1994.

Chaliand, Gerard & Rageau, Jean-Pierre: *The Penguin Atlas of Diasporas*, Penguin, London 1997.

Coetzee, J M: *Disgrace*, Secker & Warburg, London, 1999.

Conrad, Joseph: *Heart of Darkness*, Penguin, London, 1989.

Davidson, Basil: *Discovering Africa's Past*, Longman, London 1978.

Davidson, Basil: *The Story of Africa*, Mitchell Beazley Publishers, London, 1984

Fanon, Frantz: *The Wretched of the Earth*, Penguin, London 1990.

Foden, Giles: *The Last King of Scotland*, Faber & Faber, London, 1998.

Gallmann, Kuki: *Night of the Lions*, Penguin, London, 2000.

Godwin, Peter: *Mukiwa, A White Boy in Africa*, Macmillan, London 1996.

Gourevitch, Philip: *We Wish to Inform you that Tomorrow we will be Killed with our Families*, Macmillan, London, 1999.

Greene, Graham: *The Heart of the Matter*, Penguin, London 1971.

Harden, Blaine: *Africa: Dispatches from a Fragile Continent*, HarperCollins, London, 1993.

Harrison, David: *The White Tribe of Africa*, Macmillan South Africa, Johannesburg, 1981.

Kingsolver, Barbara: *The Poisonwood Bible*, Faber & Faber, London, 2000.

Kaplan, Robert: *The Ends of the Earth*, Macmillan, London 1997.

Kyemba, Henry: *A State of Blood*, Fountain Publishers, Kampala, 1997.

Lamb, Christina: *The Africa House*, Penguin, London, 2000.

Lamb, David: *The Africans*, Vintage Books, New York, 1987.

Lelyveld, Joseph: *Move Your Shadow*, Abacus, London 1997.

Malan, Rian: *My Traitor's Heart*, Bodley Head, London, 1990.

Mandela, Nelson: *Long Walk to Freedom*, Little, Brown, London 1994.

Meredith, Martin: *The Past is Another Country*, Pan Books, London 1980.

Morris, Jan: *Farewell the Trumpets*, Penguin, London, 1979.

Munnion, Chris: *Banana Sunday: Datelines from Africa*, William Waterman Publications, Rivonia, 1993.

Museveni, Yoweri: *Sowing the Mustard Seed*, Macmillan, London, 1997.

Naipaul, Shiva: *North of South*, Penguin, London, 1980.

Naipaul, V. S.: *A Bend in the River*, Penguin, London, 1980.

Okri, Ben: *An African Elegy*, Jonathan Cape, London, 1992.

Omaar, Rakiya: *Rwanda: Death, Despair and Defiance*, African Rights, London, 1995.

Pakenham, Thomas: *The Scramble for Africa*, Abacus, London, 1992.

Paton, Alan: *Cry the Beloved Country*, Penguin, London, 1980.

Peterson, Scott: *Me Against My Brother*, Routledge, London, 2000.

Phillips, Caryl: *Crossing the River*, Faber & Faber, London 2000.

Reader, John: *Africa: A Biography of a Continent*, Penguin, London, 1998.

Richburg, Keith: *Out of America: A Black Man Confronts Africa*, HarperCollins, New York, 1997.

Robbins, David: *Aspects of Africa*, Penguin, London, 1995.

Royle, Trevor: *Winds of Change*, John Murray Publishers, London, 1996.

Russell, Alec: *Big Men, Little People*, Macmillan, London, 1999.

Sampson, Anthony: *Mandela*, HarperCollins, London, 1999.

Segal, Ronald: *The Black Diaspora*, Faber & Faber, London, 1995.

Shaw, Angus: *Kandaya*, Baobab Books, Harare, 1993.

Slovo, Gillian: *Every Secret Thing*, Little, Brown, London, 1997.

Slovo, Joe: *The Unfinished Autobiography*, Ravan Press, Randburg, 1995.

Smith, David & Simpson, Colin: *Mugabe*, Pioneer Head, Harare, 1981.

Sparks, Allister: *The Mind of South Africa*, Mandarin Paperbacks, London, 1991.

Sparks, Allister: *Tomorrow is Another Country*, Struik Publishing, Sandton, 1995.

Tutu, Desmond: *No Future Without Forgiveness*, Rider, London, 1999.

Verrier, Anthony: *The Road to Zimbabwe*, Jonathan Cape, London, 1986.

Vittachi, Tarzie: *Emergency '58: The Story of the Ceylon Race Riots*, André Deutsch, London.

Watkins, Kevin & Fowler, Penny: *Rigged Rules and Double Standards*, Oxfam, Oxford, 2002.

Wrong, Michela: *In the Footsteps of Mr Kurtz*, Fourth Estate Ltd, London, 2000.

Index